CONFLICTING VIEWS

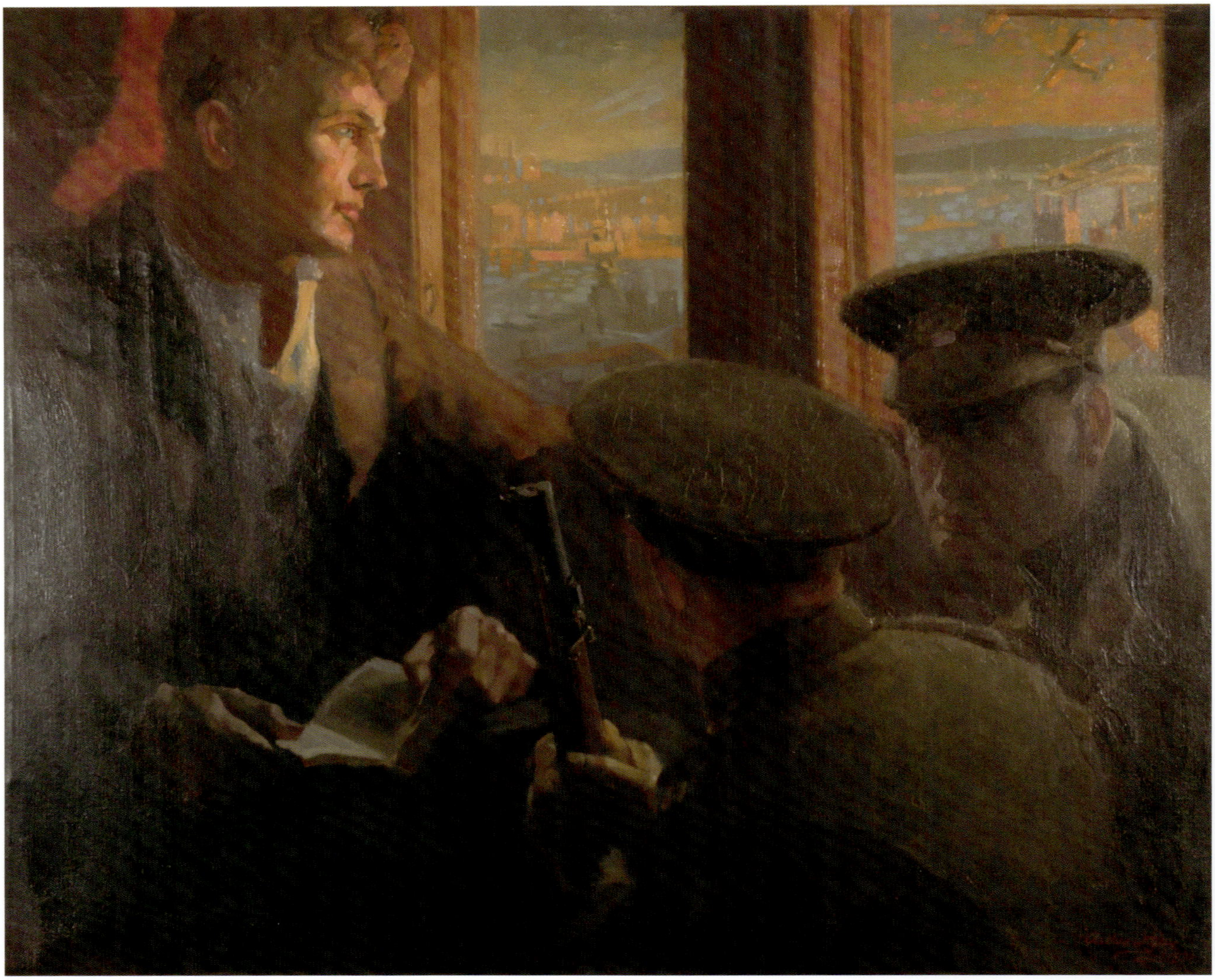

CONFLICTING VIEWS

PACIFIST ARTISTS

Gill Clarke

gill clarke

Sansom & Company

First published in 2018 by Sansom and Company
A publishing imprint of Redcliffe Press Ltd.
81g Pembroke Road, Bristol BS8 3EA
www.sansomandcompany.co.uk
info@sansomandcompany.co.uk

ISBN 978-1-911408-31-4
British Library Cataloguing-in-Publication Data
A catalogue record for this book is available from the British Library.

Design and typesetting by Design Deluxe, Bath
Printed and bound by Zenith Media, Pontypool

MIX
Paper from responsible sources
FSC® C010353

Front cover: Eric Robertson, *Shellburst*, c.1919, Oil on canvas, 71.2 x 83.8 cm, City Art Centre, Museums & Galleries, Edinburgh

Frontispiece: Arthur Wilson Gay, *The Conchie*, 1931, Oil on canvas, 69 x 84 cm, © Penny Gay, The Peace Museum, Bradford

Rear cover: Gordon Scott, *Portrait of a Conscientious Objector*, Undated, Oil on canvas, 58 x 38 cm, © Darnley Fine Art

Published to coincide with the exhibition
'Conflicting Views: Pacifist Artists' at The Otter Gallery, 25 June–7 October 2018
University of Chichester, College Lane, Chichester PO19 6PE
www.chi.ac.uk/ottergallery

MARC FITCH FUND

CONTENTS

FOREWORD

Conflicting Views: Pacifist Artists examines the experiences of British painters and sculptors, both well and lesser-known, who were conscientious objectors and pacifists in the First and Second World Wars. A biographical approach has been adopted to portray these individual accounts, which often are obscured by other debates, thereby offering new insights into the artists' varied artwork, motivations and treatment during the two great twentieth-century conflicts. Given their highly individual nature, these are presented alphabetically and by the relevant conflict. Images of the artists' work and the impact of the war on their pacifist positions and on their careers in the art world are considered. In so doing *Conflicting Views: Pacifist Artists* draws on a range of material including official documents,[1] diaries, letters, newspapers, autobiographies and writings on war, art and the peace movement.

Parts I and II focus respectively on the First and Second World Wars outlining initially the introduction and impact of conscription for the first time in British history in 1916 (partway through the First World War) and its reintroduction in September 1939 on the outbreak of the Second World War. The attention then turns to examine in detail the experiences of selected artists in each conflict who refused to undertake compulsory military service on the grounds of conscience, be it religious, political, or purely ethical and intellectual. It describes their appearances before various Tribunals in the First and Second World War to present their personal cases for exemption. The outcome of these tribunals and the subsequent treatment of individual artists and its impact on their diverse artistic practice are outlined.

Coda: The Legacy of War and Peace demonstrates the profound impact of two global conflicts and 'man's' inhumanity to 'man' on future generations through consideration of lifelong pacifist William Crozier's powerful painting *Bourlon Wood*, the site of one of the bloodiest battles in the First World War. The appearance of skeletal figures in his landscapes during the 1960s and 1970s as in *Bourlon Wood* shows Crozier's continuing preoccupation with the horrors of warfare: horrors which continue to be witnessed and recorded by contemporary artists. ◆◆◆

NOTE

1. In 1921 the government ordered that all documents relating to local and appeals tribunals be destroyed considering they were of insufficient public value to justify preservation, excepting those for Middlesex and the Central Appeal Tribunal in London and Lothian and Peebles which were retained as examples. Accordingly records are varied and incomplete. However, the records held by the Library of the Religious Society of Friends (Quakers) of the Friends Ambulance Unit has been particularly valuable as has the ground-breaking work by Cyril Pearce in authoring the Pearce Register of British Conscientious Objectors available online via the Imperial War Museums Lives of the First World War website.

FIRST WORLD WAR

CONSCRIPTION AND CONSCIENCE
DISSENTING VOICES, PACIFIST ARTISTS

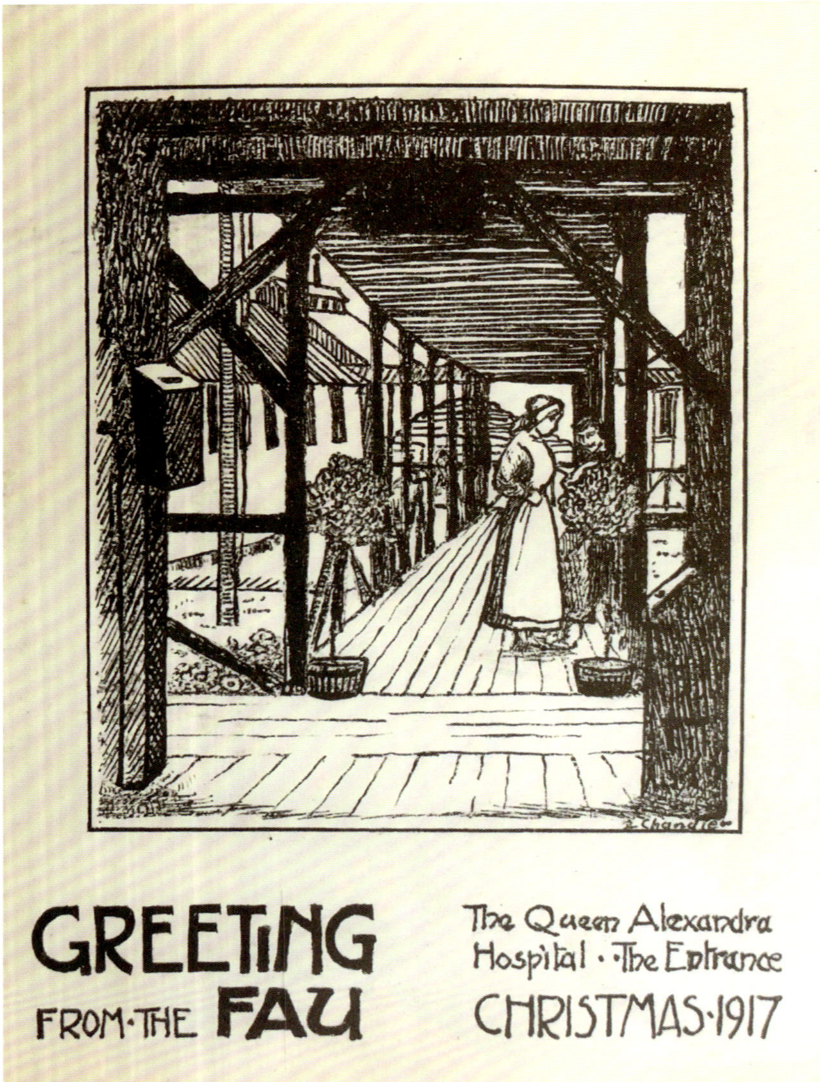

Allen Chandler | *Friends Ambulance Unit Christmas Card,* 1917
From Molly Evans' Nursing Scrapbook (Courtesy www.morganfourman.com)

AN INTRODUCTION

In January 1916 some 16 months after the outbreak of War and after much wrangling about British freedoms and in spite of deep divisions, the government led by Liberal Prime Minister Herbert Asquith passed the Military Service Act (MSA). This heralded a radical shift in national politics and life, imposing for the first time conscription on all single men 'or widowers without any child dependent on them' aged between 18–41.[1] Operative from 2 March it uniquely contained a 'Conscience Clause' for those who objected to combatant service and allowed for an individual to apply to his Local Tribunal for a certificate of exemption. Also eligible for exemption were those who were classed as more useful to the Nation in their present employment; those for whom it would cause serious economic hardship; and those who were ill or infirm. In May the MSA was extended to include married men and two years later further extended to those aged up to 51. The distinguished painter Joseph Southall actively campaigned against conscription and regularly attended conscientious objectors' tribunals. Aged 54 he was from the outset too old to be called-up. His younger friend and fellow artist Maxwell Armfield, also a pacifist, narrowly missed being conscripted having sailed for America at the end of 1915.

The MSA was viewed by many as a 'shirker's charter'; 'solid local worthies'[2] were appointed to local tribunals to judge the sincerity and genuineness of those seeking exemption. Applicants were frequently vilified as cowards and lampooned as 'not real men' not only in the press, but also in hostile, scornful local communities as is evidenced in some of the pacifist artists' biographical accounts that follow.[3] The composition and size of the circa 2000 Tribunals varied,[4] although they included a Military Representative. Tribunal reports in the press indicated variation too in the responses of the members to conscientious objectors' (COs) individual motives. The ambiguity of the Act's wording compromised the consistency of decisions made and members were largely ill equipped and prepared for such complexities with few having any legal experience or training. Appeal could be made to the County Tribunal (or equivalent in Scotland), of which there were approximately 70; Sheriffs headed these in Scotland and Judges in England.[5] The sheer number of hearings frequently overstretched local tribunals, with urban areas in particular giving little time to scrutinise cases. Camberwell's tribunal at one stage was sitting in relays from 11a.m.–9.30p.m., often four times a week.[6] Those who applied on religious grounds were generally more favourably received than those who applied on moral or other grounds.

For those 17,400[7] men who applied for exemption on the grounds of conscience there were four options open to the tribunals. They could refuse exemption; grant absolute or unconditional exemption so that the applicant would be free to go about their lives as they wished; grant exemption conditional upon undertaking work of national importance; or grant exemption from combatant service. To deal with the latter, the Non-Combatant Corps (NCC) was created in March 1916 to build roads, erect hutted camps, undertake quarrying, 'sanitary work' (burning excreta), and handling supplies. Subject to military discipline and drill they were not however given weapons training. NCC members were frequently subject to ridicule and 'scorn from regular soldiers, and outright revulsion from some of the Officers and NCOs told they had to run it.'[8] Their NCC cap badges and shoulder titles with the initials NCC were deliberately misinterpreted as 'No Courage Corps.'[9] There were approximately 3,000 members including COs Adrian Allinson, James Cowie and Job Nixon.

A man who joined a non-combatant organisation such as the Red Cross or the Friends Ambulance Unit (FAU) before 1916 was not necessarily required to subject his views to a tribunal when conscription was introduced, thereby potentially denying them the 'status' of a CO.[10] The formation of an ambulance unit of young Friends (Quakers) for service on one of the Allied fronts was first mooted in early August 1914. The first training camp was attended by about 60 male volunteers, mostly Quakers, at Jordans, Buckinghamshire, a centre for Quakers since the seventeenth century, and laid the foundations for the Unit. Twenty-one training camps were ultimately held. At the end of October 1914 the first FAU party left for Dunkirk. Arthur Cotterell an early FAU member joined them in December; and Allen Chandler[11] and Donald Wood the following year. Chandler, an architect and talented amateur painter later produced the FAU Christmas card. Following the imposition of conscription Ernest Procter, Eric Robertson and Ronald Ossory Dunlop joined in 1916. Procter and Robertson were posted to Dunkirk respectively in June and October where the work was often dangerous; Dunlop was however assigned to the General Service Section (Agriculture) remaining in England.

Towards the end of March 1916 the government created a committee supervised by the Board of Trade to find suitable civilian work (and willing employers) for COs prepared to undertake 'work of national importance'. Chaired by the Honorable T. W. H. Pelham it became known as the Pelham Committee and dealt with around 4,000 cases.[12] Among the occupations assigned by the Committee were agriculture, which constituted the largest number (approximately 1 in 4); forestry; food manufacture and distribution; textiles; government contractors; hospitals and 'asylums'.

While 'objectors came from a range of social, economic and educational backgrounds,'[13] there were broadly speaking two categories of COs 'alternativists' and 'absolutists'. Alternativists rejected military service but were prepared to accept alternative forms of service including the NCC, for example serving in the Royal Army Medical Corps as did pacifists Haydn Mackey and Walter Spradbery from 1914, or taking up civilian work of national importance and humanitarian relief work. The majority of artists from 1916 identified as COs undertook agricultural work including Claude Barry, Duncan Grant, Leslie Hunter, Harold Knight and Ethelbert White. Mark Gertler who described himself as 'Passivist' did not receive his call-up papers until 1918; he too was ultimately directed to undertake agricultural work.

Absolutists Percy Horton, William McCance, George Peace Micklewright and Claughton Pellew were unwilling to help the war effort in any way including accepting alternative, non-military compulsory service.[14] Their applications for absolute or unconditional exemption from military service were rejected and they were repeatedly court martialled, imprisoned and subjected to hard labour. *The Conchie* (1931) by Arthur Gay[15] is a powerful depiction of an Absolutist in military custody being escorted by two armed soldiers. Bible in hand he gazes out of the window to a town below, lost in thought. His freedom is about to be curtailed. The government had not expected such obdurate resistance from COs; thousands refused recognition by Military Service Tribunals continued to clog up civil prisons. The Home Office Scheme (HOS) was designed to solve this and release COs from prison to undertake civilian work unconnected with the war effort in assigned Work Centres/Camps. A committee was established in August 1916 under former miners' leader and Labour M.P. William Brace, to allocate 'genuine' COs (adjudged by the Central Tribunal in London at Wormwood Scrubs and Barlinnie Prison, Glasgow) to the Scheme. Nearly 6,000 cases were reviewed including McCance, Micklewright and Pellew who accepted this compromise.

The Armistice in 1918 did not lead to the immediate release of COs; this commenced the following April and took until late July 1919 to be completed. This did not include the last of the men serving in the NCC who were finally released in January 1920. Employment for COs post-war was not easy to come by; some were refused reinstatement in their old jobs on the railways or with public educational bodies. A similar situation operated within some Civil Service departments and in the Post Office. Further, those COs who had refused to accept work of national service were disenfranchised from voting in local and national elections for five years after the war ended. ◆◆◆

REFERENCES AND NOTES

1. The MSA did not apply to Ireland. Asquith resigned in December 1916; the populist Lloyd George replaced him as Prime Minister.
2. Marwick, A. (1965) *The Deluge: British Society and the First World War*, London: Bodley Head, p.81.
3. A notable exception is *Comrades in Conscience*, in which Cyril Pearce (2001/14) tells *The Story of an English Community's Opposition to the Great War* and challenges the idea of the unpopularity of COs.
4. See McDermott, J. (2011) *British Military Service Tribunals, 1916–1918: 'A Very Much Abused Body of Men'*, Manchester: Manchester University Press, p.15.
5. Kennedy, T. (1981) *The Hound of Conscience. A History of the No-Conscription Fellowship 1914–1919*, Fayetteville: University of Arkansas Press, p.89.
6. See Rae, J. (1970) *Conscience & Politics. The British Government and the Conscientious Objector to Military Service 1916–1919*, London: Oxford University Press, p.98.
7. See The Conscientious Objector's Register 1914–1918 compiled by Cyril Pearce.
8. Ellsworth-Jones, W. (2008) *We Will Not Fight. The Untold Story of World War One's Conscientious Objectors*, London: Aurum Press, p.93.
9. Rae (1970) Op. cit., p.194.
10. See Rae (1970) Op. cit.
11. Allen Chandler (1887–1969) a Quaker, served with the FAU as a cook for 4 years from Jan. 1915. His postings included periods in Dunkirk and Ypres, where he sketched the busy Dressing Station at Augustine Straat on Whit Monday, 1915. He also served with Ambulance Train 16 from Aug. 1915–Jan. 1916. Chandler likely made the acquaintance of Molly Evans, a highly experienced volunteer nurse serving with the VADS, who had arrived in Dunkirk on 14 Sept. 1917. I am grateful to the Morgan family for permission to reproduce the FAU card from her scrapbook, which also contains drawings by Ernest Procter.
12. Kennedy (1981) Op. cit., p.87. Pelham died in Dec. 1916 and was succeeded by Col. Sir Hildred Carlisle, M.P.
13. Bibbings, L.S. (2009) *Telling Tales about Men: Conceptions of Conscientious Objectors to Military Service during the First World War*, Manchester: Manchester University Press, p.37.
14. George Demaine (1892–1966) a RCA scholarship student, studying sculpture, was also an Absolutist. He joined the College Christian Union and became a member of the No-Conscription Fellowship (Horton also belonged). The war interrupted College life, rooms were requisitioned, students made clothes for the troops and conscription impacted on students and staff alike. Repeatedly imprisoned and sentenced to lengthy periods of hard labour for refusing to accept work under the Home Office Scheme, Demaine was released on 16 April 1919. He received his RCA diploma in 1921.
15. Arthur Gay (1901–58) was a devout Baptist, he studied at the Municipal School of Art in Bristol and exhibited mostly portraits and some landscapes at the Royal West of England Academy (RWA) from 1925–49. *The Conchie* was first exhibited in 1931 at the RWA, priced £35, it received a sympathetic public reception: a response that would have been unlikely during the height of the First World War. Gay was only 13 when war was declared, his daughter Penny Gay recalled that he 'wasn't ever involved in any official action taken in the cause of Pacifism – but it was clearly a cause about which he felt deeply – and which inspired him to paint *The Conchie*.' Gay served in a non-combatant unit in the Second World War. (Pers. comm. to the author February 2018).

    David Jagger (1891–1958) painted a striking portrait of a CO in 1917, shown at the RA summer exhibition the *Derby Daily Telegraph* reported 'Jagger's "Conscientious Objector" need not have been named. There he is to the life, with his haggard cheeks, dogged, argumentative face, and pink comforter.' (Cited in 'Catalogue' by Patrick Elliott in Elliott, P. and Llewellyn, S. (2017) *True to Life: British Realist Painting in the 1920s & 1930s*, Edinburgh: National Galleries of Scotland, p.96. Owing to the legacy of 'a severe childhood illness' Jagger was not conscripted, his pacifist beliefs 'caused considerable friction between himself and his elder brother and sister'. See http://thejaggerfamily.co.uk/david-jagger/4592835798 accessed 25 April 18. His brother Charles Sargeant Jagger (1885–1934) became a distinguished sculptor and his sister Edith (1880–1977) a gifted painter.

ADRIAN ALLINSON

(1890–1959)

Allinson initially studied medicine at the Middlesex Hospital Medical School before entering the Slade in 1910; something of a maverick he had been expelled aged fourteen from Wycliffe College in Gloucestershire for his atheism. He described himself as 'probably as aggressive and objectionable a young art student as could be found'. Henry Tonks, Head of the Slade, who had abandoned a successful career as a surgeon described Allinson as having 'a dangerous talent'.[1] This was recognised by his winning of a coveted scholarship (alongside Stanley Spencer) at the end of his first year for his 'imagination'. Allinson was a member of the Slade Coster Gang, which included amongst its members Gertler, Wadsworth, Nevinson, Currie and David Sassoon; so called as they aped the dress and tough behaviour of costermongers who sold fruit and vegetables from handcarts on the street. In his unpublished autobiography written in 1941 Allinson refers to Gertler, Wadsworth, Nevinson and Sassoon in musical terms:

> *These four and I formed a quintet that became inseparable in work and play. Nevinson and Wadsworth, as first and second violins led, Gertler and I followed as viola and cello, with Sassoon occasionally audible in the background in the part of the double bass.*[2]

Currie (c.1884–1914), a close friend of both Gertler and Allinson painted the nucleus of the gang in early Italian Renaissance-style together with the proprietor of the Petit Savoyard Café, which they frequented in Soho. Currie exhibited the result at the New English Art Club, entitled *Some Later Primitives and Madame Tisceron* (1912) it reflected the gang's metamorphosis into the short-lived Neo-Primitive group. Allinson, Gertler and Schwabe painted large panels on Madame Tisceron's walls but these disappeared when, as Schwabe later recalled, the place became rather smart during the war.[3] Allinson continued his studies in Germany and on Wadsworth's recommendation enrolled at the Knirrschule in Munich staying for some nine months where he found the time to ski, an activity he excelled at and which remained a passion.[4] The Académie de la Grande Chaumière in Paris provided the next location for his studies. In the summer of 1914 Allinson joined Walter Sickert in Dieppe returning home just before the start of the First World War.

The Café Royal, on Regent Street near Piccadilly Circus, with its marble-topped tables and sawdust-strewn floor remained a haunt for writers and artists and their models. Fellow artist Nina Hamnett remembered the high-spirited side-whiskered Allinson arriving on his motorcycle, wearing checked trousers, frilled shirt, velvet coat with a huge black stock. He was one of many artists to paint the gilded splendour of the Domino Room; his version completed in 1916 was described as one of the finest paintings executed during the war. Many of its frequenters can be recognised including Allinson seated to the right of the pillar, Dorelia and Augustus John, the standing figure David Sampson is talking to art critic, P. G. Konody. In the foreground is Nancy Cunard, the heiress, writer and later political activist.

Allinson, like Cunard, had a political conscience, his mixed parentage (his mother was Jewish and from Berlin) and non-conformist upbringing, impacted on his outspoken pacifist stance. His father, equally forthright, held advanced views on vegetarianism and contraception, which appear to have led to his being struck off the Medical Register. Allinson at his Tribunal in London in April 1916 gave his motivation for seeking exemption from Combatant Service as being vegetarian and humanitarian. The conductor Thomas Beecham (1879–1961) spoke in support of his application for exemption at the Tribunal. Allinson was working for him as a stage designer for the Beecham Opera Company having been introduced to him by his friend Philip Heseltine, a composer and music critic. Exemption was granted with a recommendation that Allinson join the Non-Combatant Corps. Later declared medically unfit (he had a chronic gastric weakness), he seems to have been largely left alone by the authorities. Although Allinson had always been something of an outsider he was not immune

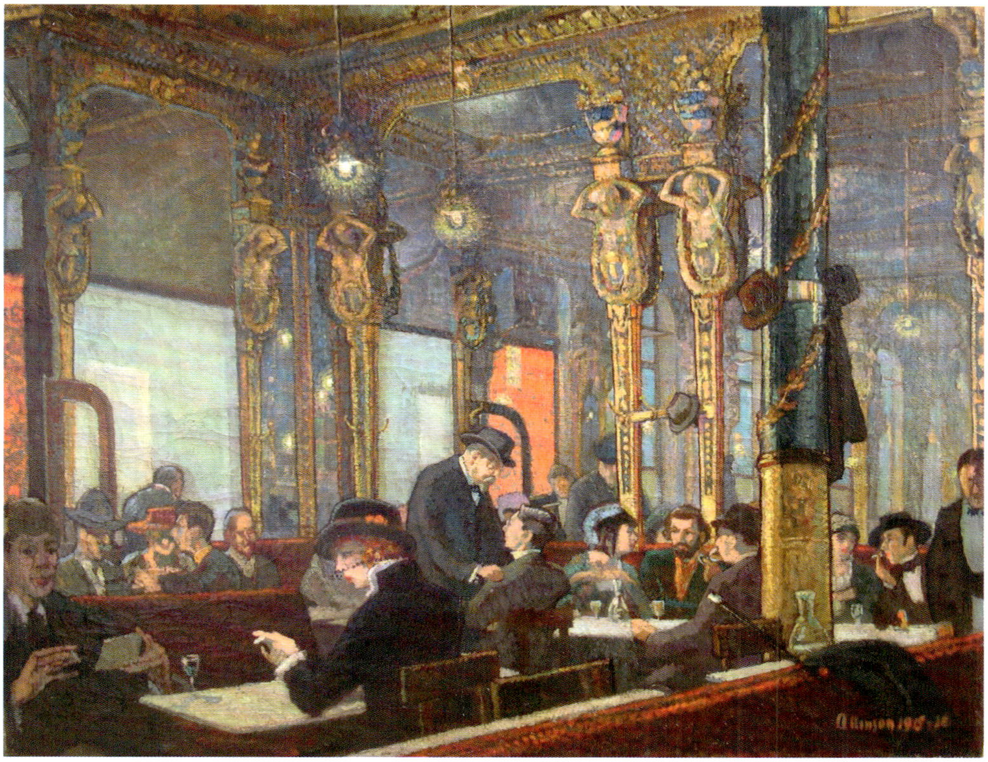

Adrian Allinson | *The Café Royal* | 1915, Oil on canvas, 99 x 125 cm | © The Estate of the Artist to the social ostracism that most conscientious objectors experienced, indeed he and Heseltine (known by the pseudonym Peter Warlock) also a conscientious objector, escaped the previous year to the Cotswolds to get away from the war fever in London.[5] Such attitudes were reflected in the stance adopted by Goupil Gallery owner William Marchant. He issued an ultimatum to the London Group stating that should the Group have members who were 'enemy aliens, conscientious objectors or sympathisers with the enemy' they would not be permitted to exhibit in his galleries and if the group contained any of these his walls would be closed to them.[6] Allinson had been elected in 1914 and matched all three categories so abhorred by Marchant, Gertler was also implicated. The American-born painter and hostess Ethel Sands (1873–1962) who had nursed wounded soldiers in France was present at a specially convened meeting of the London Group to decide how to respond to Marchant. The Group rejected Marchant's terms unanimously and accepted Ambrose Heal's offer of his Mansard Gallery for future exhibitions. During the war Allinson's drawing skill (and sense of humour) were employed to good effect in the caricatures he drew for the *Daily Express*. He also contributed illustrations to *Coterie*, one of the new avant-garde magazines that appeared for a brief period after the war. Between 1919–20 he designed a number of covers for titles in the series *Impressions of the Russian Ballet* published by balletomane Cyril Beaumont. Prior to this Allinson had produced the initial designs for wooden figures of principal dancers of Diaghilev's Ballets Russes to be sold as souvenirs to enthusiasts.[7]

Allinson lived in Switzerland for three years from 1920 where his preoccupation with painting glaciers was much evidenced, before being drawn to Italy, France and Spain and other countries where his landscapes showed a richness of colour and pattern. Allinson also loved the English countryside, painting many fine atmospheric landscapes, and designed posters for the Empire Marketing Board, London Transport and the main-line railways. During the Second World War, Allinson's *The AFS Dig For Victory in St James's Square* (1942), which depicted members of the Auxiliary Fire Service tending vegetable plots as part of the home front food campaign, was acquired under the War Artists Scheme. ◆◆◆

MAXWELL ARMFIELD

(1881–1972)

Armfield was born into a Quaker family in Ringwood, Hampshire and attended the Friends' Schools at Sidcot, Somerset and Leighton Park, near Reading before studying at Birmingham School of Art from 1899, being attracted by its reputation as a leading centre of the Arts and Crafts. In 1902 he moved to Paris to further his studies at the Académie de la Grande Chaumière and Académie Colarossi returning to London in 1905. He would visit Joseph Southall, who became a lifelong friend in Edgbaston to learn more about the technique of tempera. Two years later in 1907 he exhibited with Southall and other members of the Birmingham Painters and Craftsmen at the Fine Art Society in London alongside his former art school teachers Henry Payne (1868–1939) and Arthur Gaskin (1862–1948) with whom he had also formed a strong friendship. Armfield's work was praised in *The Tribune* for its precision and beauty of design.

In January 1909 Armfield married Birmingham-born Constance Smedley (1876–1941)[8] who had also studied at Birmingham School of Art; a successful writer (and illustrator) and committed suffragist she shared his interest and involvement in the theatre. They were to work closely until her death in 1941. Armfield through her influence became a Christian Scientist. In September 1911 they helped stage the outdoor 'Pageant of Progress' at Stroud which focused on the idea of progress and liberty. Its cast of over 1,100 were according to the *Gloucester Citizen* 'mainly members of the working classes'; also involved were numerous horses and flocks of sheep. Armfield and Smedley's 'dramatic aspirations' led them to decide to take their ideas for 'Little Theatres and Community Drama' to America. Smedley, in her reminiscences *Crusaders* (1929), explained:

> *The chaos and turmoil into which the world was plunged only made us feel a more urgent and passionate need for some language of communication for all peoples, whereby and wherein they might meet and understand each other and work together. Though art and artists at the moment seemed swept into futility and oblivion, we had never felt them to be more important…*

Prior to going to America they moved to London taking a studio in Chelsea, making contact with Margaret Morris and 'played a prominent part in an avant-garde, anti-war community centred on her theatre on the King's Road'.[9] This community bore some similarities to the Bloomsbury Group. Morris agreed to their plays being performed in her theatre.

Armfield and Smedley held fortnightly discussions in their studio with upwards of fifty people largely artists, journalists, writers and politicians trying to find out the truth about the conflict. On one occasion Geoffrey Whitworth, the honorary secretary and founder of the British Drama League, failed to attend a meeting as his guest, the exiled Tomas Masaryk (1850–1937), later first 'President of the Tcheko-Slav Republic',[10] was under police surveillance. Whitworth did not want to bring unwarranted (and official) attention to the private meetings. These meetings brought them into contact with Violet Paget whom they had asked to speak but rather than give a political speech she wrote and read a 'scene-plot' from *The Ballet of the Nations. A Present-day Morality* (1915), which she wrote under the pseudonym Vernon Lee. Lee was keen to get it published and illustrated but felt that 'there was no chance of a pacific publication at this time'.[11] Subsequently she read it at Morris's theatre where they invited several publishers with the result that it was commissioned by Chatto and Windus and published later in the year with Armfield providing the illustrations to match the satirical text that featured the Ballet-Master Death and Satan, the World's immortal Impresario.

Not long afterwards Armfield and Smedley landed in New York in 1916,[12] Armfield having been somewhat unexpectedly granted a passport. The move to America enabled him to continue with his work. Given the impending

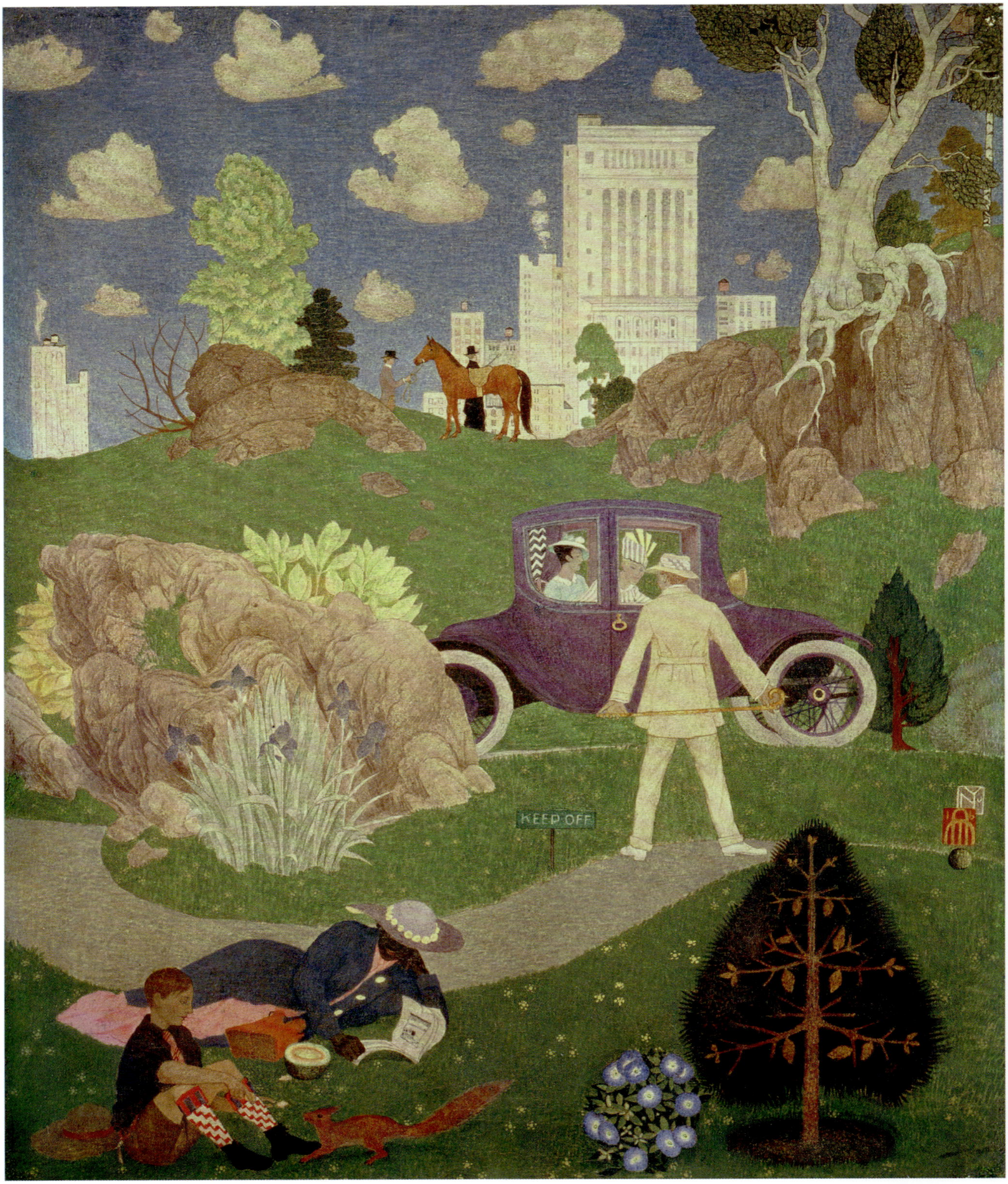

Maxwell Armfield | *Central Park, New York* | c.1916, Tempera on canvas, 64.2 x 39 cm | © Southampton City Art Gallery / Bridgeman Images introduction of conscription it is likely that the pacifist Armfield would have registered as a conscientious objector and run the risk of imprisonment and curtailment of his work had they remained in England. They stayed in America for seven years. Shortly after their arrival Armfield completed in tempera *Central Park, New York.*[13] 'The strange stark forms of New York ... reminiscent of Egyptian architecture, and the ethereal crystalline atmosphere ... appeal[ed]' as Smedley recalled to her husband. Armfield devoted his first year in America to painting.

Armfield and Smedley returned to England in 1922 founding the New Forest Group of Painters in 1924. Mockbeggar, close to Ringwood where they built a house began to feel rather isolated and they were pleasantly surprised to find that Bournemouth 'Instead of a comatose district inhabited by invalids... [was] brimming with artistic interest and activity...'. Nonetheless, in April 1927 with his work (and sales) tending to fall out of favour they returned to London and opened the Greenleaf Theatre Studio in Kensington. In 1930 Armfield wrote the well-received *Manual of Tempera Painting*, which he dedicated to Southall. With the outbreak of the Second World War they rented part of an old inn at West Wycombe, Buckinghamshire. After Smedley's death Armfield moved back to the New Forest, gave up his Christian Science beliefs and studied the occult and theosophy. His political and pacifist conscience remained; in 1943 he painted *This England: Portrait of an Owner.* Armfield described it as a satirical view of industrial society, which he loathed, and saw personified in the figure of the small industrialist.[14] The following year he was asked to complete the last painting in tempera that Southall was working on when he died: a memorial portrait of the Bradford MP, Frederick William Jowett (1864–1944), a founder member of the Independent Labour Party. In the portrait Jowett is depicted reading a political pamphlet while on the table in front of him lies a copy of the Independent Labour Party newspaper with a headline 'IS THIS WHAT YOUR MEN FIGHT FOR?' Armfield must have approved the sitter and subsequently completed it for presentation to the City of Bradford.[15] In 1945 he designed the cover for John Moxford's *The Coming of Peace*, which was published by Pentagon Press. Armfield lived to see a revival of interest in his work before his death in January 1972. ◆◆◆

CLAUDE FRANCIS BARRY

(1883–1970)

Barry completed his formal schooling at Harrow School in 1899, after which his wealthy aristocratic background enabled him to travel in Italy for six months with a tutor. Contrary to his parents' wishes, he attended Bournemouth School of Art for some months in 1900, where he most likely developed his interest in etching. He studied in Newlyn from 1905 and was tutored by Alfred East (1844–1913), which left a lasting impact in the realm of landscape, where he was taught 'to simplify; to concentrate on the overall form rather than the detail'. The following year he had his first painting accepted at the Royal Academy (RA).[16] In 1908 Barry moved to St Ives where he became an active member of the Art Club.

An avowed pacifist Barry refused to fight in the First World War and while little is known about his war resistance, it has been suggested that his father, who was serving with the Berkshire Yeomanry training troops, got him exempted on the grounds of ill health.[17] He spent the early part of the war near his family's home in Windsor where Barry's exemption took the form of agricultural labour picking potatoes, which he described as 'the worst six months of my life.'[18] During the war years he took printmaking lessons from Frank Brangwyn. Despite his anti-war sentiments Barry was inspired by the conflict, which resulted in some of his best work. In 1917 he settled in St Ives again and two years later submitted *London and Wartime: Nocturne* to the RA. Barry also completed *Fires of Victory* and *Trafalgar Square Peace Night* which celebrate the end of the war and contain elements of Vorticism with the diagonal lines of the searchlights criss-crossing the night sky and also demonstrate his grounding in the pointillism of the French Post-Impressionists. Barry spent months in London waiting for peace to be declared, and this culminated in his spending the evening of 19 July 1919 amongst the crowds in Trafalgar Square making notes showing them 'madly jazzing under the shadow of Nelson's monument' with the scene illuminated by a magnificent firework display.[19] It was one of a series of celebrations to mark the end of the war, which had officially ended only on 28 June with the signing of the Treaty of Versailles.

On the outbreak of the Second World War Barry returned reluctantly from living in Europe to St Ives and rented East's former studio on Porthmeor Beach where he concentrated on working on oils having given up etching. His dramatic paintings produced in the freedom of a large studio again show his mastery of pointillism and Vorticist framing. Notable works included *Blitz on St Paul's* (1942), and *Tower Bridge, London: A War-Time Nocturne*. A lover of Italy (the bulk of his etchings were produced at a printers in Milan which was destroyed, along with all the plates, in an American bombing raid in August 1944), he responded to the Battle of Monte Cassino in 1944 with a number of evocative paintings. With the end of hostilities he moved to Jersey. His work continued to evolve and he concentrated largely on more figurative paintings and working in a minimalist style into his late eighties. Barry inherited the family baronetcy title in 1949 and thereafter expected to be addressed as 'Sir Francis'.[20] ◆◆◆

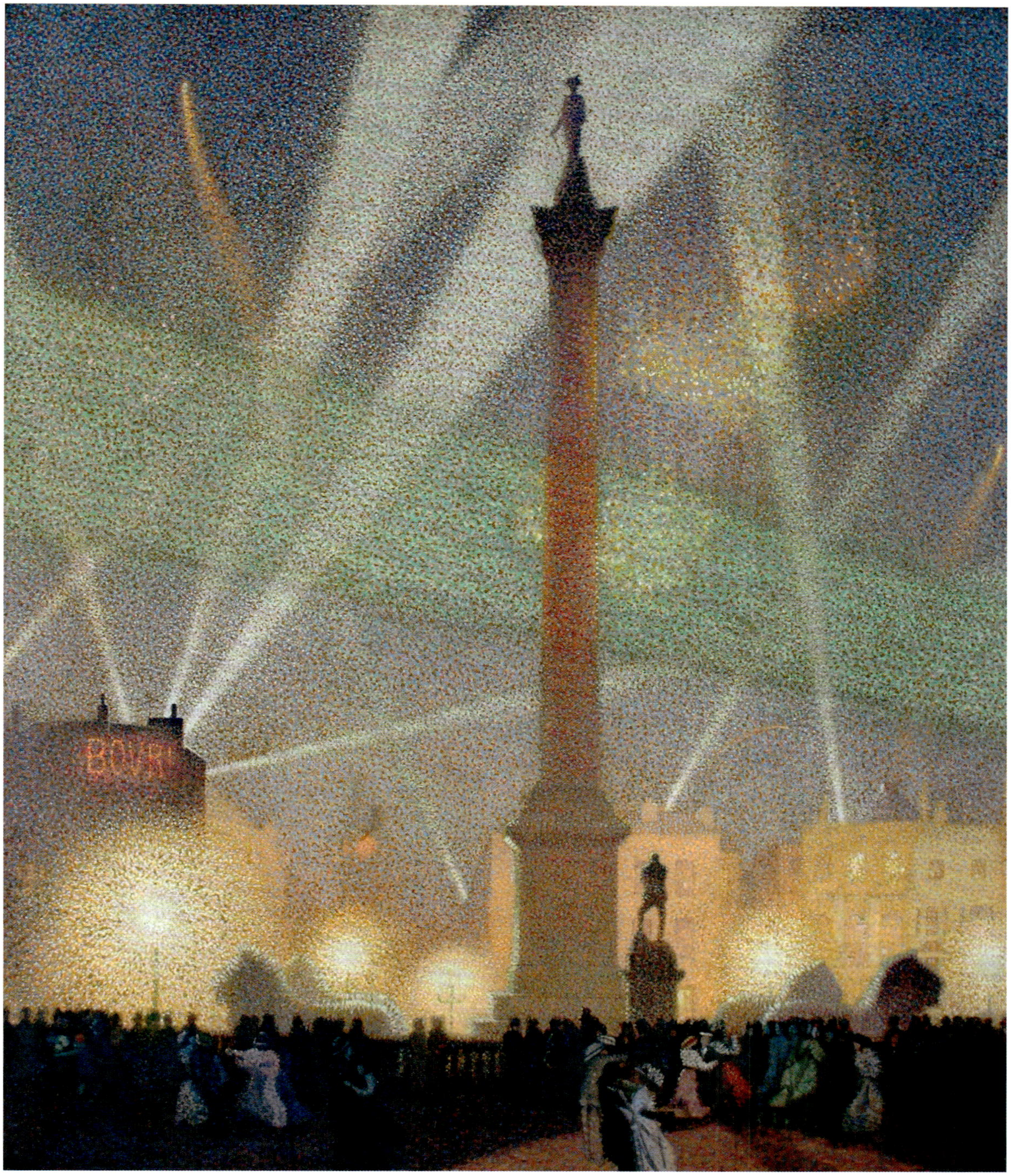

Claude Francis Barry | *Trafalgar Square Peace Night* | 1919, Oil on canvas, 200 x 162.5 cm

ARTHUR COTTERELL

(1885–1961)

Cotterell attended Bootham School, an independent Quaker boarding school in York. He was employed in the family's wallpaper manufacturing business, which had been founded in 1844. The nature and place of Cotterell's pre-war artistic training is unknown.

At the outbreak of war Cotterell was living in Bristol and attended monthly Quaker meetings in Bristol and Frenchay. A conscientious objector, he was an early member of the Friends Ambulance Unit (FAU) which he joined in December 1914. He spent the next four years or so working largely as an ambulance driver, he was first stationed at Headquarters in the Kursaal, Malo-les-Bains near Dunkirk. In December 1916 he worked briefly on a converted barge hospital on the Dunkirk canal.

In April 1917 Cotterell was assigned to Section Sanitaire Anglaise 13 (SSA, Motor Ambulance Convoy)[21] where he served alongside Eric Robertson until both were demobilised on 19 January 1919. Using one of the Unit's vehicles, they went on several hazardous sketching trips when there was a lull in the shelling. The scenes of destruction were recorded by both artists. In Nieuport (now Nieuwpoort), they clambered over the ruins of the 'great church' coming across 'sacred stones, fragments of china Madonnas and bones thrown up from the surrounding graves by the violent undreamed of resurrection which had followed centuries of calm.'[22]

Cotterell made numerous sketches of his stations, including a field kitchen in Verdun in 1917 and dug-outs. Towards the end of the war he was stationed near Reims in the small village of Treslon where his drawings included aid posts and a church interior.[23] *Muizon on the Vesle, Reims, October, 1918: Cars of the Section Sanitaire Anglaise 13* is one of the few watercolours by Cotterell; set against the backdrop of the shelled village are the cars of SSA, all 'Vulcans', presented to the British Red Cross Society by the Nottinghamshire and Derbyshire Coal Miners and Owners. Laurence Cadbury, a founder member of the FAU and former Officer-in-Charge of SSA 13 (until September 1916 when he was sent to HQ at Malo-les-Bains), purchased six drawings of the convoy from Cotterell in June 1918 (he also acquired some from Ernest Procter).

Following his demobilisation in 1919 Cotterell returned to Bristol. He exhibited with the Royal West of England Academy (RWA) until 1921 showing mainly landscapes in oils and watercolours. At the annual exhibition in 1919 he exhibited several works executed in France including *Ruins of Pouilly Church, near Rheims*, *An Ambulance Convoy in a French Village* and *Ay, near Epernay, France*. All were priced at three guineas. ◆◆◆

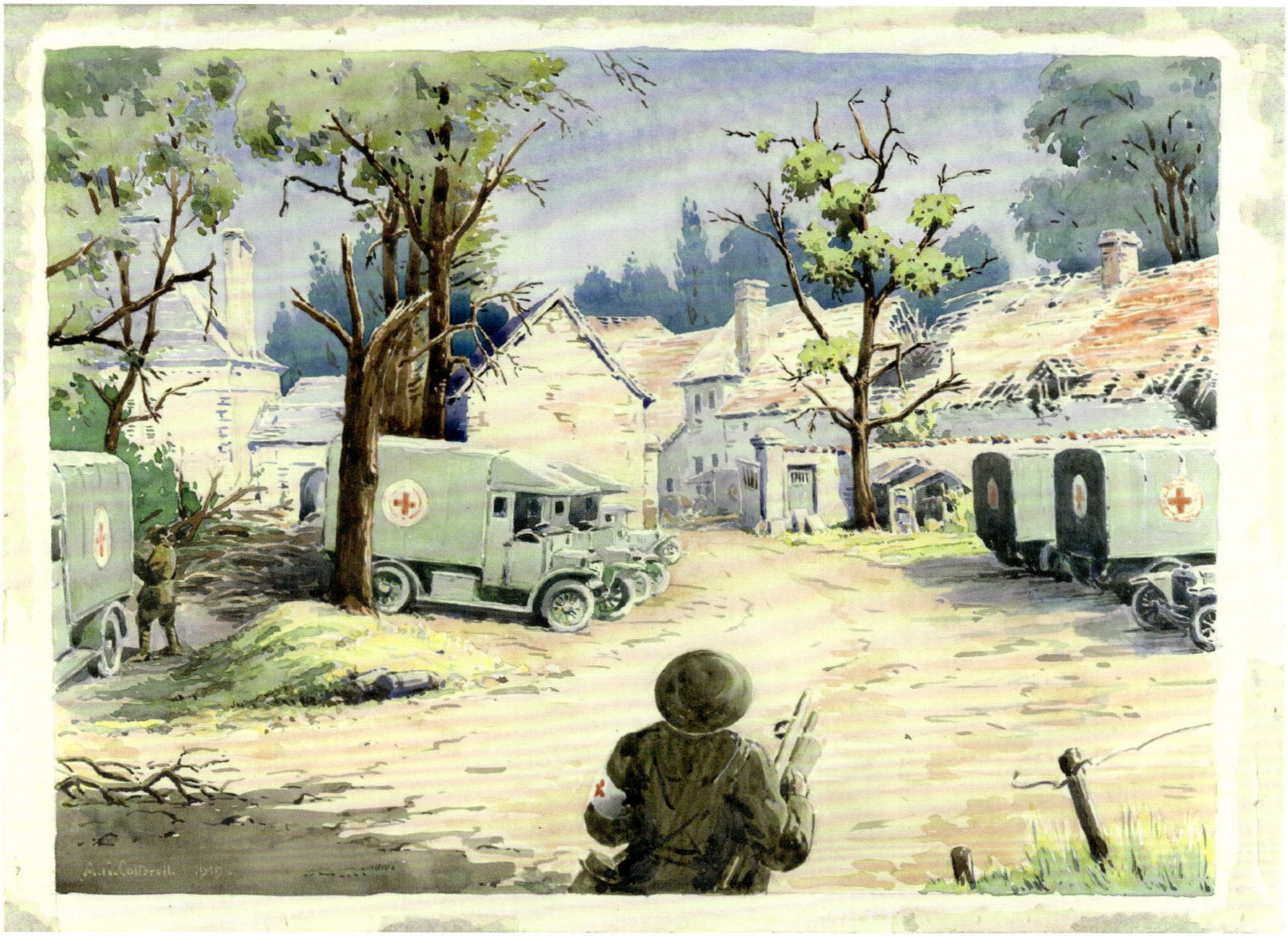

Arthur N. Cotterell | *Muizon on the Vesle, Reims, October, 1918: Cars of the Section Sanitaire Anglaise 13*
1919, Watercolour, 27.3 x 36.8 cm | © Imperial War Museum Art.IWMART LD1844

JAMES COWIE

(1886–1956)

A contemporary of William McCance at Glasgow School of Art from 1912 Cowie's route to studying art was somewhat different. His ancestors were non-conformist farmers and the young Cowie was expected to follow suit but he was determined to pursue other avenues and indeed he spent much of his life as an outsider in the Scottish art world; some of his contemporaries seeing him as an academic reactionary and maverick. Initially he studied English at Aberdeen University while also enrolled at the United Free Church Training College where he was taught art by James Hector (1868–1940) who recognised his prodigious talent. Cowie finished his course (but not the degree) with a distinction in drawing and for a brief period taught art at Fraserburgh Academy before taking his Diploma course in two years rather than the customary three as he could not afford the expense: 'Fra' Newbery (1855–1946) having seen his portfolio allowed him to do so.

Shortly before the outbreak of war Cowie was appointed art master at Bellshill Academy in Lanarkshire some ten miles east of Glasgow. A conscientious objector he appeared before the Glasgow Military Service Tribunal, in July 1916 it disposed of 6,145 cases.[24] Cowie was granted exemption from Combatant Service accepting a call-up into the Non-Combatant Corps (NCC). Cowie laboured from a base camp near Edinburgh before being assigned from October 1917 to the Agricultural Company Gordon Highlanders, whose work on the land was vital given the labour and food shortages.[25] In the same year he exhibited two works at the Royal Scottish Academy (RSA) but nothing again until 1921.

Following the end of the war Cowie returned to teaching at Bellshill Academy until 1935, when he left to become head of painting at Gray's School of Art in Aberdeen. In 1937 he moved to Arbroath as Warden of Hospitalfield College of Art succeeding the English sculptor Frank Dobson (1888–1963) and stayed until he retired in 1948. An influential teacher he had a profound impact on those he taught including the two Roberts, Colquhoun (1914–62) and MacBryde (1913–66), and Joan Eardley (1921–63); it was a period when he too was most productive. A fine draughtsman, Cowie's meticulous approach resulted in some of his strongest work while at Hospitalfield. A stiff formality in some of his compositions gave way to an interest in Surrealism although he eschewed participation in any surrealist groups.

During the war Cowie ran a drawing class at the local Royal Naval Volunteer station. In October 1941 he was commissioned by the War Artists' Advisory Committee to produce a portrait of a Scottish Civil Defence worker, which he submitted in the spring of 1944. In the same year he completed his large and ambitious metaphysical oil painting *Evening Star* which he had been working on intermittently from 1937: with its subtleties of tone and surreal motifs it was he believed his 'most profound and important statement … [combining] all the elements that had obsessed him through many years.'[26] It shows the influence of Paul Nash whose work he discovered in the mid-1920s; traces of this debt are also discernible in *Still Life with Glass, Apple and Spoon* (1944). 'Cowie admired Paul Nash and the English painter's example might well lie behind his habit of placing objects enigmatically in the foreground of a landscape as he does in *Still Life with Glass, Apple and Spoon* … These odd juxtapositions and the consequent disjunctions of scale create a sense of mystery.'[27]

Cowie moved to Edinburgh in 1948 when he became secretary of the RSA. His career came to an abrupt close when he suffered a major stroke, dying three and half years later. ◆◆◆

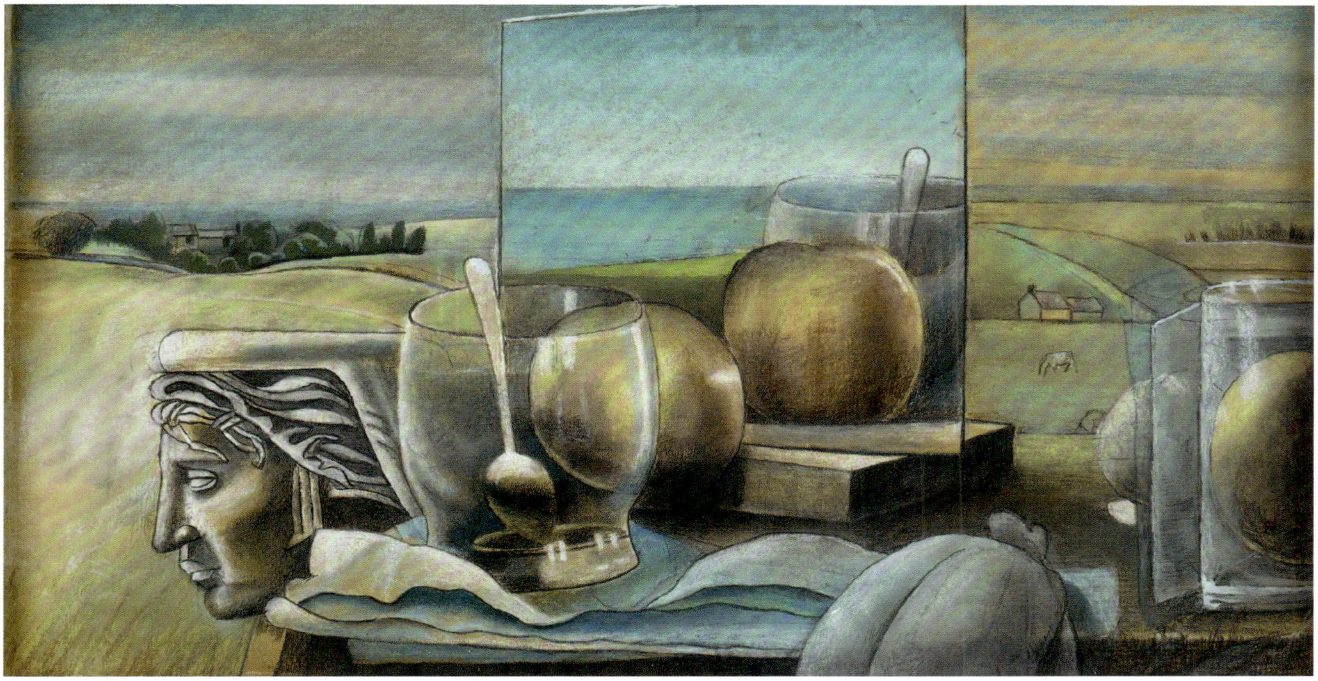

James Cowie | *Still Life with Glass, Apple and Spoon* | 1944, Mixed media, 25 x 47 cm | © Ruth Christie / The Scottish Gallery

RONALD OSSORY DUNLOP

(1894–1973)

Dunlop who was born in Dublin came from an artistic Irish-Scottish Quaker family; the son of watercolour artist Eleanor Fitzpatrick and theosophist and artist Daniel Nicol Dunlop. He attended evening classes at Manchester Art School. A conscientious objector, Dunlop appeared before a Tribunal hearing in Wimbledon on 10 July 1916, which focused on his Quaker roots; his occupation was listed as Advertisement Writer and Designer. The Tribunal exempted him from Combatant Service provided he joined the Friends Ambulance Unit where he was assigned to undertake Agricultural Work. From September 1916 his work on the land comprised spells at Jordans, Buckinghamshire; Lutterworth, Lincolnshire and some seven months in Mapletons' factory, Garston some ten miles from Liverpool. The company, founded by Hugh Mapleton a Quaker in c.1903, was a pioneer in the manufacture of health foods particularly nut products. From there he went to Abrams Hale, Cheshire and Nixon & Co., Altrincham before being demobilised on 1 February 1919.

Post-First World War Dunlop studied at Wimbledon Art School under the guidance of landscape painter, Alfred James Collister. Dunlop felt he received his first really sound training in art and began to explore there his feeling for the poetic moods of nature. In 1923 Dunlop founded, with several poets and other literary friends, the short-lived Emotionist Group. A prolific exhibitor, he had his first solo show in 1928 at the Redfern Gallery.

Struggling with Paint, his autobiography published in 1956, traces his difficulties producing works of art and explains that he did not believe in going into detail about personal matters. Instead Dunlop points out that 'there are many things that happen which have a distinct bearing upon the development of one's life as a painter.'[28] The reader is left to intuit what bearing his wartime work on the land had. During the Second World War Dunlop continued to paint albeit he had difficulty getting permission to paint landscapes on the Thames. Frequently accosted by the Home Guard and River Police he allayed their suspicions only on production of his identity card and Ministry of Information permit. At the end of war Dunlop moved from London to the south coast to the village of Barnham. He was attracted to the light of West Sussex, finding it more intense and diffuse than the grey light of Surrey. He continued to write and paint landscape and seascape, portraiture and still life, and was elected a Royal Academician in 1950. ◆◆◆

MARK GERTLER

(1891–1939)

Gertler was born into a poor Jewish family in Spitalfields, London but by the time of his suicide in 1939 his death was front-page news. Prodigiously talented he commenced art classes at Regent Street Polytechnic in 1906 before attending the Slade from 1908 supported by The Jewish Educational Society. He studied when the Slade was at its zenith alongside an exceptionally talented generation of young artists including Bomberg, Nash, Nevinson, Wadsworth and Dora Carrington. Gertler's protracted relationship with Carrington and his 'unrequited passion'[29] for her was to cause him much tumult. Regarded as the best draughtsman since Augustus John, Gertler won a Slade scholarship (1909) and various prizes (1910) culminating with the award of a British Institution scholarship when he left in 1912.

Gertler's artistic talents were recognised by civil servant and arts patron Edward 'Eddie' Marsh (1872–1973) who had been introduced to him by the painter John Currie (c.1884–1914) and sculptor Henri Gaudier-Brzeska (1891–1915) at the Allied Artists exhibition at the Albert Hall in summer 1913. In addition to buying Gertler's work which he found highly original he provided him with a regular allowance, which was crucial to his early career. Lady Ottoline Morrell (1873–1938), the literary hostess, also became a friend and staunch supporter, taking Gertler under her wing towards the end of the following year and introducing him into her world. They had been introduced by Gilbert Cannan (1884–1939)[30] who wanted Ottoline to see Gertler's paintings as she was the official buyer for a six-month period for the Contemporary Art Society. Gertler later painted *Gilbert Cannan at his Mill* in Cholesbury, Hertfordshire following visits during 1915–16.

The outbreak of war had little impact on Gertler and moreover he believed that the best way to help was to *paint*.[31] In 1915 he moved to Rudall Crescent in Hampstead where he lived and worked for the next seventeen years. However, he was troubled by his financial dependency on Marsh and their opposing views of the war, which Gertler shared with many of his friends. Gertler wrote to Marsh on 19 October 1915 explaining that he did not want to hurt him as he recognised that his help had enabled him to do far, far better work than previously but he had:

> *.... come to the conclusion we two are too fundamentally different to continue to be friends. Since the war, you have gone in one direction and I in another. ... I am I believe what you call a 'Passivist'. I don't know exactly what that means, but I just hate this war and should really loathe to help in it. I wanted to do some war-work simply because the hateful atmosphere had got into me and it seemed difficult to create at such a time. But now I've changed my mind I shall paint as long as I can. As long as I am not forced into this horrible atmosphere I shall work away.*[32]

Gertler continued to work away but with the advent of conscription in January 1916 he remained fearful of 'being dragged away into this war'. He gave expression to these 'nightmare[s]' in a letter on 3 February to Samuel 'Kot' Koteliansky (1880–1955), the literary translator, expressing his fear that he would have to give up his studio when all he wanted to do was 'paint and paint'. Gertler was working feverishly hard throughout May on his large oil painting *Merry-Go-Round*, which was to be his masterpiece, although in a letter to Lytton Strachey that month he described it as *very unsaleable* and explained that he hoped to finish it in a few weeks. A study in red chalk by Gertler shows the profile of six female heads roughly stepped; of these three face right and three left, all with opened mouths and a separate study of an ear. The woman depicted in the top left-hand corner appears to relate to the innermost female rider in the upper, left-hand corner of the finished painting.[33] Strachey duly went to see Gertler's 'whirligig picture' and, writing to Ottoline Morrell on 3 July, he explained how if he were to look at it for any length of time, despite his admiration he would 'be carried away, suffering from shell-shock. ... but as for *liking* it, one might as well think of liking a machine-gun'.[34]

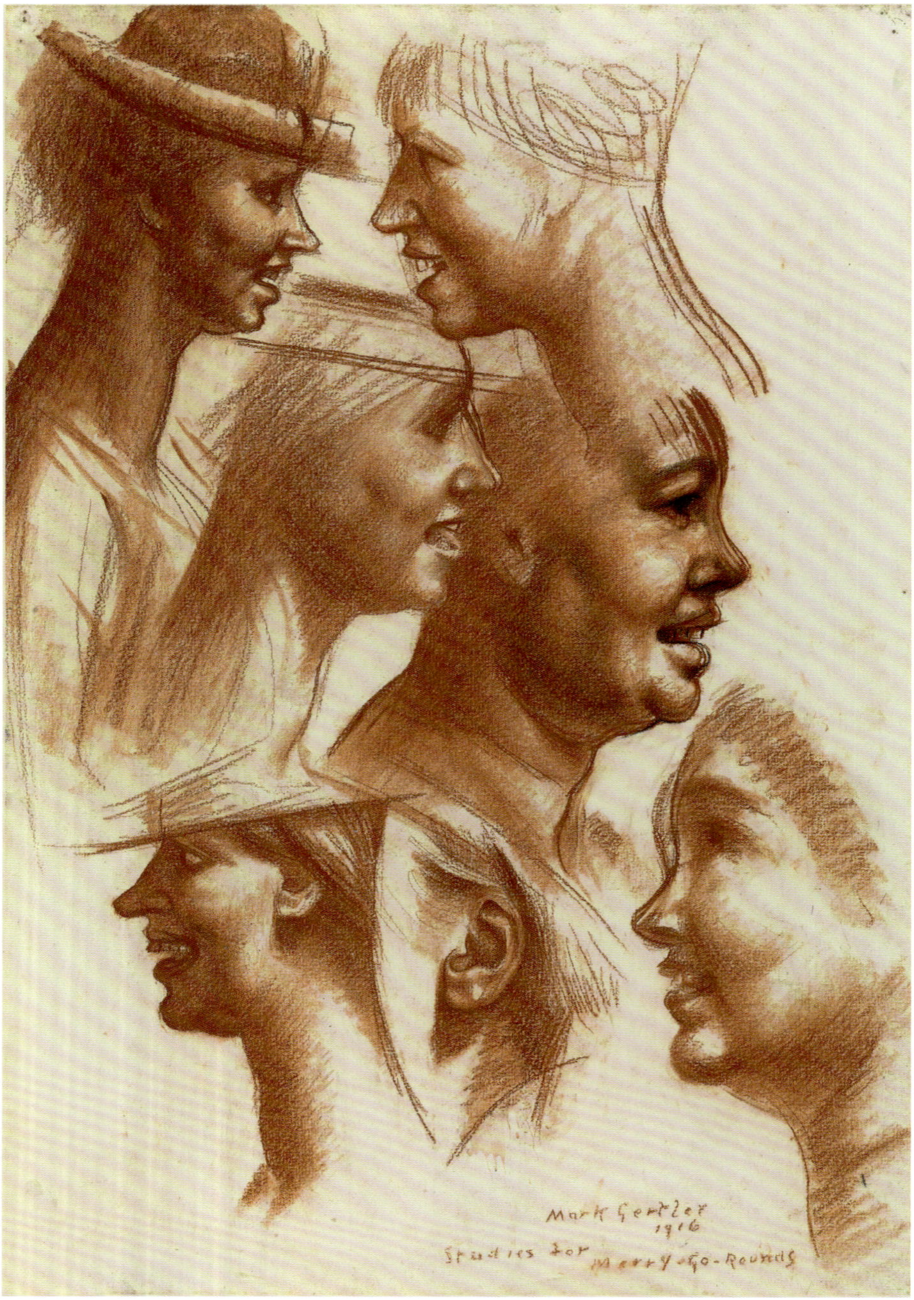

Mark Gertler | *Studies for Merry-Go-Rounds* [sic] | 1916, Red chalk on paper, 56 x 38 cm
Courtesy of Piano Nobile, Robert Travers (Works of Art) Ltd. | Private Collection

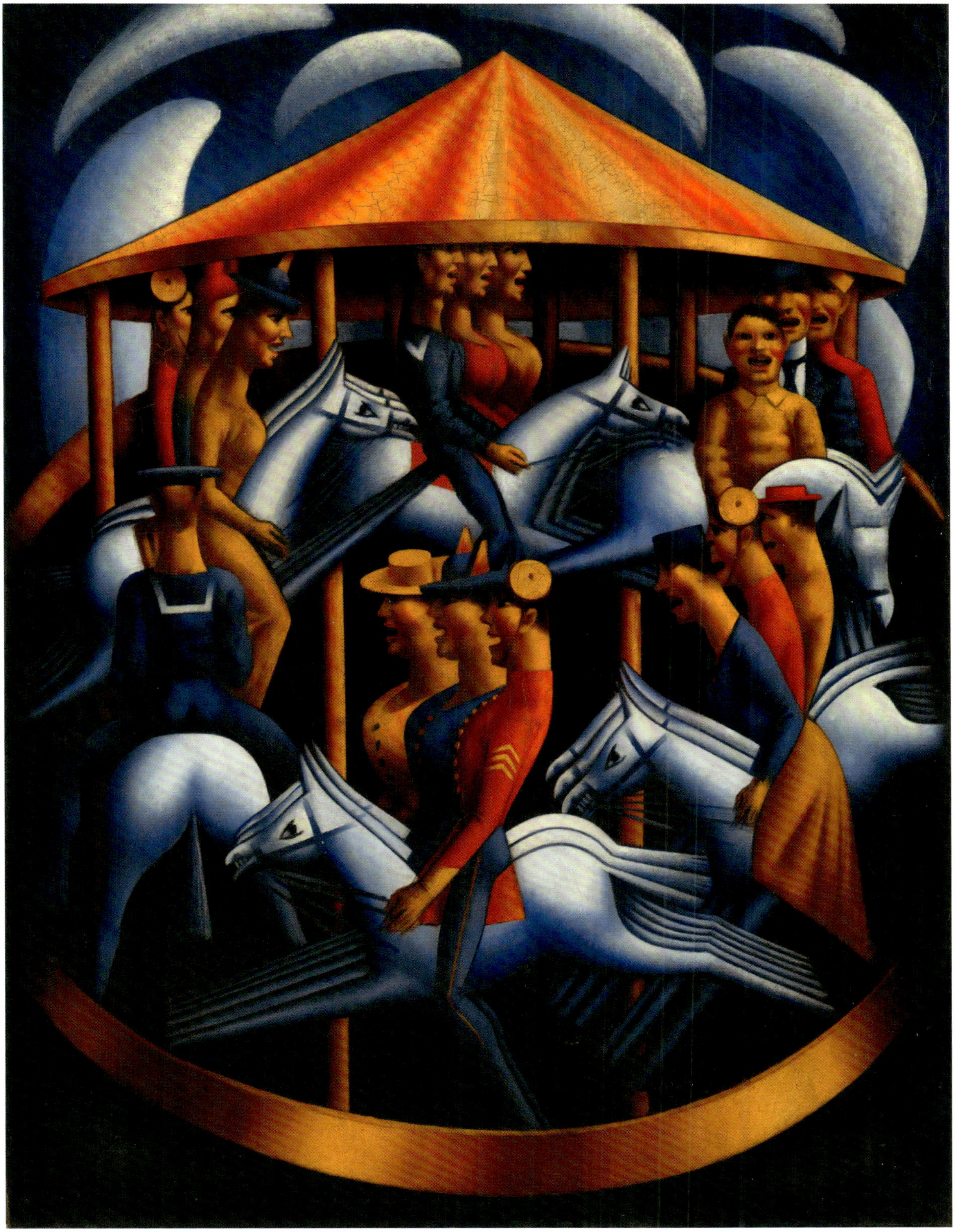

Mark Gertler | *Merry-Go-Round* | 1916, Oil on canvas, 189.2 x 142.2 cm | Photograph: © Tate London 2018

The annual fair on Hampstead Heath inspired Gertler's striking anti-war painting but his sentiments were not made explicit in either private or public at the time. The highly stylised satirical painting with uniformed soldiers and sailors and civilian 'riders' with mouths fixed in some rictus scream sit stiffly on the carousel's wooden horses as if imprisoned within it. Its structure conveys a feeling of a grotesque, violent world spinning out of control. It is a powerful projection of 'Bloomsbury's unease about the threat posed by war to independent thought, and the brutality underlying the rhetoric of heroism.'[35]

The eminent barrister St. John (Jack) Hutchinson (1884–1942) wrote to Gertler asking if it was wise to show *Merry-Go-Round* at the London Group exhibition. He had represented several writers who were conscientious objectors and was doubtless aware of Gertler's likely conscription and warned that there could be a tremendous outcry:

> *... the old, the wise, the professional critic will go mad with anger and righteous indignation – and what strikes me is that these symptoms may drive them to write all sorts of rubbish about German art and German artists in their papers and may raise the question acutely and publicly to our position.*

Exhibited at the London Group's show at the Mansard Gallery of Messrs. Heal and Son from April–May 1917 the comments levelled at *Merry-Go-Round* made no reference to war. Frank Rutter, the *Sunday Times* critic praised Gertler claiming he is:

> *at his brazen best ... a joyous clash of metallic blues and shrill orange yellows, a riot we almost hear when we enter the gallery. It is the apotheosis of the steam organ in paint, and a style of decoration admirably fitted for the adornment of a popular restaurant.*

D.H. Lawrence to whom Gertler sent a photograph of the painting, found it anything but joyous describing it as 'terrible and dreadful' and was deeply affected by it recognising Gertler's anguish and seeing it as related to his Jewish roots. He wrote on 9 October 1916:

> *... it is the best modern picture I have seen ... But it is horrible and terrifying. I'm not sure I wouldn't be too frightened to come and look at the original.*
>
> *.... in this combination of blaze, and violent mechanised rotation and complex involution, and ghastly, utterly mindless human intensity of sensational extremity, you have made a real and ultimate revelation. I think this picture is your arrival – it marks a great arrival. I believe there was something in Pompeian art, of this terrible and soul-tearing obscenity Also I could sit down and howl beneath it like Kot's dog, in soul-lacerating despair. I realise how superficial your human relationships must be, what a violent maelström of destruction and horror your inner soul must be ... It would take a Jew to paint this picture. It would need your national history to get you here, without disintegrating you first ...*
>
> *You are twenty-five, and have painted this picture – I tell you, it takes three thousand years to get where this picture is – and we Christians haven't got two thousand years behind us yet.*

Nearly two decades later Gertler admitted to Hampstead neighbour and fellow-artist Randolph Schwabe (1885–1948) with whom he regularly walked on the Heath on Sundays that he kept *Merry-Go-Round* as it represented something to him such that he neither sold nor painted over it like those he didn't like.[36]

For Gertler work was his salvation from his troubles; another 'escape' was Garsington, the Morrells' home near Oxford but both were disrupted at the end of February 1918 when he received his 'calling up papers'. He told Carrington that he rushed immediately from his studio to the Recruiting Office in London but found that this time it was no mistake. Gertler appealed the next day and completed the form over lunch with Hutchinson and

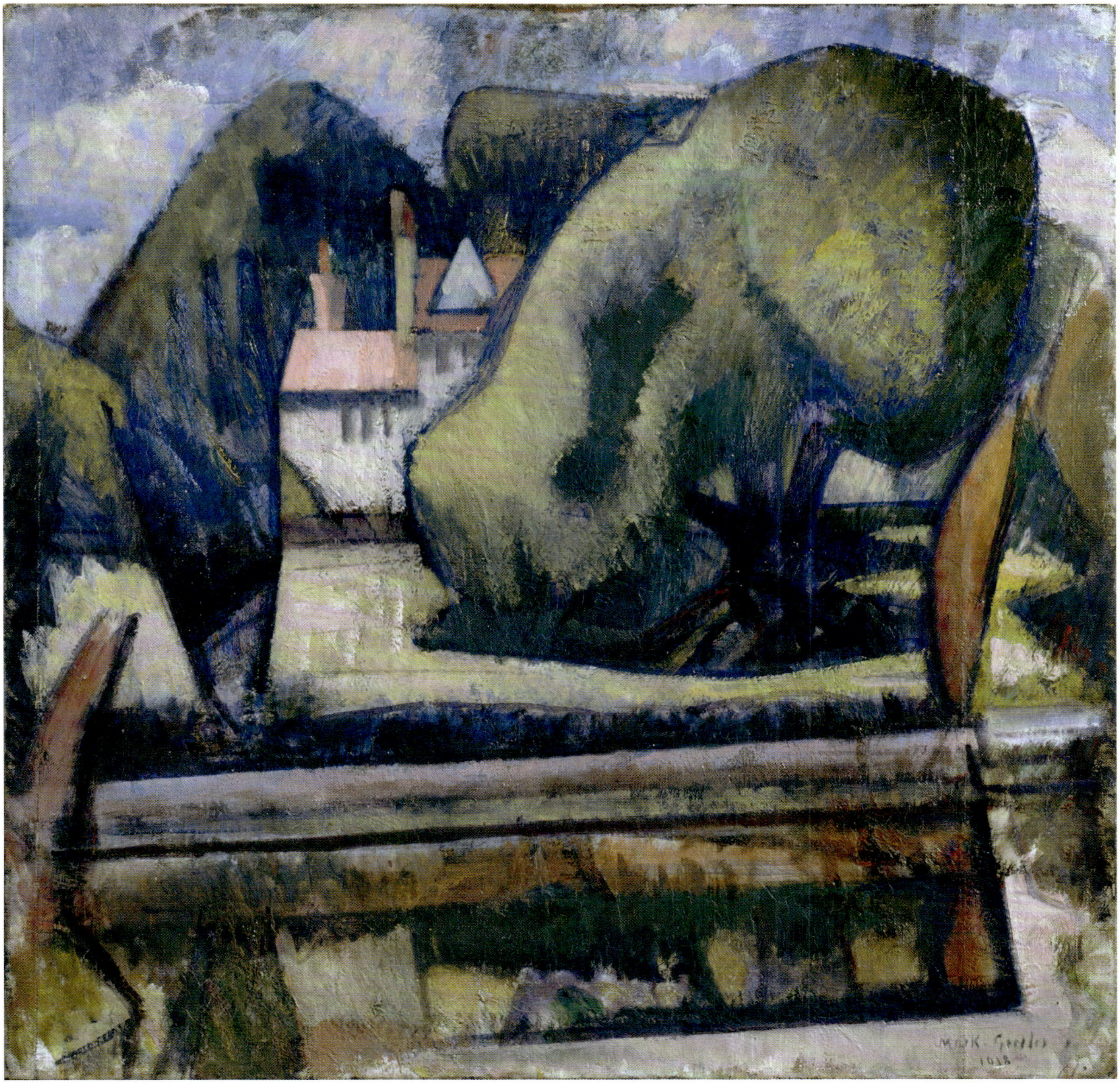

Mark Gertler | *The Pool at Garsington* | 1918, Oil on canvas, 75 x 75 cm | Photograph credit: Government Art Collections 2018

Monty Shearman, also a barrister and art collector, objecting on the grounds of his Austrian parentage but agreeing to do work of national importance.[37] He believed it hopeless to try and get off altogether. Gertler hoped the tribunal might let him work at Garsington; Ottoline had previously offered him employment and a studio should the need arise. Meanwhile Desmond MacCarthy (1877–1952), the literary critic and journalist, was trying to get Gertler work, as was Lady Tredegar. Their efforts ceased when it emerged that Gertler, following a medical, was rejected as unfit and as a consequence he was directed to work on Philip Morrell's farm, which had become a refuge for conscientious objectors. Around this time Gertler was offered a commission as a war artist by Alfred Yockney (1879–1963), former editor of the *Art Journal*, who was now employed by the Ministry of Information. The commission was for a scene on the London tube during an air-raid. It was finally cancelled as Gertler, bored by the whole thing, produced little or nothing.

Three years after the ending of the war Gertler had his first solo show at the Goupil Gallery but tuberculosis was never far away and resulted in his spending time in sanatoriums. He continued to paint and exhibit at the Goupil, his work showing the influence of Cézanne and Renoir; from 1927–31 he exhibited with the Leicester Galleries. Ill health and the effects of the economic depression marred the last decade of Gertler's life. From 1931 he taught part-time at the Westminster Technical Institute. His work was less popular and his show at the Leicester Gallery in 1934 failed. Always sensitive about his work and beset by money worries Gertler attempted suicide in summer 1936. The papers reported his death on Monday 26 June 1939. Schwabe learned of his suicide the previous Saturday from Daphne Charlton, and reported this at length in his diary commenting:

> *I am sorry that any man should be so miserable as one must be to put one's head in a gas oven. Gertler was an egomaniac: he felt the failure of his last show at Lefevre's (which nevertheless got good notices in the Press).*
> *He was bothered about tuberculosis: and his wife had left him. I think his work had been getting worse. Altogether a pitiable end for man of a real objective representational talent. … In our personal relations we got on well, I'm glad to say.*[38] ◆◆◆

DUNCAN GRANT

(1885–1978)

Duncan Grant spent his early childhood in India and Burma where his father's regiment was stationed. Aged 8 he was sent to school in England leaving early to study at the Westminster School of Art and later the Slade where he attended intermittently. In 1906 Grant studied for a year in Paris at Jacques-Émile Blanche's school, returning to France in 1909 when he visited Matisse and Picasso.

In 1913 Grant and Vanessa Bell (née Stephen, 1879–1961) became directors of the Omega Workshops in Fitzroy Square, London having been invited by the painter and art critic Roger Fry (1866–1934) the director and driving force behind it. He remained associated with it until 1919 and believed that designing for the workshops between 1913–15 helped him with ideas and experiments with materials. The results such as *Abstract Collage*, c.1915 were striking.

Grant, a central figure in the Bloomsbury Group, like most of the members believed the war to be wrong. Vanessa Bell, a member of the No-Conscription Fellowship, played a significant role in turning the group against the war.[39] Her collage known by the title *Triple Alliance* includes a fragment from *The Times* dated 1 September 1914 and may be alluding to contemporary events.[40] With conscription increasingly likely Grant was convinced by his friend the economist Maynard Keynes (1883–1946), who was working at the Treasury, that he and his friend and lover David Garnett (1892–1981) would have greater likelihood of exemption if they moved from London and worked on the land. Garnett's experiences with the Friends' War Victims' Relief Mission in France in 1915 had led him to become a pacifist. Clive Bell's (1881–1964) controversial pamphlet *Peace at Once* (1915) which was banned by the Lord Mayor of London as 'anti-patriotic' and later destroyed strengthened Garnett's beliefs (Vanessa Bell endorsed it though questioned whether the world would take it seriously) and he was in agreement with Bell's main arguments that war should be brought to an end as quickly as possible by a negotiated peace with Germany.[41]

Wissett Lodge in a remote village in Suffolk, a few miles from the market town of Halesworth, was to provide a temporary solution as it offered a location for them to work on the land. A cousin of Grant's mother Miss Florence Ewebank had recently died; her house was empty and the gardens and orchard neglected and in need of cultivating. Bell and her sons Julian and Quentin joined them in spring 1916 along with her cook and their nursemaid. A talented artist she painted with Grant on the limited occasions when he was not working in the mornings or afternoon and completed the bedhead *Nude with Poppies* (1916). Grant conceded that digging afforded him some time to think about paintings and his approach.

The locals viewed Garnett's and Grant's fledgling efforts as fruit farmers with much disdain and suspicion and in early May 1916 Grant and Garnett (known as Bunny to his friends) were required to attend the Blything Military Service Tribunal in nearby Bulcamp. Despite the attendance of their influential friends, specifically Keynes and Philip Morrell MP,[42] testifying as to the sincerity of their convictions the case was dismissed. Bell wrote to her sister Virginia Woolf (1882–1941) shortly after describing the Tribunal as consisting 'of perfectly bovine country bumpkins, whose skulls couldn't be penetrated at all. They would hardly listen to anything and one felt at once that it was quite hopeless.'[43] The Appeal, two weeks later in Ipswich was a very different affair with Keynes adopting an adversarial approach and in his prefatory remarks making plain the need for a swift hearing as he was required back in London at the Treasury to attend to more important matters. The Tribunal duly granted Grant and Garnett exemption from Combatant Service conditional on their confirming that they were undertaking work of national importance. A local representative of the Board of Agriculture visited them at Wissett but refused to confirm the work was of national importance concluding that they were doing the work of two women.[44] Clive Bell[45] who stayed with them on the fruit farm wrote to avowed pacifist and Quaker Edmund Harvey (1875–1955),

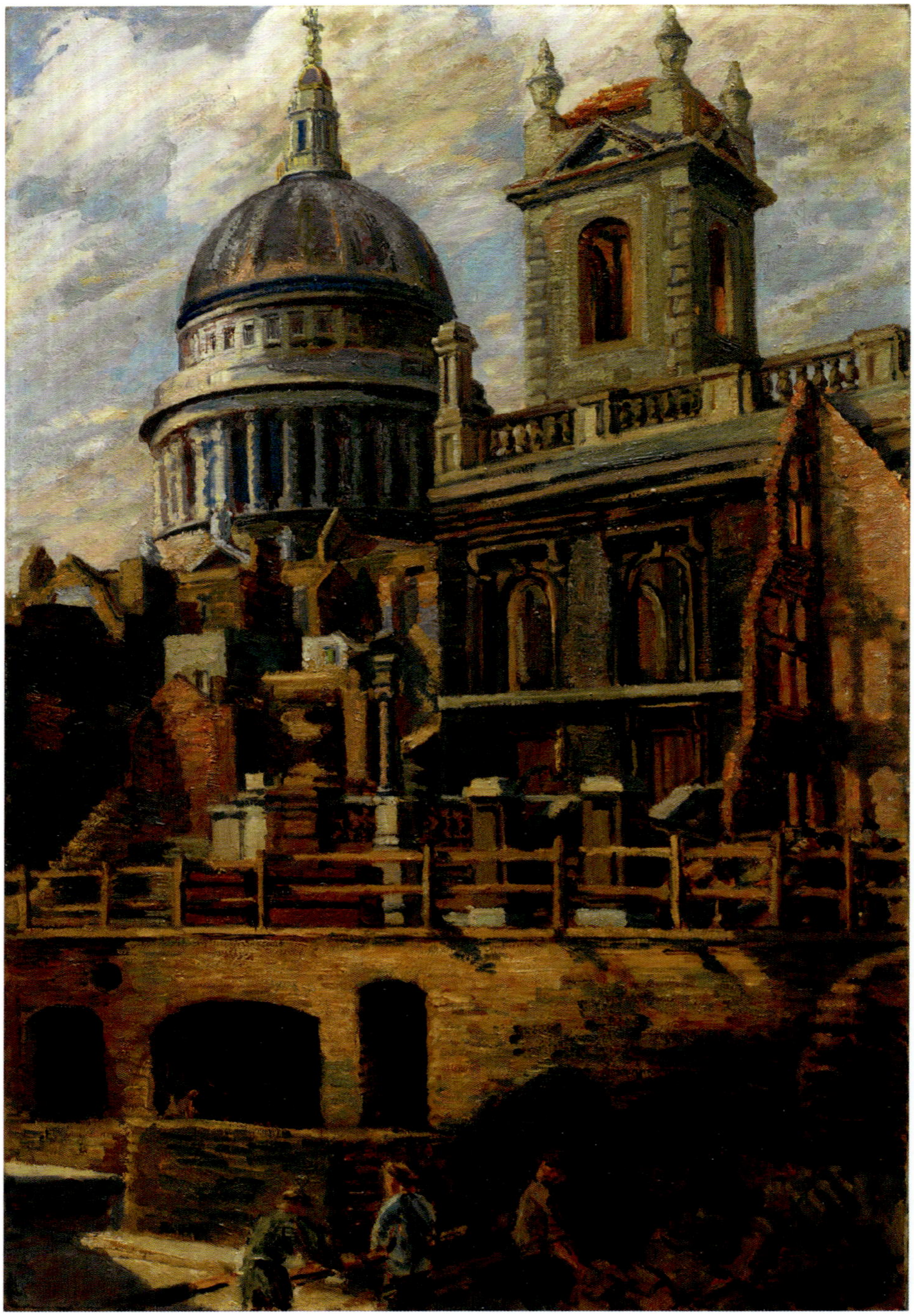

Duncan Grant | *St Paul's* | 1941, Oil on canvas, 91.4 x 60.9 cm
© Imperial War Museum Art.IWMART LD1844

the Liberal MP for West Leeds and member of the Pelham Committee and who was largely responsible for ensuring that the so-called 'conscience clause' was enacted in the Military Service Act 1916 to plead their case. Of Duncan Grant he said:

> *... [he] is, in the judgement of many competent critics, the best painter in England. He is doing work for which he is quite unfit, for which he does not much care, and which keeps him away from his home and friends; so I hope I am not committing a very bad indiscretion in suggesting to you, privately, that he is already sufficiently uncomfortable without further molestation. ... Is this a too testy letter? But to think that here at last is the Englishman who might be creating the masterpiece, for which we have all been waiting so long – and we set him to grow black-currants – not very well!*[46]

In September at a further Tribunal Grant and Garnett were given more time to find work that would satisfy the Pelham Committee, as they could not be their own employers as at Wissett.

Vanessa Bell found work for Grant and Garnett with a young tenant farmer Mr Hecks who needed help to run the 120 acres or so that made up New House Farm on Lord Gage's Estate on the Sussex Downs. Hecks agreed to employ them as labourers working a 7½-hour day on weekdays with a half-day on Saturdays at a wage of 12/6d. a week plus 5 pence an hour extra if they worked overtime. Bell rented Charleston Farmhouse, near Firle on the estate for them to live in, which was close to her sister Virginia's house, Asheham in Beddingham, near Lewes.

Grant found the endless work exhausting and the meagre diet insufficient such that he suffered in the second winter a severe attack of rheumatism. Shortly afterwards Grant met Robert Ross the art critic and dealer in London who was also a pacifist but declined a commission as an official war artist he was privately offered as he did not wish to join the Army, wear uniform and become a Major as was customary.[47] Unsurprisingly Grant produced relatively few pictures between 1916–18 these being largely still-lifes and studies at Charleston such as *Interior* painted in early 1918; its title 'pithily conveys the painting's inward-looking design and mood.'[48] After the war and free to paint again Grant's palette gave way to more rich and vibrant colours, which he handled assuredly, his popularity at its height in the 1920s and 30s 'remained buoyant' with the advent of war.[49]

In the Second World War Grant joined the Home Guard and accepted employment by the War Artists' Advisory Committee (WAAC) 'to undertake a few specific works, spasmodically or over a short period of time' as he believed the war justified. *Study for 'The Gunnery Lesson'* was undertaken in Plymouth in 1940 rather than Rosyth as first suggested as Grant thought the climate preferable to that on Scotland's east coast.

Sir Kenneth Clark in a letter to Grant in July 1941, observing that he had painted St Paul's many times, wondered if he would mind painting it once more:

> *... because I don't think it has ever looked more beautiful than it does rising out of this sort of Pompeii in the foreground and the Pompeii has all the elements of colour which I think you enjoy painting.*[50]

Grant who admired its design by Wren and dominant position accepted but was asked by E. M. O'Rourke Dickey, secretary to the Committee to let him know where he wanted to paint from so that the Home Security people could inform the police. Grant visited St Paul's but subsequently saw a photograph in *The Times*, which he felt, was observed from a better view and contacted the photographer to find out where he took it. Grant succeeded in capturing the indomitable spirit and splendour of St Paul's finally painting it from the basement of a bombed building nearby, and as Virginia Woolf wrote, over a decade earlier 'it looms over us, huge and menacing'. It was a place that much-inspired Grant and following his death in May 1978 was the setting for his memorial service. ◆◆◆

PERCY HORTON

(1897–1970)

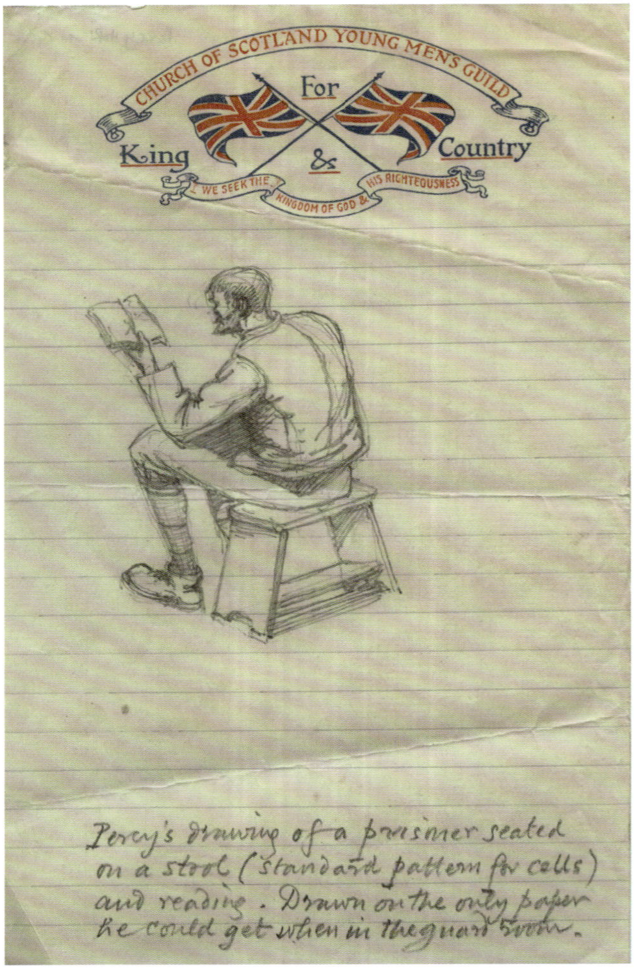

Percy Horton | *Sketch of Seated Prisoner* | c.1917, Pen and ink
© The Estate of Percy Horton / Liddle Archive, University of Leeds Library Special Collections

A scholarship student at Brighton School of Art Horton from 1912 studied on the south coast for nearly four years, under the painter and stained glass designer Louis Ginnett (1875–1946), before Ginnett enlisted in 1915 with other artists from the St John's Wood Arts Club.[51] Horton, a talented and prize-winning student passed the Department of Education Drawing Examination with distinction in 1914. While studying he joined the Labour Party and was to become an ardent socialist. Horton's opposition to the First World War led him and his best friend among the art students Royle Richmond (c.1891–1917), to join the pacifist No-Conscription Fellowship (NCF) in 1916. Founded in November 1914 the NCF was arguably the most important of the anti-war movement organisations. Its Statement of Faith declared it an organisation of men 'who will refuse from conscientious motives to bear arms, because they consider human life to be sacred and cannot therefore assume the responsibility of inflicting death'.[52]

Horton and Richmond regularly attended the weekly meetings of the Brighton Branch of the NCF, meeting Lydia Smith (1886–c.1970) a local teacher, Quaker and former suffragette who was Branch secretary and engaged to Richmond.[53] From late 1917 Smith was editor of the NCF's weekly journal *The Tribunal*, a potent symbol of war resistance from its first edition on 8 March 1916, such that the police actively sought to close it down. With the passing of the Military Service Act in January 1916 Horton and Richmond became liable for conscription. As conscientious objectors (COs) both had to appear before Military Service Tribunals to present their case for absolute exemption. Horton's took place in Brighton on 21 March 1916: he was refused and exempted only from combatant service. His case was reported in the *West Sussex Daily News* the following day under the sub-heading 'HOW TO PROVE SINCERITY.' He was quoted as saying:

The really sincere man is prepared to suffer rather than to act against his principles, and is not out to save his own skin. ... If I fail to get absolute exemption ... I shall appeal ... I cannot abandon my convictions, and must take any consequences which may arise from refusing to comply with the Military Service Act.

Consequences there were. Granted exemption from combatant service only, his appeal on 14 April was rejected and his exemption withdrawn, which resulted in his call up to the 27th Royal Fusiliers. He failed to report, was arrested in Brighton and taken under duress to Chichester Barracks. Taken by train to Edinburgh 'in irons and kit' where the Fusiliers were stationed; he was subjected to verbal abuse by all and sundry at Chichester station and only saved from being 'roughed up' by fellow recruits through the intervention of the duty sergeants. Refusing to put on his uniform he was forcibly dressed in khaki and a cycle of three Court Martials in Edinburgh ensued, the first on 7 August when he was sentenced to two years hard labour in Calton Jail in the city. Conditions were grim and insanitary, Calton having first received prisoners in 1817.[54] Horton later recalled the cold, silent and fortress-like prison with its lack of fresh air and poor food consisting almost entirely of porridge and sour milk and soup and bread, only on a Friday anything remotely like 'solid food' was consumed when prisoners were given potatoes. This together with Horton's first 13 weeks being spent in solitary confinement in a small semi-dark bare cell that was unlocked only for the short period of daily exercise or the delivery of food did little to maintain his spirits. Although he suffered no serious set-backs to his health at that stage, he felt his mind and memory rather deadened, as he had no material to read or draw with. Later scraps of paper and stubs of pencil were smuggled in by the Quaker Minister, Charles Thomson, who risked a fine by doing so, and was his sole visitor.

Horton remained in prison having been court-martialled for the third time on 17 May 1917 when he again outlined his objections to military service:

... I am strongly convinced of the sanctity of human life, and of the underlying spiritual unity of mankind. Believing that force, though it may appear to be an expedient, is in reality no argument or remedy. I look upon war as being not only immoral, but also absolutely irrational and futile as a method of deciding disputes between nations. ... It is my firm conviction that no righteous cause can be forwarded by violence, and that truth and falsehood cannot both use the same weapons ... I am prepared to return to further incarceration with perfect equanimity, knowing from experience that confinement of the body cannot affect the liberty of the soul.[55]

Stitching mailbags and mat-making during Horton's prolonged incarceration led to the development of a large ganglion on his wrist. In an article in *The Tribunal* on 13 December 1917 captioned 'Notes on Life in a Scottish Prison', the unknown prisoner (generally considered to be Horton) describes how the monotony was almost intolerable making over 1,000 mats containing 40,000 figures all stitched together in the same way. He described how his fingers felt 'dead' at times and that he had often sat down to draw and found no feeling in them. Horton had been taken to Edinburgh Royal Infirmary in November for an operation on his wrist where limited access to materials gave him the opportunity to make rough drawings of nurses and patients. These caught the attention of Scottish artist Edward Arthur Walton (1860–1922), a member of the Glasgow Boys who had moved to Edinburgh in 1904. Walton, a Quaker, who had visited Horton in prison offered to take him into his home to convalesce when he was released on medical grounds in early 1918, 'although still liable thereafter for military service in case of health recovery.'[56] Horton's release followed the Home Office's compiling of a list in response to adverse publicity about those COs considered 'at risk' of being too unfit to withstand the regime of prison life. Horton stayed for several months before returning to his parents in Brighton. In July 1921 Horton and Lydia Smith were married at St Pancras Registry Office.

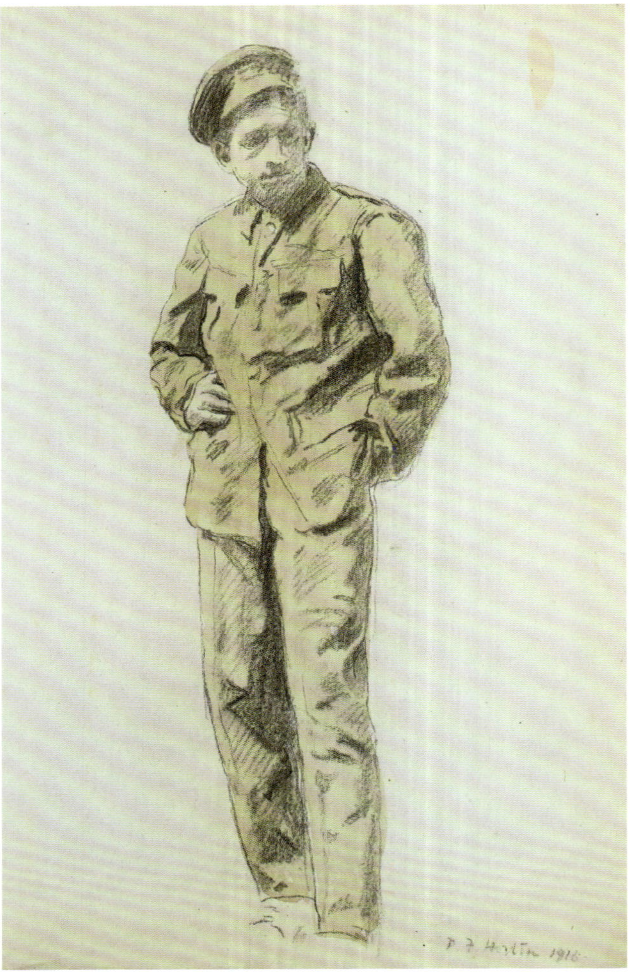

Percy Horton | *Portrait of a Private*
1916, Watercolour over charcoal, 37.5 x 25.5 cm
Courtesy of Sir Peter and Lady Coulson

Horton recommenced studying first at the Central School of Arts and Crafts and was much influenced by Archibald Standish Hartrick and then at the Royal College of Art (RCA) alongside Henry Moore, Edward Bawden and Eric Ravilious. He was awarded his Diploma with a distinction in painting in 1924. The following year he was appointed art master at Bishop's Stortford College; the headmaster was sympathetic to former COs having two others on his staff, unlike many other educators. In the 1930s Horton, who came from a working class background, taught three evenings a week at the Working Men's College in London. Horton's work 'shows a humane concern for ordinary people whom [he] depicted with dignity in a range of social roles. … *The Unemployed Man* (Sheffield City Art Galleries) [is] typical of his artistic, political, and social concerns.'[57]

Aside from his own painting Horton contributed regularly to *Left Review*, which before its demise in May 1938; 'provided the leading voice for the "art as propaganda" school of leftist literary thought … [and] attempted to confront seriously the aesthetic issues raised by political art'.[58] Writing under the pseudonym 'Toros', Horton implored artists to become socially committed. Horton also taught at the RCA from 1930–49, including five years in Ambleside in the Lake District when the College was evacuated in the Second World War. An active member of the Artists International Association from its inception in 1933, Horton was vehemently opposed to Fascism and revised his anti-war stance and joined the Grasmere Home Guard, participating in night patrols, he found the arms drill a bore. He was employed by the War Artists' Advisory Committee to undertake several commissions including *Blind Men Working on War Production, Lucas Factory, Birmingham* (1942/3). In 1949 Horton was elected Ruskin Master of Drawing at Oxford University and remained in this post until retiring in 1964. ◆◆◆

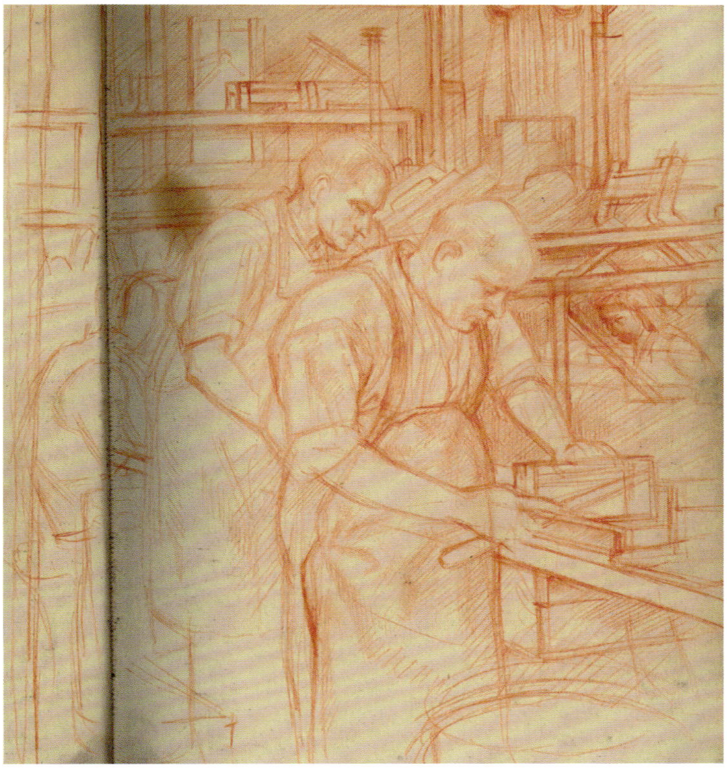
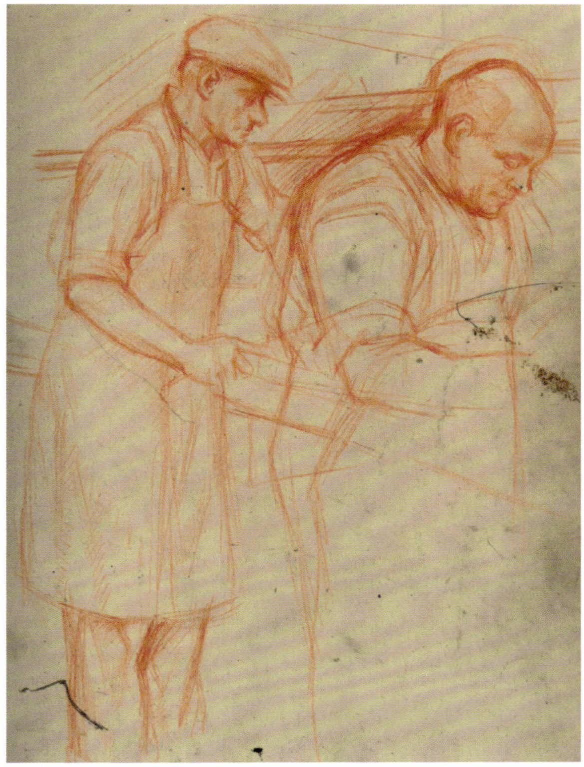
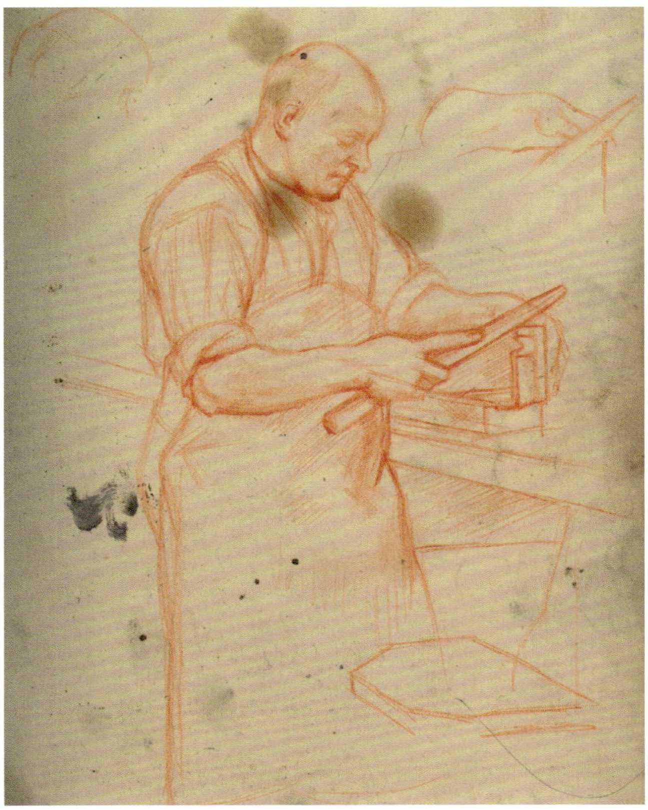
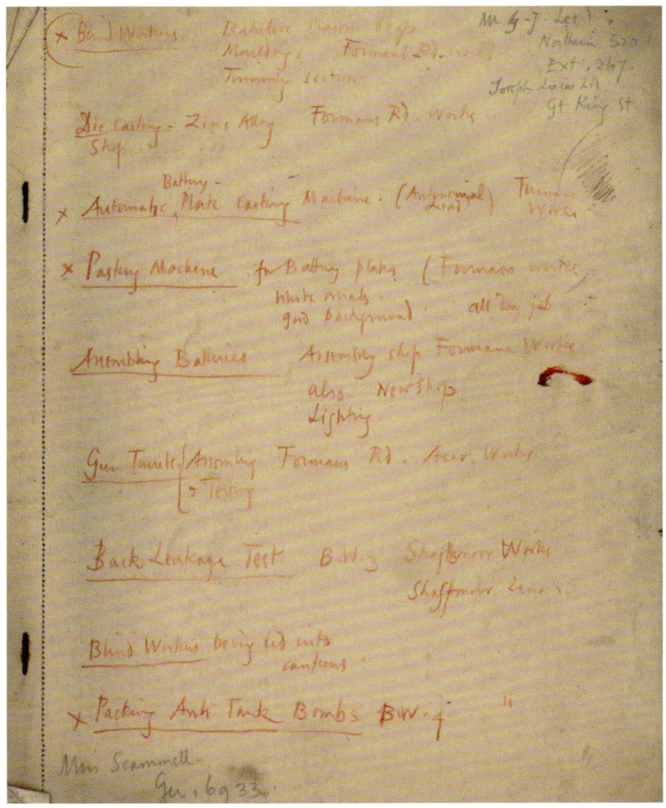

Percy Horton | Studies for *Blind Workers in a Birmingham Factory*, c.1942
Image courtesy Liss Llewellyn Fine Art | © The Estate of Percy Horton

(GEORGE) LESLIE HUNTER

(1877–1931)

Hunter was largely self-taught as an artist; he adopted the name Leslie when living in the United States, his family having emigrated when he was 15. Following a devastating earthquake and fire in San Francisco in April 1906 that destroyed his studio the day before his first one-man exhibition, Hunter returned permanently to Scotland where he worked in Glasgow as a magazine illustrator.

In 1914 Hunter revisited Paris and was greatly influenced by the Impressionists, especially Cézanne. He returned to Glasgow on the outbreak of war having been greatly distressed by being arrested in Étaples in August while on a sketching holiday and fled to Paris. From 1916 until the end of the war he worked on a mixed farm previously owned by his uncle at Millburn, near the small village of Larkhall in South Lanarkshire, although liable to conscription.[59] He appears not to have been 'pursued' selecting to do such work, which would have addressed the official direction, to undertake work of national importance. His biographer Tom Honeyman (1937), who later became Director of Glasgow Art Gallery, explains that Hunter 'could not fit himself into the idea of being an instrument for the infliction of hurt or death to another human being.'

Hunter painted in his spare time producing some fine and precise still lifes and interiors of the farm kitchen typified by *Cupboard and Kitchen Utensils*, (c.1914–18),[60] some developed from earlier sketches. He had the use of a large room on the first floor of the farmhouse and when not painting in the kitchen would work in the boiler room where he could set up a still-life composition.[61] Hunter held his second show with Alexander Reid, the internationally known Glasgow dealer, in March 1916. This received generally favourable comments in the press singling out his still-lifes that showed his interest in Dutch painting and his mastery of colour and form. Thirteen works were sold. He returned to Glasgow when the war ended and never returned to the farm.

It was not until the 1920s that Hunter established his reputation. Associated with the Edinburgh-based Scottish Colourists[62] he exhibited with Samuel John Peploe (1871–1935) and Francis Cadell (1883–1937) in 1923 and in Paris in 1924 when work by John Duncan Fergusson (1874–1961) was included. The work of all four was shown the following year in the Leicester Galleries in 1925.[63] His erratic life-style impacted on his work and in 1927 he returned to France where unsettled he moved frequently, returning to Glasgow two years later in poor health. He intended moving to London seeing it as more lively but died in December 1931. ♦♦♦

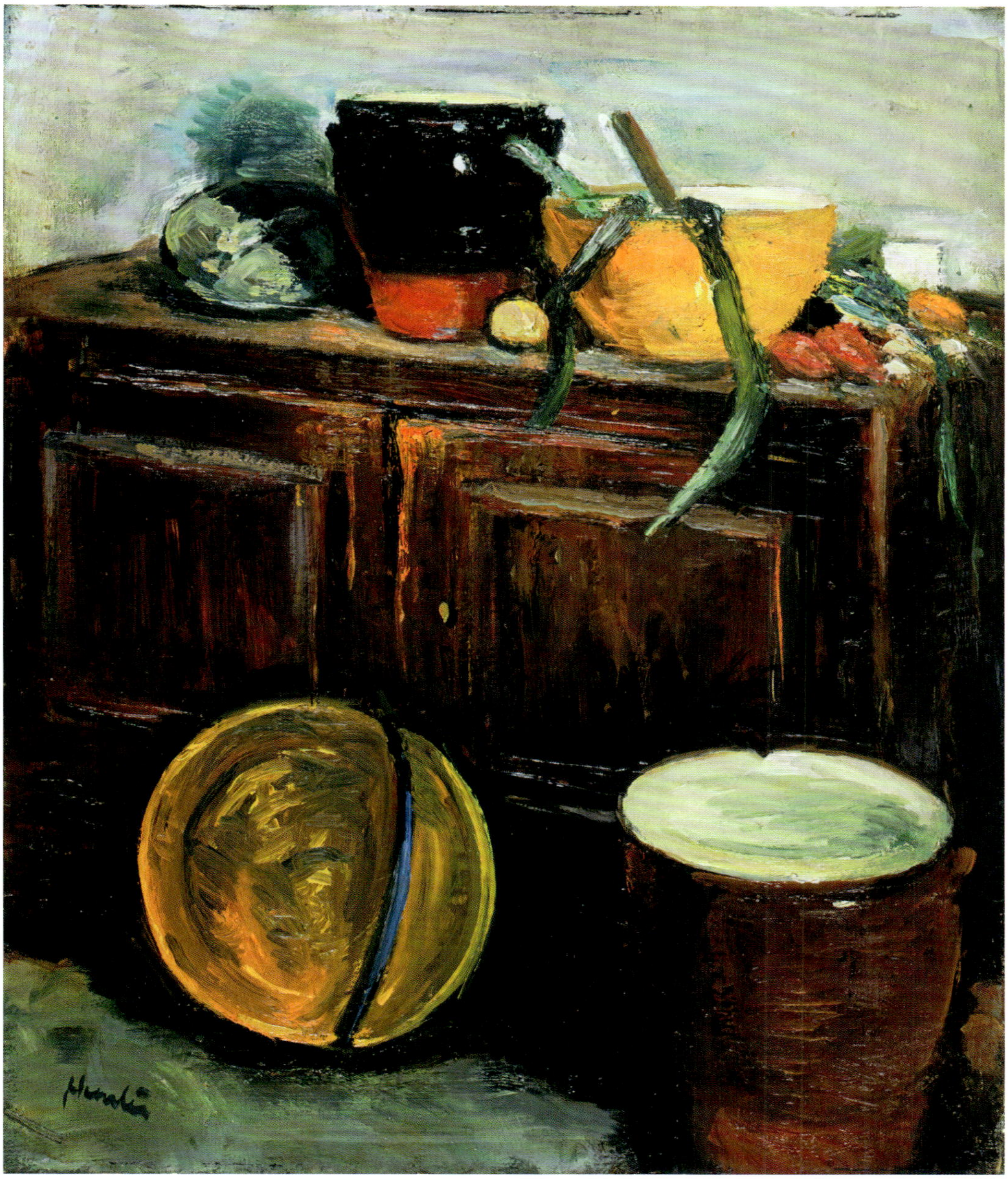

Leslie Hunter | *Kitchen Utensils* | c.1914-18, Oil on plywood, 45.7 x 38.1 cm
Tate, Presented by William McInnes 1935 | Photograph: © Tate London 2018

HAROLD KNIGHT

(1874–1961)

Harold Knight studied at Nottingham School of Art under Wilson Foster, an austere but influential teacher who had recently returned from working in ateliers in Paris and Antwerp, and who had a meticulous knowledge of anatomy. A 'star student' Knight won a number of competitions and a British Institute Scholarship which enabled him to study in Paris in 1896 where he attended the Académie Julian, training under Jean-Paul Laurens and Benjamin Constant. He later settled in Staithes as part of the small and rather scattered artists' community on the North Yorkshire coast painting local fisher folk. In June 1903 he married Laura Johnson whom he had met while a student in Nottingham and who had invited him to join her and her sister in Staithes. 'Their long, individual careers from this point onwards were closely connected …'.[64] They stayed in Holland for extended periods studying the Dutch masters, particularly Rembrandt and Vermeer and in 1906 the Leicester Galleries gave them a joint show in London which focused on 'Dutch Life and Landscape'. In 1907 they left Staithes for the warmth and light they had been assured they would find in Cornwall, going first to Newlyn before moving some years later to Oakhill, Lamorna Gate, a few miles south of Penzance.

The Knights' comparatively remote location meant their life at the outset of war was not greatly impacted. However, amendments to the Defence of the Realm Act 1914 which had given the government wide-ranging powers just four days after war was declared to help prevent invasion and maintain morale led to restrictions being placed on artists' activities. In 1915 painting any part of the coast-line was forbidden; restrictions were tightened further making it virtually impossible for the Knights who frequently worked *en plein* air to continue to do so.[65] There were fears that the Germans would invade. It was a difficult time for artists to sell work and with their savings diminished the Knights sold their Belsize car and moved from Oakhill to cheaper lodgings near St Ives.

A quiet reserved man, Harold Knight held strong convictions about the wrongness of war and killing and registered as a conscientious objector believing that nations' disputes could be settled by peaceful means. His pacifist views made him unpopular amongst the local community, many of whom shunned him viewing his behaviour as cowardly and selfish, particularly given distressing reports from the front. Knight's stance tested even long-standing friendships such as that with Samuel John (Lamorna) Birch. Birch was one of the first artists to settle in Lamorna and founded his own colony of artists and while too old to enlist had joined a local volunteer force. This involved his guarding Newlyn harbour and in view of the food shortage he also undertook agricultural work.[66] Knight, not a well man, refused to pre-empt any call-up by undergoing an army medical that would likely have declared him unfit to serve.

Knight's appearance before the West Penwith Military Service Tribunal on 6 June 1918 was reported in the *Western Times* on 8 June and the *Cornishman* on 12 June. A detailed report in the latter was captioned:

> *PENZANCE ARTIST CONSCIENTIOUSLY OBJECTS*
> *TO COMBATANT SERVICE*

Various questions had been submitted to Knight on paper beforehand to which he replied in writing. The *Cornishman* reported:

> *He objected to combatant service because he believed a human being was the highest manifestation of God on earth and to destroy even a body of a human being was to destroy a part of God. He believed killing man would be wrong to do as an individual, and equally wrong in obedience to an order from the Government. He did not object to non-combatant service. He objected to participating in the use of arms of any dispute, whatever the circumstances and however just, in his opinion, the cause. He would be willing to join some branch of service engaged in the saving of life but not military service, his objection to which was that to do*

so would be to become part of the military organisation, and perhaps be expected to obey orders which might be against his conscience. He had held these views since 1912. He was of the Christian faith but not a member of a recognised religious body. He was baptised and confirmed as a member of the Church of England but had ceased to be a member and had joined no other religious body. He had been offered work under the ministry of information for war records purposes which he had accepted. He was quite prepared to place his services as an artist at the disposal of the nation. He was quite willing to do agricultural work.

The work Knight had been offered by the Ministry of Information was to paint seaplanes at Newlyn harbour. Later Knight declined to carry out the work as he learned that it might be used for propaganda purposes.

At the tribunal Knight was asked to state any sacrifice he had made because of his conscientious objections. He explained that he had lost valued friendships and his career as a portrait painter had been prejudiced by the attitude towards the war he had felt compelled to take. In 1916 Knight painted a portrait of the Welsh poet W.H. Davies, who had been introduced to the Knights by the Icelandic poet Hamar. The group used to meet at the Café Royal. Knight was also asked if subsequent to the outbreak of war he had engaged in any form of philanthropic work for the good of the community. Knight informed the tribunal that he had painted a portrait for the Canadian War Records Office.

Supporting Knight's appeal was the philosopher Alfred Sidgwick who lived in St Buryan and had known Knight for some years who expressed in writing his conviction that his views were not for shirking duty although he disagreed with their lack of practicality. Bernard Walke, vicar of St Hilary (1912–36), a great lover of the arts, another supporter of Knight wrote that he had known him for the past four years and he held conscientious objections to military service in any form both on religious and ethical grounds and as such he could not accept military service without violating his convictions.

Tribunal members questioned Knight at length. The exchanges reveal a vivid picture of attitudes to and the processes COs were subject to (Knight's replies are italicised):

MR LAITY: You are a great friend of Mr Walke's aren't you?
– *Yes.*

MR LAITY: You were at a pacifist meeting with him?
– *Yes.*

MR LAITY: I take it for granted you are a pacifist as well.
– *Well, naturally.*

MR LAITY: I look upon a pacifist as a Pro-German.
– *That is not so.*

MR LAITY: He that is not for Me is against Me, surely?
– *I am willing to serve my country, but not in this particular way.*

MR LAITY: Then you would like to escape military service and allow another man to lay down his life for your freedom, and you are not plucky enough to help them?
– *From my point of view it would not be helping, because I think fighting wrong.*

MR LAITY: Then if other men acted on your principle the Germans would be here and we should be under the Kaiser?
– *That I cannot say. As I understand the teachings of Christ in the sermon on the Mount.*

MR LAITY: A lot of people bring in Christ as a side issue.

THE CHAIRMAN: If you saw a bully thrashing a woman, what would you do?
– *I should prevent him as far as I could, but not to the extent of taking his life.*

MR LAITY: Is it not a fact that you paint portraits and pictures for officers at Porthcurno?
– *I see no objection to that.*

MR LAITY: Of course not, it means a bit for yourself. I think you have been under the tuition of Mr Walke.

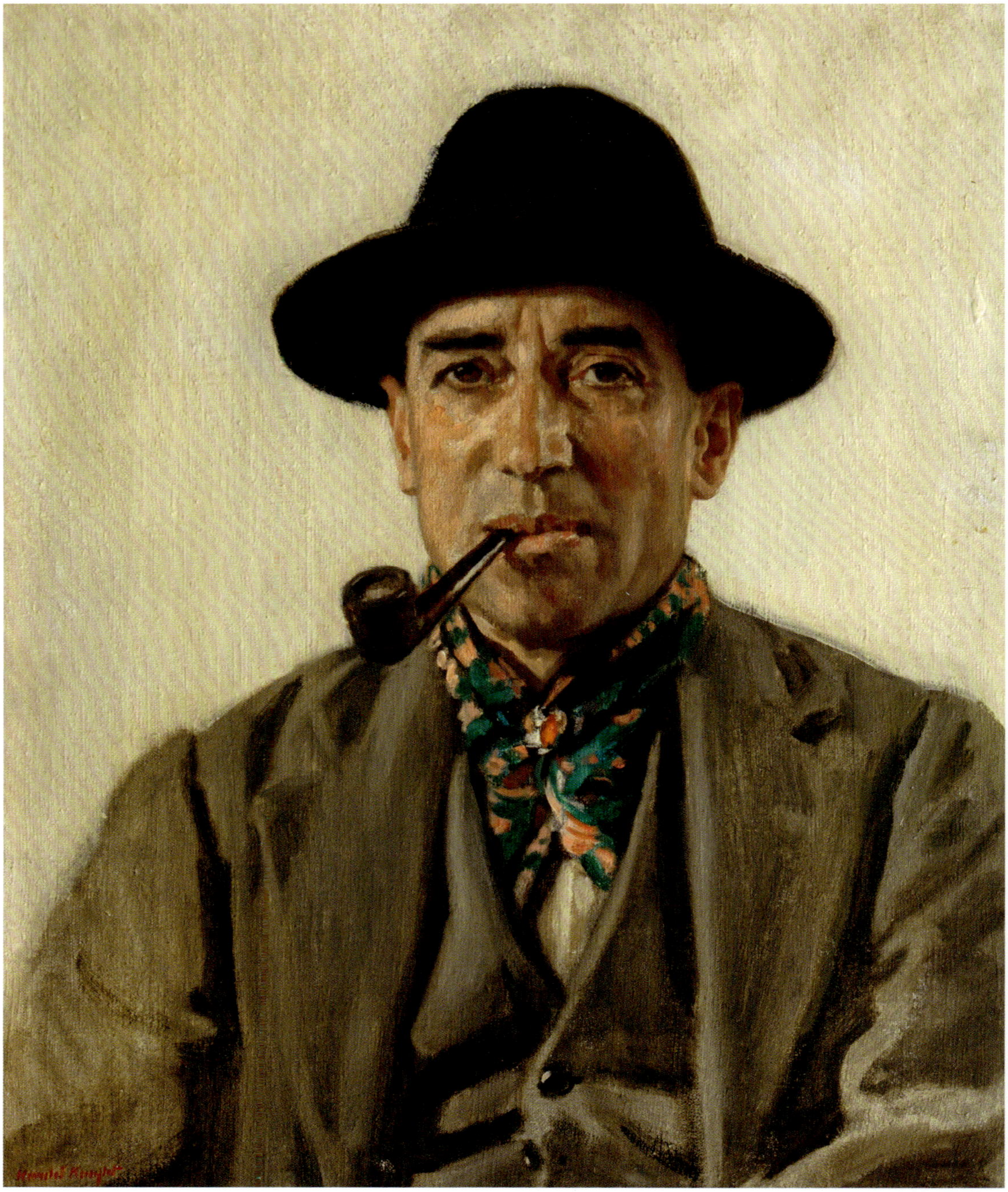

Harold Knight | *W. H. Davies in Cornwall* | 1916, Oil on canvas, 60 x 49.5 cm | © Reproduced with permission of The Estate of Dame Laura Knight DBE RA 2018 | Reproduced by permission of Cyfarthfa Castle Museum & Art Gallery

– I do not think so. If you mean Mr Walke has dictated my opinions to me, that is not so. I held them before I knew Mr Walke.

MR E. R. CARE: Can you tell us why you have not assisted in some work to help your country since the war started? *– I have had my own living to make.*

MR CARE: The Government would provide you with a living.

MR KNIGHT: *I have subscribed to the Red Cross and that sort of thing.*

MR LAITY: Mr Knight doesn't seem to care a hang who fights so long as he is clear.

The *Western Times* additionally reported that a tribunal member suggested that this was a fine opportunity for Mr Knight to go to Princetown (where fellow artist Claughton Pellew was imprisoned) to paint the portraits of the conscientious objectors there. The tribunal dismissed the appeal, the chairman remarking that if Mr Knight desired to get clear he would have to appeal to a higher authority.

Knight worked on a farm by the village of Zennor on the north Cornish coast helping to bring the harvest in when that was finished he worked alone engaged in the monotonous task of hoeing often in bitterly cold weather. As a result Knight's hands became blistered and calloused and for a time he was unable to paint. These experiences did little to assuage his depression and sense of isolation and rejection.

In January 1919 the Knights made London their base. For Harold it was an opportunity to pursue his future as a portrait artist and to escape the ill feeling experienced in Lamorna. Knight's greatest successes were in portraiture, some commissions coming from abroad, and for which he was best known. His 'safe' approach to painting contributed to his being somewhat overshadowed by Laura who was more outgoing and colourful in her work. Knight was elected to the Royal Academy in 1937, the year after Laura became the first woman so honoured. Knight died in Colwall, Worcestershire on 3 October 1961 at the Park Hotel, where he and Laura were now spending most of their time. ◆◆◆

HAYDN MACKEY

(1881–1979)

Mackey trained briefly at the Slade and at Langham Art Club in London. While teaching figure drawing part-time at Walthamstow School of Art in 1906 he met Walter Spradbery with whom he became lifelong friends. During the First World War Mackey served alongside Spradbery, whose pacifist views he shared, as a medical orderly with the 3rd East Anglian Field Ambulance, Royal Army Medical Corps (RAMC). Both enlisted on 14 September 1914.

While stationed outside Peterborough in January 1915 both friends exhibited in the Minster Precincts. Mackey, known as 'Mac' to his friends, included an unfinished portrait in oils of their then commanding officer Lt. Colonel Josiah Oldfield (1863–1953). The local newspaper reporter described the portrait as very life-like. His skills and those of Spradbery were noted with wry amusement in *A Record of the 3rd East Anglian Field Ambulance during the Great War* (1919). The compiler noted the joy of Mackey and Spradbery when in training at Thetford:

> *The craze for camouflage came along. Mackey in dirty canvas suit, big pipe in mouth and squashed cap on the back of his head; armed with a long-handled tar brush and several pails of different colour distemper, was a sight that few, who saw it, will ever forget.*[67]

Mackey served in France with the 36th Field Ambulance and on 26 August 1918 won the Military Medal near Mametz. When things were quiet on the battlefront he and Spradbery trundled an old handcart with their paints and brushes around and made notes and sketches.[68] *Epéhy*, was one of only a few paintings to be completed in situ. Another oil painting of Epéhy is dated 20 September, it was completed just a day after the short battle ended and the village was captured. Post-war Mackey worked many of these sketches up alongside a dozen or so artists who had served in the RAMC including Spradbery and Austin Spare (whose *Times* obituary he later wrote) in a studio in the Fulham Road, London under Lieutenant-Colonel Brereton. 'Working together in the studio, they would use each other as models for wounded soldiers, posing in bandages.'[69] Paintings, sculptures and models of their records of service were subsequently exhibited at the Imperial War Museum, Crystal Palace in June 1920. Mackey showed several sketches and his paint palette, which was much the worse for shrapnel fire, Spradbery's series of pictures depicted the actual fighting around Mailly-Maillet.[70]

Mackey established himself as a fine illustrator and was a close friend of many well known artists and literary figures including Frank Brangwyn, Dylan Thomas and G. K. Chesterton. Active in the local arts community as well as exhibiting widely Mackey took over the Presidency of the Essex Art Club in 1970, following the death of Spradbery, until he too died in 1979. ◆◆◆

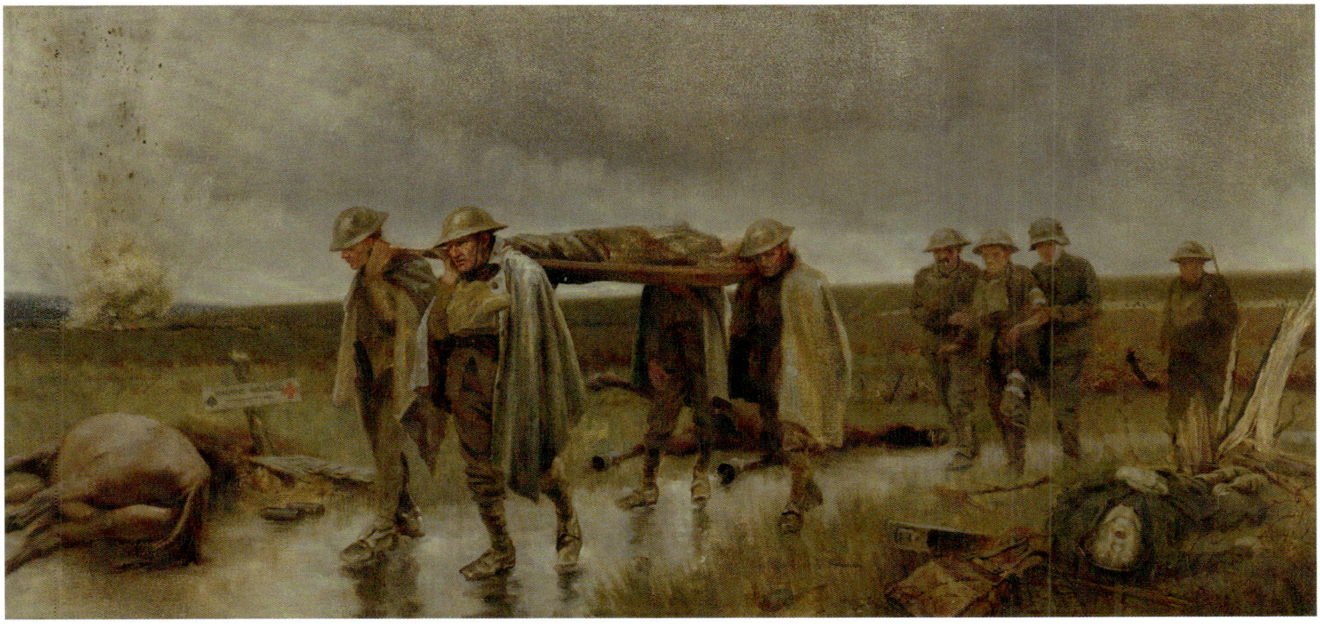

Haydn Reynolds Mackey | *Epéhy* | 1918, Oil on canvas, 75.7 x 145.1 cm | © Helen Power | © Imperial War Museum Art.IWMART LD3653

WILLIAM McCANCE

(1894–1970)

McCance entered Glasgow School of Art in 1911 on a scholarship, the same year that his father died in a coal mining accident. He spent four years training under the Director 'Fra' Newbery and was taught amongst others by Robert Anning Bell (1863–1933) and the Belgium painter Maurice Greiffenhagen (1862–1931). McCance was awarded the Haldane travelling scholarship in his final year in 1915; his examiners included the eminent Irish artist William Orpen (1878–1931). After graduating he embarked on a year-long teacher training course at Glasgow's Kennedy Street School and a teaching career beckoned but was interrupted by the war.

McCance, a conscientious objector, refused to go on parade with the Cameronians (Scottish Rifles) at Hamilton Barracks and was court martialled on 30 November 1917. He was sentenced to 112 days hard labour and sent to Wormwood Scrubs Prison in west London. In 1918 he was transferred to Knutsford Work Centre, Cheshire under the Home Office Scheme having appeared before the Central Tribunal at the 'Scrubs.' Knutsford, previously a prison had been cleared of ordinary prisoners to accommodate conscientious objectors. This involved removing locks on cell doors and renaming them rooms and allowing inmates to wear civilian clothes (warders wore plain clothes), and go outside in the evenings until 9.30 and on Sundays but the prison atmosphere remained. McCance was also imprisoned in Warwick Work Centre where similar changes occurred and prison regulations suspended; his art training led to him being put in charge of the re-painting of buildings.[71] He was given leave to marry fellow student Agnes Miller Parker (1895–1980), the wedding took place on 6 July 1918 in Bucklow,[72] despite her conservative father being unimpressed on meeting McCance seeing him as idealistic and opinionated.[73]

Discharged in 1919,[74] McCance and Miller Parker moved to London later that year where they spent the next 10 years living initially in Earls Court, where fellow artist William Roberts rented a room in their flat. They later moved to Chiswick staying there until 1929 where their neighbours included like-minded artists, writers and politicians. The series of semi-abstract and dramatic anti-war paintings including *Heavy Structures in a Landscape Setting* which suggests a military gun battery and *Conflict* that McCance produced c.1922 owe much to his social and political milieu and the influence of Wyndham Lewis, William Roberts and the Vorticists. The bright, garish colours of these highly stylized paintings show something of his radical modernist vision. The mechanical forms in *Conflict* exude tension and a feeling that something sinister and threatening is about to happen; a tall primeval-like being menacingly towers over other multi-faceted, angular grotesque forms. Conflict could erupt dramatically at any moment.

From 1923–26 McCance wrote regularly for *The Spectator*, pronouncing incisively on a variety of topics including modern painters, pottery, printmaking and architecture. Although he did not return to Scotland until 1960 he was an ardent supporter of the Scottish Renaissance, which had been established in the 1920s by poet and Scottish nationalist Hugh MacDiarmid (born Christopher Murray Grieve, 1892–1978) and was largely a literary movement although its influence was much wider. McCance also contributed articles and illustrations to MacDiarmid's short-lived literary, cultural and political journal the *Scottish Nation* which was devoted to Scottish interests.

In 1930 McCance became Controller of the Gregynog Press in rural mid-Wales which had been established in 1922 by Margaret and Gwendoline Davies. Blair Hughes Stanton (1902–81) became principal engraver and his wife Gertrude Hermes (1901–83) together with Agnes Miller Parker, both gifted wood engravers, were employed on a salary. The private press produced nine high quality limited edition books and scores of pamphlets during the three years McCance was controller but such was the workload that he stopped painting.

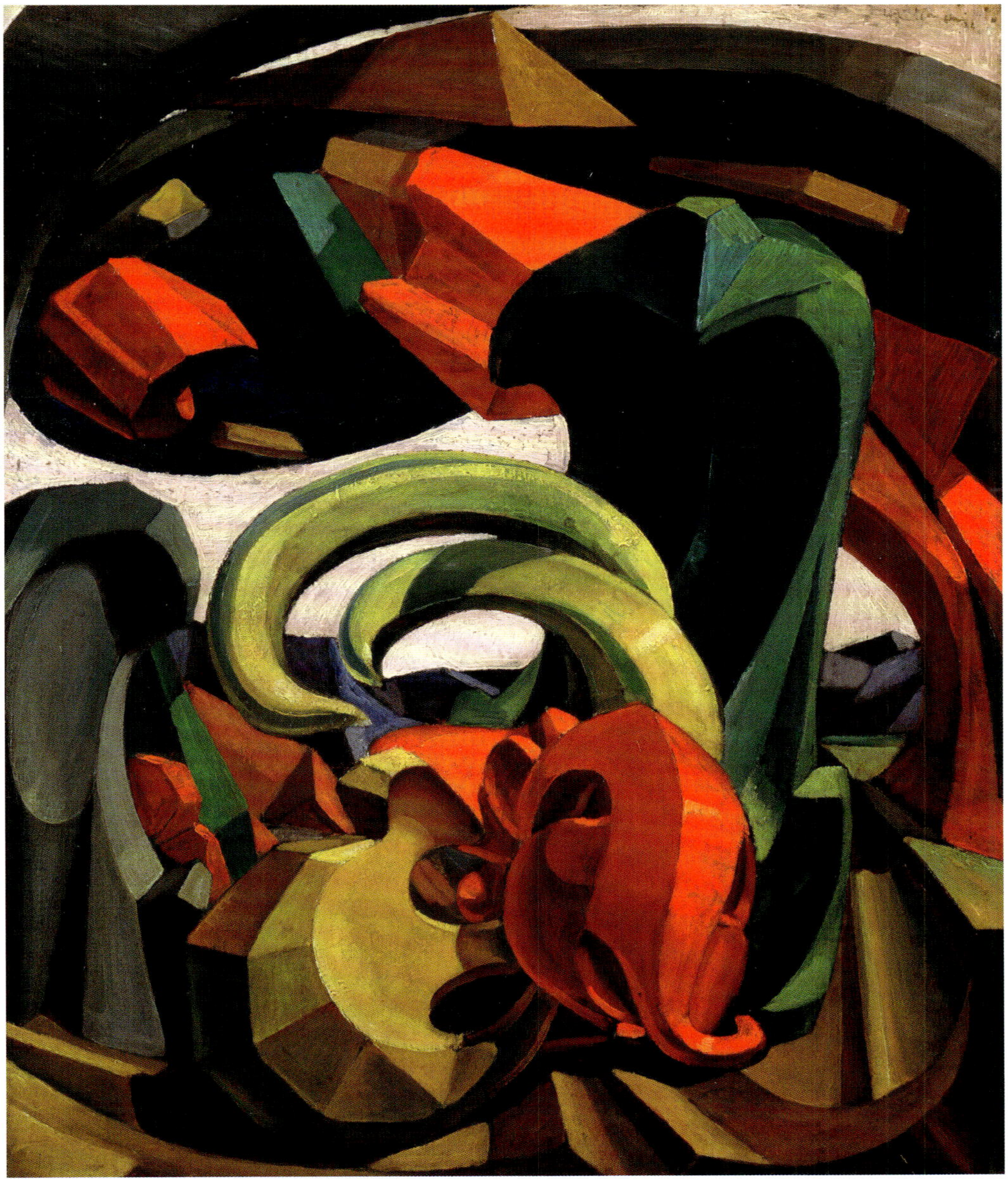

William McCance | *Conflict* | 1922, Oil on canvas, 76 x 63.5 cm | © Margaret McCance / Glasgow Museums

McCance resumed his art criticism in 1936 writing for *Picture Post, Reynolds News* and *News Chronicle* amongst other publications. He continued to paint, print and sculpt. Earlier he had written on matters related to the economy, becoming involved with the Douglas Social Credit Group the goal of which was a radical change in the credit policy of banks. McCance remained concerned for national issues whether economic, social or political.

In 1943–44 McCance succeeded artist, author and wood engraver Robert Gibbings (1889–1959) at Reading University, where he lectured on typography and book production in the School of Art. His paintings of this period once more responded to the horrors of a world at War, most notably *Hiroshima*. From 1960 he returned to Scotland settling in Girvan in Ayrshire. While he rarely exhibited he remains one of the most inventive British artists of the 1920s. ◆◆◆

GEORGE PEACE MICKLEWRIGHT

(1893–1951)

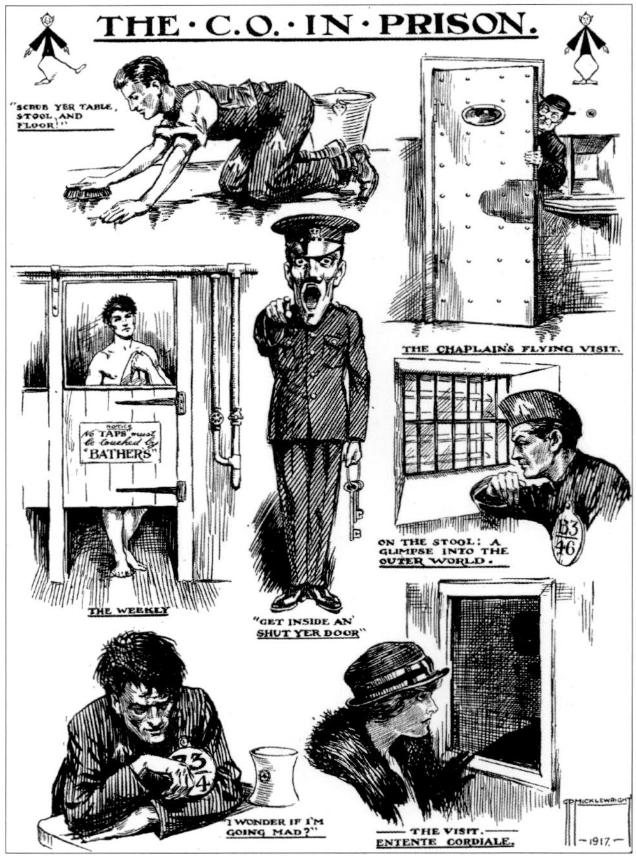

G. P. Micklewright | *The C.O. in Prison, the Ideal,* 1917
© Reserved, from the collections of the
Religious Society of Friends (Quakers) in Britain

Micklewright was born in West Bromwich and attended Ryland Memorial School of Art in Lodge Road in the town. He furthered his studies like many other young artists by going to Paris. Little is known however about the specifics of his training and/or career.

Micklewright, in all likelihood a Quaker, appeared before a local tribunal in summer 1916 to apply for exemption from military service on the grounds of being a conscientious objector (CO). His arrest is reported on 29 August 1916. The Magistrates Court comments are recorded as 'Absentee': Micklewright had failed to answer his call-up. This led to Court Martial at the Lichfield Barracks; the Depot of the South Staffordshire Regiment on 31 August. Micklewright was sentenced to 84 days hard labour, which was commuted to 56 to be served at Wormwood Scrubs. The cycle continued; on 27 September he appeared before the Central Tribunal at 'the Scrubs' and was recognised as a genuine conscientious objector, class A and offered admission to the Home Office Scheme. This entailed Micklewright agreeing to undertake civilian work under civilian control in specially created Work Centres. He was sent initially to Warwick on 27 October 1916 where he remained for nearly a year before being transferred to Princetown Work Centre on 28 August 1917. Like many COs, Micklewright was not allowed to work near his family. In 1917, while at Princetown he drew a memorable series of cartoons of COs for which he is best known, these provide a vivid portrayal of how his fellow war resisters were viewed by their pro-war contemporaries. At Dartmoor, (where Claughton Pellew was also transferred on the same day), Micklewright continued working on the drawings of COs. *What a C.O. Feels Like* appeared in a Home Office Work Camp newsletter. *The C.O. in Prison* another in his series gives a view of the harsh life inside experienced, and *C.O.s at Dartmoor* parodies work on the land.

Post-war Micklewright established something of a reputation for his designs for book jackets, which were largely for novels, including adventures, westerns and mysteries. ◆◆◆

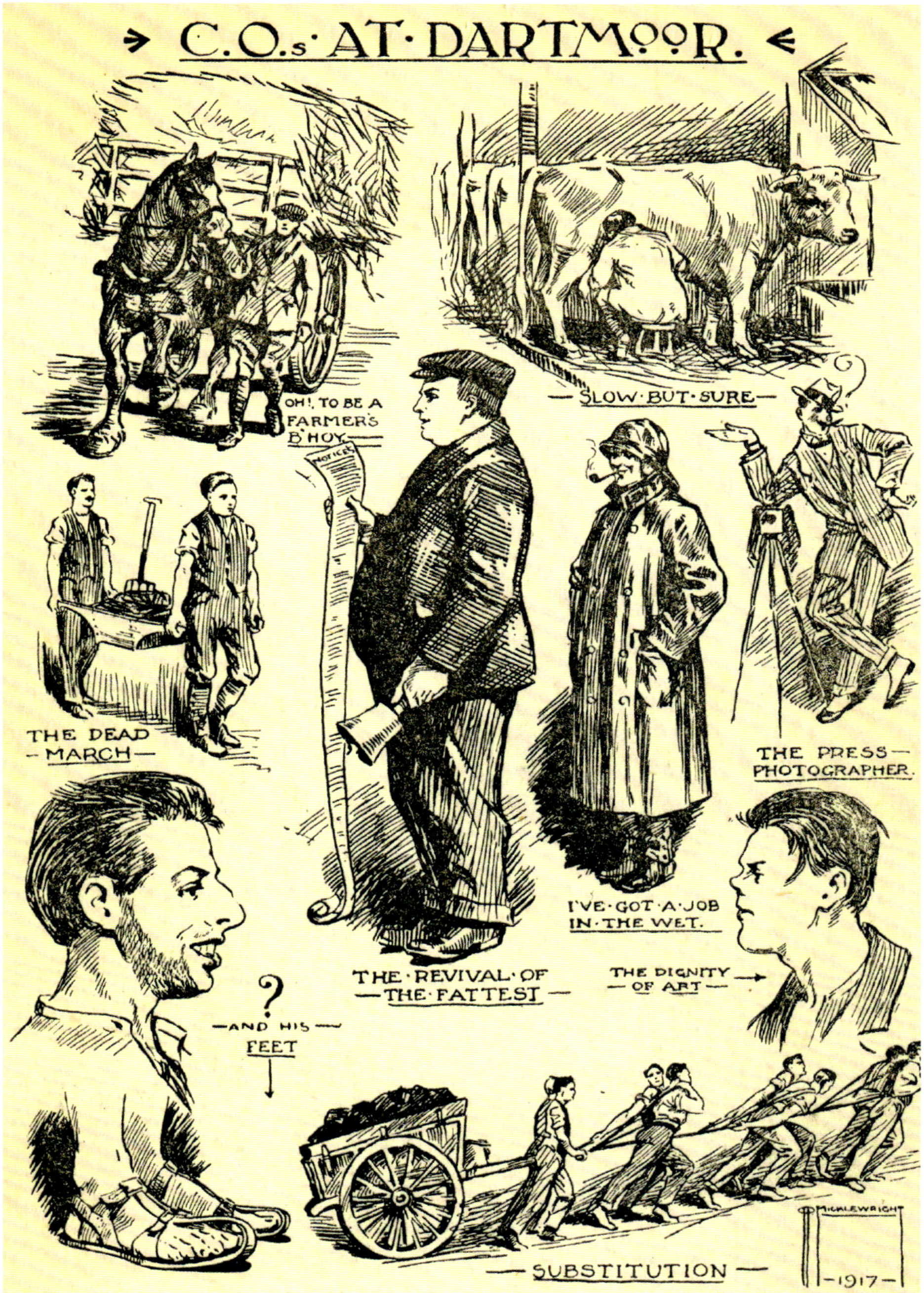

G. P. Micklewright | *C.O.s at Dartmoor,* 1917 | © Reserved, from the collections of the Religious Society of Friends (Quakers) in Britain

JOB NIXON

(1891–1938)

Nixon aged 20 studied at Burslem School of Art, prior to which he had been 'apprenticed to a local engraver who supplied copper plates for transfer printing to local pottery manufacturers.'[75] He won a scholarship to the Royal College of Art (RCA) before entering the Slade, which he thought the best art school in the world. In 1915, while still a student he was successful at the Royal Academy.

The war interrupted Nixon's studies; a conscientious objector he gave his motivation as Church of England. Granted exemption from Combatant Service he was directed to the Non-Combatant Corps in May 1916 and assigned to the Eastern Command until demobilized on 17 January 1919.

Returning to his studies Nixon won the first Prix de Rome for Engraving in 1923 and was elected ARE. While in Italy he produced the large plate *An Italian Festa* which when exhibited in England was regarded as a technical and artistic triumph. Nixon painted in oil and watercolour, but is best known for his etchings, drypoints and line engravings, which he produced from 1913. He taught at the RCA where he was assistant to Malcolm Osborne (1880–1963) in the Engraving School. In 1928 he began to exhibit watercolours with the Royal Watercolour Society, becoming an associate member in 1934.

In 1931 Nixon and his wife the artist Nina Berry were persuaded by John Birch to move to Cornwall, settling in Lamorna; hard up he was supported by Eric and Dod Procter and Laura Knight. Nixon moved to St Ives in 1934, he briefly ran a School of Painting, offering two weekly evening sessions. He returned to teach at the Slade in 1935. Nixon died suddenly, on holiday in 1938. ◆◆◆

CLAUGHTON PELLEW (HARVEY)

(1890–1966)

Pellew studied at the Slade School of Fine Art, London (1907–11) alongside an exceptionally talented group of contemporaries including Paul Nash, Mark Gertler, Edward Wadsworth and Stanley Spencer where he was taught by Henry Tonks, Frederick Brown and Wilson Steer. Pellew (he later dropped the name Harvey) spent much of his childhood in Canada where his parents emigrated to; his father was a mining engineer. Paul Nash and his brother John became good friends with Pellew. Paul first staying with the Pellew family in 1910, the following year Pellew stayed at Iver Heath in Buckinghamshire at the Nashes where he tried to interest him in specific features of the countryside such as ricks and stooks of corn. Paul Nash recalled Pellew's poetic mind and his own difficulty at that time understanding Pellew's almost devotional approach and rhapsody on the beauty of form.[76] In Nash's autobiography *Outline* (1949) he acknowledges the searching intensity of Pellew's work, which he found revelatory.

In 1912 Pellew made his first visit to Europe to see the great art masterpieces he had studied. During the year both Nash brothers holidayed in Norfolk with Pellew who had lodgings at Mundesley-on-Sea. John, encouraged by Pellew, made methodical visual notes for several watercolours that he completed after their walking holiday in 1914.

Increasingly drawn to Roman Catholicism Pellew stayed for several months with Father Harold Shelley Squirrell, in The Presbytery in Cromer, Norfolk where he was priest at Our Lady of Refuge. Pellew was received into the Roman Catholic Church in 1914. The previous autumn he had spent an extended period of time in Assisi in central Italy and this no doubt influenced his decision. His painting of *San Francesco Assisi* was exhibited at the New English Art Club in the summer of 1914. Squirrell's attitudes towards the impending war and more importantly his support for peace would have impacted on Pellew, a pacifist. Squirrell was a member of the small, short-lived Guild of the Pope's Peace founded in 1916 by conscientious objectors the poet Francis Meynell and typographer Stanley Morison, and Edward Ingram Watkin,[77] a friend of Pellew. The Guild supported Pope Benedict XV's advocacy for an immediate peace by negotiation rather than resorting to arms.[78]

Pellew appeared before the Military Service Tribunal at Greenwich at the beginning of June 1916 and was given exemption as a Non-Combatant only. Conscripted into the Non-Combatant Corps 2 Southern Company he refused to participate in any way and faced his first court martial. He was sentenced to one-year detention commuted to 112 days hard labour. At his Central Tribunal appeal held at Wormwood Scrubs on 15 August, 1916 Claughton was considered a genuine conscientious cbjector, class A, and was referred to the Home Office Scheme (HOS) administered by the Brace Committee. Harshly treated, he was moved from one prison to another including short spells in Dorchester, Winchester, Strangeways and Manchester. Released from prison to the HOS he was transferred to the remote and primitive Dyce Camp near Aberdeen on 26 August 1916 where the living conditions were dire, there was no housing other than old army bell tents condemned for use by soldiers: it closed barely two months after opening.[79] The prisoners did however manage to set up their own camp newspaper, *The Granite Echo*.

An alternative to prison, Pellew's punishment at Dyce was to break rocks initially for ten hours a day in a granite quarry for road-building alongside fellow conscientious objectors (some 250). Their presence generated strong feelings amongst the local community and an editorial in the *Aberdeen Daily Journal* branded them 'degenerates'. Pellew was transferred to the Army Reserve Class W on 22 September 1916; this new class of reserve wore no uniform and was not subject to military discipline. Nonetheless, the Army were able to recall Pellew to the Colours if he rejected or was rejected by the Home Office Scheme. From 28 August 1917 he was based in Dartmoor at the Princetown Work Centre, the largest institution it housed over 1,000 conscientious objectors. Here too many locals were hostile to their presence objecting to their supposed 'coddling' and 'pampering'; the *Daily Mail* describing them as '*Dartmoor Do-Nothings*'. Released in 1918 Pellew spent the last four months of the war working on a farm in Buckinghamshire. John Nash 'later suggested that he never fully overcame his war experiences, which left him with a permanent sense of isolation, and may have influenced his decision to settle in a remote rural area of Norfolk.'[80] Pellew's experiences were in sharp contrast to better-connected Bloomsbury Group pacifist artist Duncan Grant[81] who avoided imprisonment and those artists who benefited from state patronage as official war artists.

In 1919 Pellew married painter 'Kechie' Tennent (1888–1968), also a Slade student and who, during the War, had become a Roman Catholic. He took up wood engraving in 1923 and became highly skilled in a craft that was enjoying a revival in part due to the flourishing of a number of private presses. Over the next two decades he produced 70 plus engravings largely of tranquil rural scenes for which he is primarily known. He later provided pen-and-ink illustrations and a book jacket for *The Reward of Faith* (1950) by Elizabeth Goudge.

Following Pellow's death in 1966 John Nash wrote the Introduction to the Memorial exhibition held in Norwich 1967, in which he acknowledged the debt he owed Pellew specifically his encouragement and advice at the beginning of his career seeing him as the most modest, generous and selfless of individuals. ◆◆◆

ERNEST PROCTER

(1886–1935)

Procter came from a staunch Quaker family and was educated at Bootham, the Quaker school in York and at Leeds Art School c.1905–06. Periods of study followed in Newlyn, Cornwall at the Forbes' School of Painting, where 'students were initially required to paint with absolute fidelity to nature before developing their own individual styles'.[82] Laura Knight in her autobiography *Oil Paint and Grease Paint* (1936) recalled Procter being 'the best man student' describing him as 'a gangling, long, thin youth' whose 'black hair stood on end'. Of his work she remembered lots of sketches and compositions with cupids in them. Fellow Forbes' School student Doris ('Dod') Shaw, who became a great friend of Laura, joined him in Paris at the Académie Colarossi. The Procters held their first joint exhibition 'Watercolours' in October 1913 at the Fine Art Society (FAS), London having married the previous year at Paul church not far from Newlyn.

A Quaker and committed pacifist Ernest Procter 'attested' in autumn 1915 at a recruiting office in response to Lord Derby's scheme that eligible men aged 18–41 should enlist voluntarily or 'attest' to serve if called up; single men to be called before the youngest married volunteers. Having formally attested Procter was given a khaki cloth armband with red embroidered King's crown to wear with civilian clothes. The following year with the imposition of compulsory military service he joined the Friends Ambulance Unit (FAU) being sent on 11 April to Jordans, Buckinghamshire, for one month's training. Here he was instructed in administering first-aid to the wounded, stretcher-drill, sanitation and hygiene and field-cookery, as well as physical training, which took the form chiefly of route marches and long-distance treks to Reading and Cambridge. Procter would have felt at home on the latter as he was a great walker often being seen with his rucksack on the moors in north-eastern Cornwall.

Dunkirk was the location for Procter's first posting when he was sent to the Reserves Camp, where from 12 June 1916 he worked in the Motor School for two months. This was followed by a fortnight farming before returning to the Reserves Camp at the end of August. From 5 September Procter worked at Headquarters (HQ) as an Orderly helping doctors and nurses with various routine tasks. Thereafter his service record lists his 'Work' as 'Artist': this commenced at the Works Dept. (25.9.16) where he remained for a little over six months before a 'Visit to SSA 13, 14' (Section Sanitaire Anglaise Motor Ambulance Convoy)[83] for a week or so in mid-May 1917, Procter drew SSA 14 members at Somme Suippe including showing them arriving at the Night Post behind the trenches; he stayed the night in the concrete dug-out which was 40 feet deep.[84] Procter also found the time to decorate the Red Cross huts and paint scenery for the camp entertainment and in addition he formed a small art club. In a letter to Dod he said they are 'all [8] very keen and several worth bothering about… [we] all sit round tables drawing snow scenes and sea scapes out of our little heads.'[85]

By 25 May 1917 Procter was back at HQ where he stayed for three weeks, during which time Dunkirk was bombed. His drawing of an air raid on the night of 3 June shows the searchlight and blazing fires as a result.[86] Procter was sent on 15 June to Coxyde (now Koksijde) about 10 kilometres behind the front line, which was used for rest billets as it was only occasionally shelled. The cemetery some 500 metres from the village (which was started by French troops on the Belgian coast) was used at night for burial of the dead brought back from the front line. Procter made good use of the three days he was there producing several drawings of SSA 19 who were tending the wounded from the trenches who had been carried to the Poste de Secours. He was then stationed back at HQ (18.6.17) where he drew profusely; he told Dod that on 8 September he 'spent nine and a half hours working on a picture' he described as 'more tiring than digging dugouts. It was to be *Descent from the Cross* …'.[87] This was interrupted on 25 September when he made a three-day visit to 'Quarterly Meetings' travelling back to HQ on 28 October where he was based for over a year. Procter's

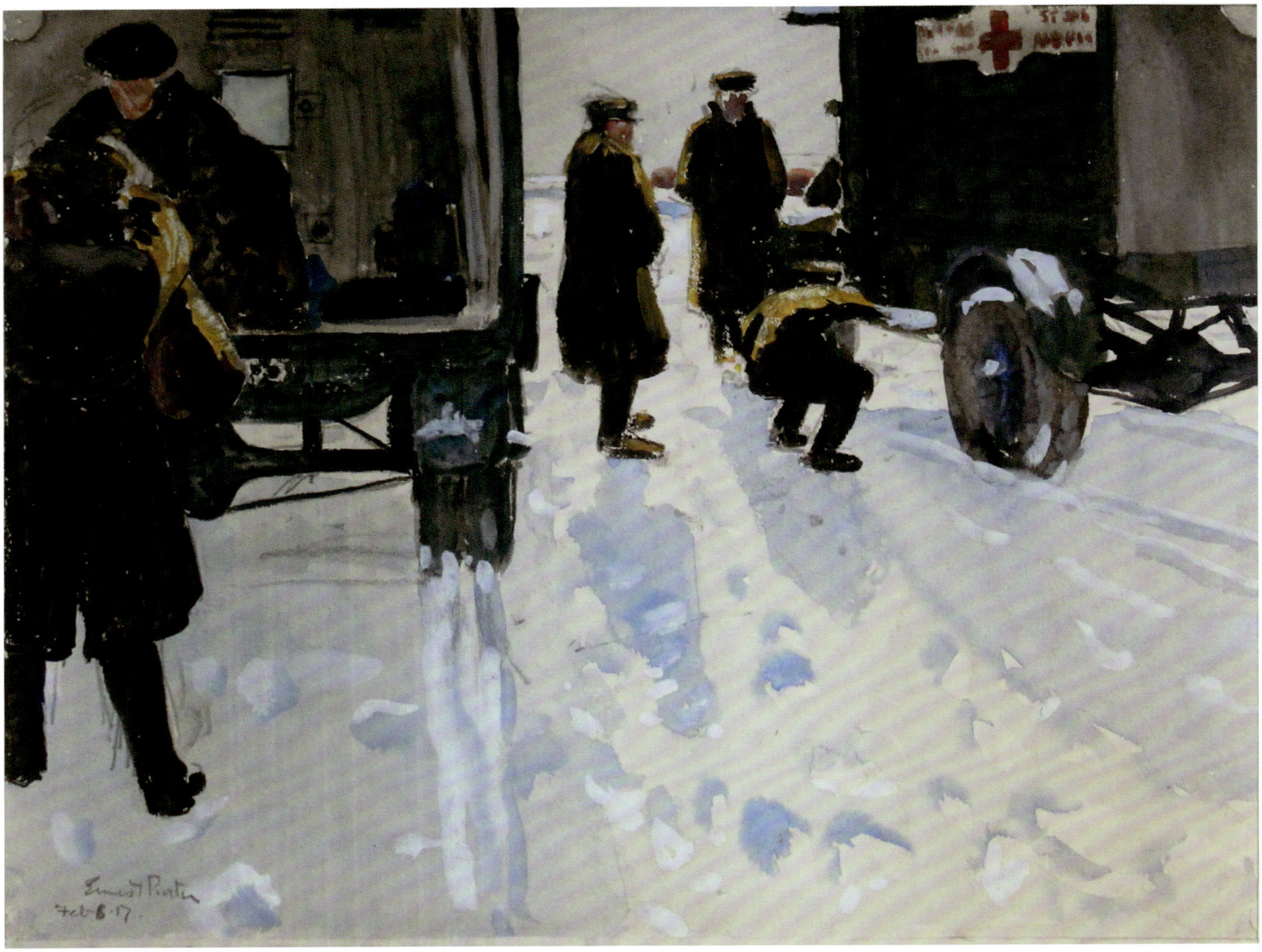

Ernest Procter | *SSA at HQ, Loading Up* | 1917, Watercolour and pencil, 50 x 65.1 cm

Service Record from 8 November 1918 under the heading 'Station' then states 'For Min. of Information' under 'Work' it again stated 'Artist'. In December 1918 Procter had written to Alfred Yockney (1879–1963), formerly editor of the *Art Journal*, now employed by the Ministry of Information and responsible for the War Artists' Committee and after some delay he was granted a permit to paint work for the Red Cross. On 2 February 1919 Procter was demobilized.

During his service Procter captured the lives of the men in the FAU, which by then was under the charge of the Red Cross in a series of sketches and watercolours.[88] The extensive body of work he produced documents the newly motorised unit taking the sick and wounded to hospitals and conveys a vivid picture of the war-torn landscape, sometimes full of cloud and snow and ruined towns of the Western Front. The risk involved and sense of danger is much in evidence despite the protection of the Red Cross emblem.

Procter returned to Newlyn from the Western Front in the spring of 1919. The Procters travelled fairly soon after to Burma to decorate the Kokine Palace in Rangoon; this experience of eastern art and design was to influence their later work. Gluck, a close friend of the Procters, visited their cottage and remembered seeing a very beautiful small panel

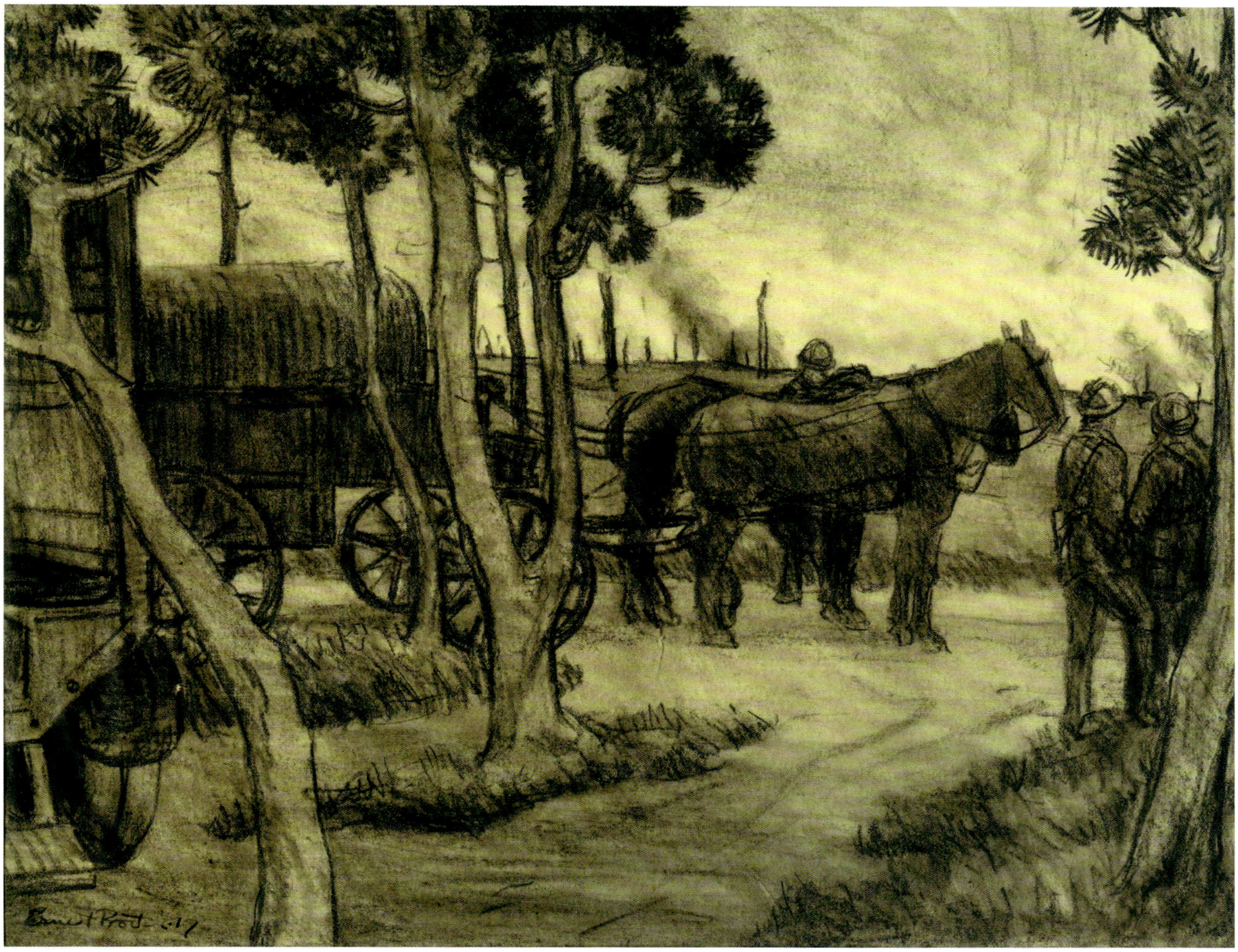

Ernest Procter | *SSA 14 at Somme Suippe* | Undated, Charcoal and pencil drawing, 49.5 x 64.6 cm

of the Crucifixion, which Ernest had done at the front. She thought it quite unlike any of his other work and reminded her of Flemish painting. Gluck also recalled being surprised by the conventional treatment of his drawings for pictures that he would turn into decorations. For her this elicited a divided response, and brought his work even more into contrast with Dod's but as she pithily said 'this did not cause disharmony, [as]he had a gentle and unaffected personality.'

In 1920 Ernest established the Harvey-Procter School of Painting in a large studio near the harbour. He and good friend Harold Harvey (1874–1941) offered tuition in oils and watercolour, studying the Figure, Still Life and Landscape. In the 1930s the Procters and a number of Newlyn artists including Harold Knight, painted religious scenes for the church of St Hilary in west Cornwall at the request of its vicar Bernard Walke. Walke in his autobiography *Twenty Years at St Hilary* (1935) singled out Ernest's contribution describing in some detail his picture of the Visitation painted on a gold background and let into a stone reredos, cunningly built as if to represent the home of the Visitation and his picture of the Deposition from the Cross, above the Altar of the Holy Souls.[89] Procter was appointed Director of Studies in Design and Craft at Glasgow School of Art in 1934. He died a year later aged forty-nine. ◆◆◆

ERIC ROBERTSON

(1887–1941)

One of the most brilliant students of his generation, Robertson studied at the newly founded Edinburgh College of Art where he was greatly influenced by the work of Dante Gabriel Rossetti and Edward Burne-Jones. He regularly visited the studio of symbolist painter John Duncan (1866–1945) in the west of the city which was something of a magnet for young artists including Cecile Walton (1891–1956) whom he later married (despite the opposition of her parents). They viewed him as 'a philanderer and a creator of decadent pictures'[90] and altogether decidedly unsuitable. Cecile was instructed to write and say that she could not meet him again as she was going to Italy. Nonetheless, on her return in 1912 Robertson and Cecile's close friend Mary Newbery were the subjects of her first major oil painting, which she completed during the summer at the house the Waltons rented annually in Wenhaston, Suffolk.[91] The couple had become engaged earlier that year on 20 May; they married on 21 January 1914 in Edinburgh at Edward Walton's studio in Belford Park.

Robertson, a conscientious objector, did not believe in bearing arms and following the introduction of conscription appeared before the Edinburgh Military Service Tribunal headed by Sheriff Maconochie on 11 August 1916 claiming exemption from Combatant Service; his 'motivation' being that his wife and relatives were Quakers. This was granted conditional on his joining the Friends Ambulance Unit (FAU), which was allied to the Red Cross. Just over a week later he attended a two-week training camp in the village of Jordans, Buckinghamshire. Robertson left for France (Dunkirk) on 9 October 1916 and initially worked at HQ, which was situated in the Grand Hotel Pyl at Malo-les-Bains, a seaside suburb of Dunkirk. Less than a month later Robertson was Chief Cook.

One of his close companions in the FAU was fellow artist Arthur Cotterell. They made numerous sketches while in France including on a dangerous trip they undertook from HQ to the ruined town of Nieuport (now Nieuwpoort) in Flanders travelling some twenty miles through ruins and devastated shell-riddled landscape. Another companion was Olaf Stapledon (1886–1950) who became a philosopher and noted author of science fiction and with whom Robertson remained friends postwar. Stapledon later wrote about his FAU experiences in *We Did Not Fight 1914–18. Experiences of War Resisters* (1935).[92] The collection of memoirs also included contributions from Siegfried Sassoon and Bertrand Russell and was edited by Julian Bell (son of Vanessa and Clive Bell). Robertson also met Procter whom he got on well with and they too spent much time together.

By March 1917 Robertson was working in the Motor Department; then following a short period of leave in London with Cecile he was ordered to join SSA 13 with whom he served from 8 April as an Orderly. SSA 13 was stationed at Villers-Marmery in north-eastern France, Robertson was assigned to an ambulance in the nearby village of Thuisy where a château was used as a temporary shelter. 'The noise of the guns was such that he feared the sky was breaking and the heavens were falling in "great sheets of shattered glass and stones." The walls of the château shook, the window frames rattled and plaster fell from the ceiling as the bombardment, which lasted ten days, continued.'[93]

SSA 13 moved several times and in July 1917 Robertson found himself in Maffrécourt in the Champagne-Ardenne region of France where he spent the next five months. During this time he produced a series of naturalistic portraits of his fellow volunteers including student George Romney Fox (b.1898), on 9 August.[94] It was a dangerous place subjected to heavy shelling with the added threat posed by gas shells. The dugouts where Robertson and Cotterell sheltered were protected by gas curtains sprayed with an anti-gas solution but on the evenings when they forgot to spray gas would creep in and they had to spend the remainder of the night wearing masks. Ferrying wounded soldiers round the clock was made increasingly difficult by the shell craters in the road and the high summer temperatures.

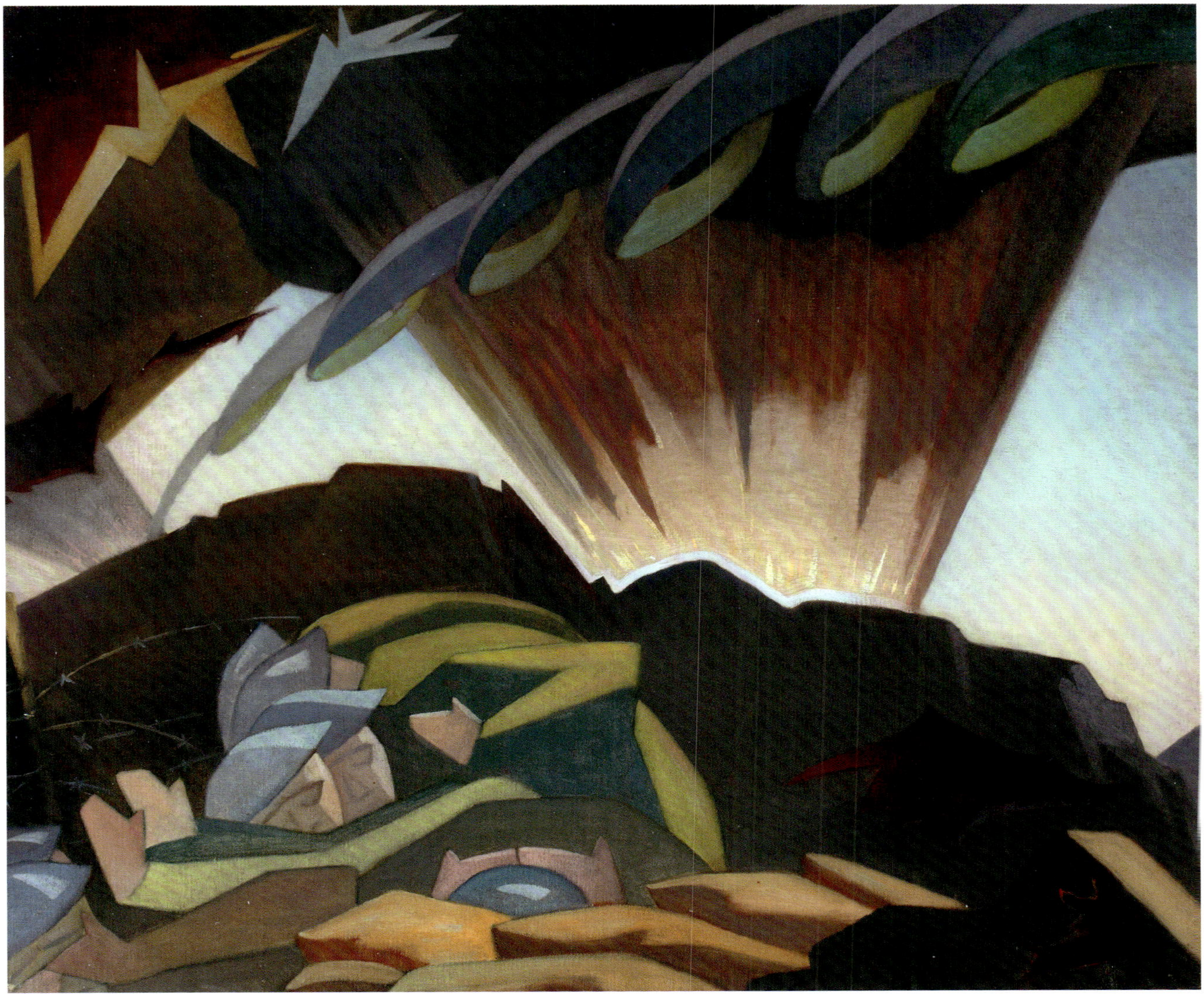

Eric Robertson | *Shellburst* | c.1919, Oil on canvas, 71.2 x 83.8 cm | City Art Centre, Museums & Galleries, Edinburgh

Robertson captured something of these experiences and their impact on his art in his diary in 1917:

> *The sound of explosions from the … hills, the wild phantom dance of dust and smoke pillars against the evening sky, seemed a perfect expression of art. So instead of hating, because of the knowledge of the horror that might be revealed when the smoke had ceased to weave its dance of death, instead of fear at our advance to where the distant terror played, I found my eyes gazing with a look of wonder and exhilaration at the beauty of the reality.*[95]

Hours of waiting afforded Robertson the opportunity to make pencil studies of the wrecked landscape though his major output was in pastels and oils. On leave in Edinburgh in 1918 he sold 35 pastel sketches (many of which were of the Champagne landscape) at five guineas each.

Robertson's harrowing experiences and the loss of human life left an indelible impression and resulted in his memorable painting *Shellburst*, completed shortly after he returned from France having been demobilised on 20 January 1919. Cotterell left the previous day. Walton had sent Robertson copies of the Vorticists' magazine *Blast*[96] that Wyndham Lewis edited containing artwork and essays inspired by the horrors of war. *Shellburst* was exhibited in November at the recently reformed Edinburgh Group's[97] first show post-war and shows the more abstract style that he briefly adopted and his debt to Vorticism.

A skilled draughtsman, Robertson was seeking new ways to express his art and beliefs. The semi-abstract *Shellburst* is a fine example of these with its violent dynamism and angular forms and strong, jagged lines recreating the effect of an explosion with columns of earth rising into the air, a situation Robertson must have witnessed many times. The huddled, helmeted soldiers crouched uneasily behind sandbags and barbed wire are illuminated by the explosion revealing them trying to protect them themselves from swirling shards of debris hurtling towards them following the brutal machine-like destruction of the landscape.

In May 1921 Robertson exhibited *Shellburst* at the 'Nameless Exhibition of Modern British Painting' at the Grosvenor Gallery, London sponsored by *The Burlington Magazine*. The poster advertising the exhibition depicted the head and shoulders of a masked man and stated 'Representative works of all contemporary movements including Royal Academicians & the extreme moderns … will be shown anonymously until the last fortnight when names will be divulged.' The work was selected independently by Charles Sims RA, Henry Tonks and Roger Fry. Desmond MacCarthy critic for *The Burlington* explained that Sims stood for the Royal Academy tradition; Tonks for the taste of the New English Art Club in its heyday and Fry for the movement dubbed vaguely Post-Impressionist.[98] *Shellburst* was in the latter section, though under the title *Bursting Shell*.

Two years later Robertson moved to Liverpool following the break-up of his marriage. In 1927 he re-married and struggled to get portrait commissions; his foray into commercial art met with little financial return. He died in the Wirral, Cheshire in 1941 of tuberculosis at the age of fifty-four. ◆◆◆

JOSEPH SOUTHALL

(1861–1944)

Joseph Southall, a lifelong Quaker and fervent pacifist, spent most of his working life in Birmingham having been educated at the Friends' schools in Ackworth, near Pontefract, West Yorkshire and Bootham, York. On leaving school he was articled to a major firm of Birmingham architects while attending evening classes at the School of Art, 1879–80. He abandoned his architectural training after four years, aged 21, finding it too restrictive. Inspired by the writings of Ruskin and William Morris he made a number of visits abroad including an extended period in Italy in 1893 when he was much taken by the Italian Primitives and egg tempera painting. In the same year he met and was influenced by Edward Burne-Jones and Morris.

A founder member of the Society of Painters in Tempera 1901, many of whom had Quaker antecedents, Southall painted largely 'mythological and romantic subjects, which often took up to two years to complete owing to their large size.'[99] He choose not to teach at Birmingham School of Art preferring to give informal lessons at his Edgbaston home. Ethelbert White took advantage of this staying for a week in 1923 when Southall gave him lessons in tempera while he painted *Five Fishermen Pushing a Boat*.

A committed socialist and prominent peace campaigner throughout the First World War, Southall, too old to be conscripted, joined the Independent Labour Party (ILP) on the outbreak of war feeling its opposition to war more akin to his own strongly held views. Shortly after joining the ILP he became chairman of the Birmingham City branch, a position he held until 1931. (He gave up his membership of the Liberal Party.) Such were his convictions that he was also chairman of the Birmingham Auxiliary of the Peace Society and a vice-president of the Birmingham and District Passive Resistance League. Despite Southall's outspoken stance against the First World War, he was commissioned to produce the fresco that stands on Birmingham Art Gallery's staircase. *Corporation Street, Birmingham in March 1914*, which he worked on, from 1915–16 'conveys its pro-peace politics by implication, providing the population with an image of their recent pre-war community life.'[100]

Southall's political activism was such that his output in tempera and watercolour was greatly reduced, as he applied his artistic skills to pamphlets, illustrated booklets, cartoons and sketches for magazines in the knowledge that they would reach a mass market. Of these outlets, the illustrations (and lettering) he produced over three months for the anti-war pamphlet *The Ghosts of the Slain: A Vision of the Future* (1915) published by the National Labour Press are some of his most powerful. Written by farmer and one-time Liberal MP Robert Leonard Outhwaite (1869–1930),[101] who later joined the ILP, the pamphlet received strident criticism in the *Morning Post*; the artwork was singled out as contemptible. Headlined 'Treason in Disguise' the reviewer declared 'it preached the most pestilential doctrine – doctrine which in some of its terms is hardly to be distinguished from treason…'.[102] Earlier in July 1915 Southall had read a paper titled *Art and Peace* at the Conference upon the Pacifist Philosophy of Life, in Caxton Hall, London. His opening line 'That the arts of Peace should be an antidote to the arts of War…'[103] sets the tenor for his thesis that art is an international language and oversteps boundaries yet he makes the point that 'the arts have been used very freely, and are now being used, to stir up martial fervour, and to excite anger.'[104]

Southall sent a copy of *The Ghosts of the Slain* to the Friends' Reference Library, the following year. In an accompanying letter he explained to the librarian, Norman Penny that it 'is one of the things that the police have spared in repeated raids on the Labour Press.'[105] Southall was unsure whether that counted for or against the work, which was a savage attack on the institutions of the state that supported the war. His illustration on the title page captioned 'Fear and hate start the conflagration of War' makes his ideological stance abundantly clear. His first illustration to Outhwaite's biblically styled text depicts 'Those who sit in the high places cast the people into the pit'. Southall uses his powers of draughtsmanship to great effect to portray a blindfolded 'Tommy' being cast over a precipice by a top-hatted

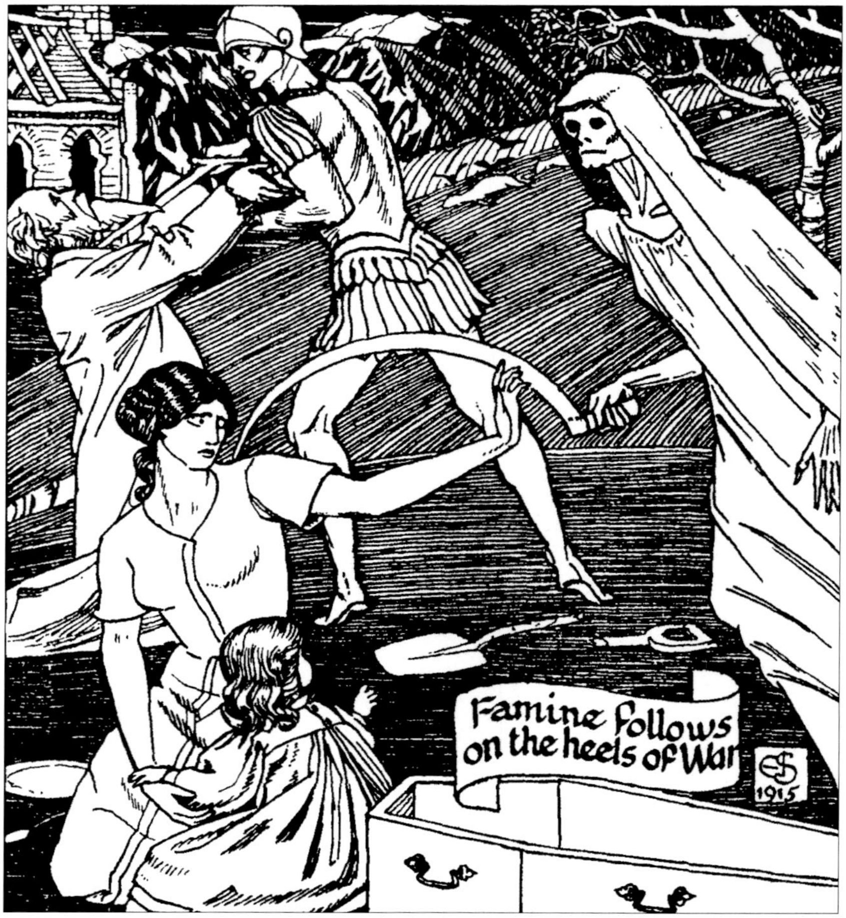

Joseph Southall | *Famine Follows on the Heels of War* | From 'The Ghosts of the Slain' (1915) | R.L. Outhwaite M.P. | National Labour Press Ltd

politician or diplomat aided by a pin-striped business man. Looking on passively is a blindfolded Archbishop who sardonically raises his hand in blessing which is witnessed by a fashionably dressed young woman representing the wealthy and powerful ruling classes who points dismissively to the abyss below. Of these only the top-hatted person has his eyes open. Next to the woman, a smiling skeleton representing Death beats a military drum only to reappear in a later illustration as the cloaked Grim Reaper wielding a scythe at a kneeling woman who puts her hand out to protect the young girl beside her and behind whom is an empty coffin.

Southall also provided anti-war illustrations for suffragette and pacifist Sylvia Pankhurst's (1882–1960) newspaper *The Woman's Dreadnought* published by the East London Federation of the Suffragettes, including in June 1917 'Peace or Famine – Which?' Pankhurst was also an accomplished and prize-winning artist, having studied at Manchester School of Art; her ambition had been to become a painter. In 1918 Southall wrote and illustrated the satirical pamphlet *Fables and Illustrations*, published by the National Labour Press. Divided into two parts, narratives and illustrations, it forcibly yet simply conveys Southall's wit and anti-war stance. The Preface expresses sarcastically 'his indebtedness to the ruling classes of Europe, whose unfailing courtesy has provided him with all the material necessary for the compilation of his work.' The image of 'The Obliterator' – an enormous smiling tank-like machine

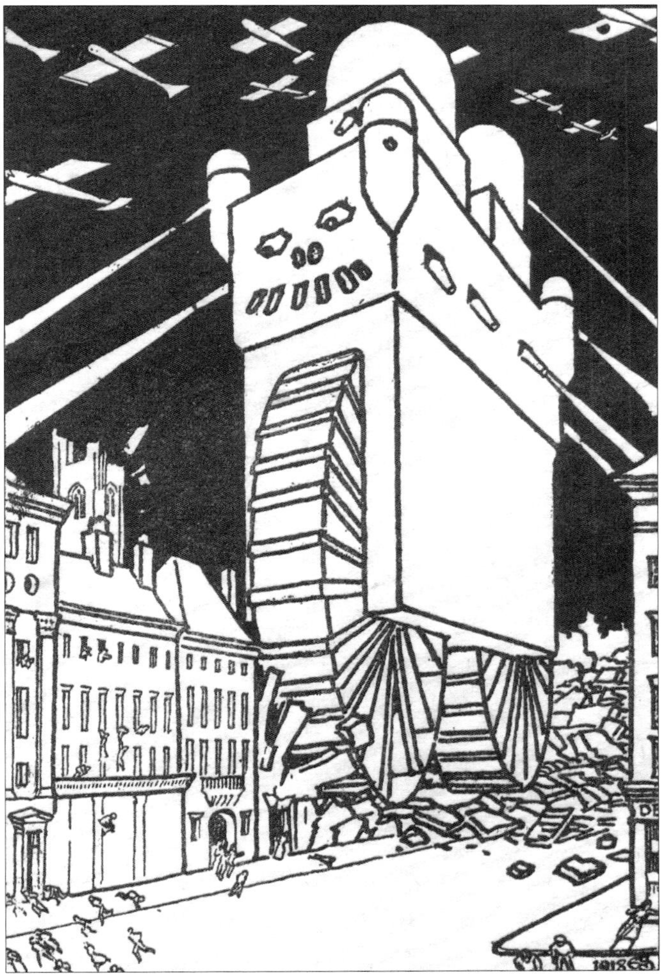

Joseph Southall | *The Obliterator* | 1918, Ink on paper

crushes all in its path appears opposite a mock sales promotion captioned 'A Trade Circular – "Obliterator" Ltd., 1925'. The text explains that it is supplied impartially to all civilised Governments, has given entire satisfaction and that it is guaranteed to leave nothing standing and nothing breathing. Southall continues:

> *For complete list of cities, towns and villages already destroyed, see our 64-page illustrated pamphlet.*
>
> *It is estimated that 'The Obliterator' has already shortened the war by at least nine years and is making a clean sweep of civilisation, thus preparing the way for clean peace. …*

In the interwar years Southall continued to exhibit and was a member of numerous art associations. Uncompromising in his pacifism he continued to oppose war, campaigning against the evils of war when his health allowed. An avid reader of *Peace News* he helped to form a Birmingham branch of the No-Conscription League in 1939. He died at home, where he had lived since the 1880s; on 10 November 1944 Southall was interred in the Friends' part of Witton Cemetery, Birmingham. ◆◆◆

WALTER SPRADBERY

(1889–1969)

Spradbery won a scholarship to Walthamstow School of Art in 1903 where he became a student-teacher aged fifteen teaching the principles of design. Here he met Mackey who came as a part-time teacher in c.1906 whom 'Sprad' (as he was later known) found to be a stimulating teacher. In the 1950s the two close friends attended the public Saturday morning Life Class held at the Sir John Cass School of Arts and Crafts in Aldgate where on occasion Austin Spare[106] and his youngest sister Nellie, an accomplished amateur artist, joined them.[107]

Spradbery voluntarily enlisted with Mackey a matter of days after the outbreak of war and served as a medical orderly with the 3rd East Anglian Field Ambulance, Royal Army Medical Corps. (RAMC). For Spradbery, a lifelong pacifist this decision was for 'humane reasons'. Towards the end of the year the unit moved from its Barracks in Walthamstow to a billet in the granary and stables of Burghley House, Stamford, the sixteenth-century country seat of the Cecil family and their descendants. Spradbery in his account of his training between 1914–15 describes the historic house and the 'charming old town' in some detail, finding it 'most paintable from several aspects, full of quaint corners and handsome courts…'.[108]

In January 1915 the unit moved some fifteen miles to Peterborough where Spradbery's landscapes and local sketches were exhibited in the Minster Precincts, alongside work by Mackey. Spradbery found 'the roughness of camp life and the constant training made [him] indifferent to painting much…'.[109] Spradbery narrowly avoided being court martialled in 1917 when in the custody of the Royal Warwickshire 3rd (Reserve) Battalion in Newport, on the Isle of Wight he was threatened with transfer to a combatant unit and ordered to remove his Red Cross armband. He later explained in *Peace News* (1952), how when, as a conscientious objector, he refused (as did Mackey who would not let him do it alone) to comply. Arguing 'it was an international symbol and a religious one overriding in significance and authority the Royal arms on [his] buttons'.[110] After a period in the Guard Room they were officially returned to the RAMC Depot in Blackpool.

Spradbery served in France with the 36th Field Ambulance until the Armistice. During that time he was a victim of a mustard gas attack in Senlis, which impacted on his eyesight and also resulted in his losing his voice for two weeks. He was awarded the Distinguished Conduct Medal for 'conspicuous gallantry and devotion to duty' for leading a stretcher party under heavy machine-gun fire for the second time to rescue a wounded N.C.O. (Non-Commissioned Officer) near Mametz on 26 August 1918. Later in the year he designed the Christmas card for the RAMC. The outwardly 'simple' card with the insignia of the RAMC on the front belies the detail inside which shows four RAMC personnel carrying a stretcher laden with Christmas fare on which a fifth soldier sits raising a glass, behind him a flag with a Red Cross on a white ground inscribed 'Bonne Santé' and intertwined with a laurel wreath. In the background visible beneath the stretcher a nocturnal scene of a battlefield with a ruined building, are cross-like forms and an ambulance.[111] The Christmas card Spradbery designed in 1940 was very different in tenor and medium. The small linocut and watercolour was produced in the midst of the Blitz nearly twenty years after he first experimented with linocutting having been encouraged by Mackey who had adopted an innovative approach to printmaking. Produced following nights of bombing raids by the Luftwaffe the image vividly demonstrates the impact of his wartime experiences and the horrors he faced as a young working-class man and his involvement in the peace movement. Replete with symbolism, the Virgin Mary stands in front of the downed plane holding the baby Jesus while offering a bowl to what could be the pilot, a helmeted skeleton beats a drum and behind this blackened figure the flag of victory teeters as the flames from ruined buildings light up the smoke-filled sky. In marked contrast to the brutalism of the 1940 Christmas card Spradbery was also working on a gentle, peaceful watercolour *Houses, Stroud* that he

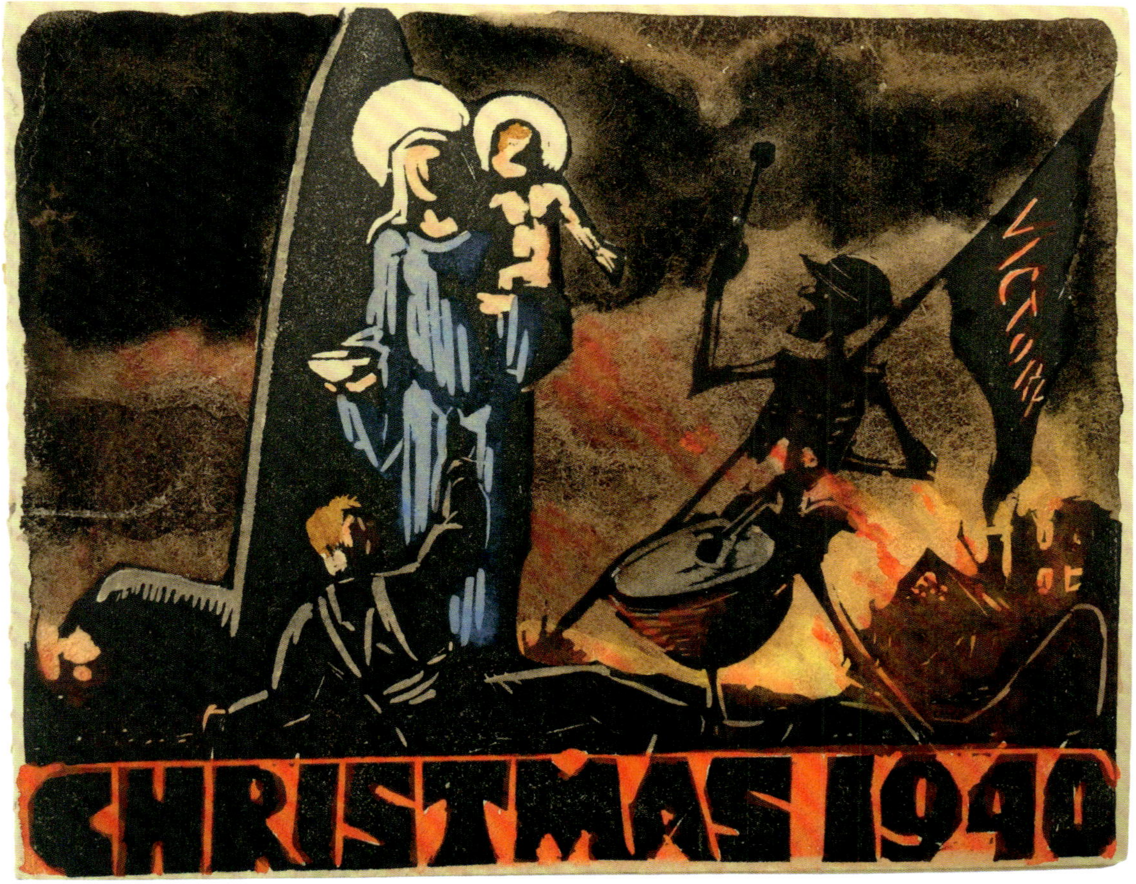

Walter Spradbery | *Christmas Card* | 1940, Linocut | © Elizabeth Malet Spradbery, courtesy William Morris Gallery

contributed to the 'Recording the Changing Face of Britain' scheme established by Sir Kenneth Clark, then Director of the National Gallery.[112] His friend artist-craftsman Frank Brangwyn (1867–1956) regarded his finest watercolours as comparable to those of the great English watercolourists of the eighteenth and nineteenth centuries.

In late 1944 Spradbery designed his last series of posters for London Transport, the first was in 1911 and was submitted to Frank Pick (1878–1941) who became Managing Director of the London Passenger Board when it was created in 1933 (before resigning in 1940). Spradbery designed 62 posters and 18 panels and it is for this body of work that he is best known. The series *The Proud City* shows his skills to great effect and portrays key London landmarks including St Paul's Cathedral, the iconic symbol of the nation's defiance, to celebrate their surviving the Blitz while at the same time boosting the morale of passengers and staff alike. Each image was accompanied by a quotation from a noted British poet or historian. Spradbery sought to convey through his designs 'the sense that havoc is itself passing and with new days come new hopes.'[113] His fears that they would be the bleakest posters he had ever designed were groundless, popular domestically, 27,000 were produced some of which were exported overseas as Allied propaganda with versions translated into Portuguese, Arabic and Farsi.

Spradbery died in December 1969 having been greatly involved in the arts in his local community. A memorial exhibition to Spradbery was held at the William Morris Gallery, in 1970. It was a fitting location as Spradbery had been active in getting the Brangwyn Gift of artworks presented to the Borough of Walthamstow in 1935–36 and played a key role in establishing the Gallery in 1950 which houses these. ◆◆◆

ETHELBERT WHITE

(1891–1972)

While studied at St John's Wood Art School in north London from 1911–12 under watercolourist and stained glass artist and principal Leonard Walker (1877–1964). 'The Wood' claimed to thoroughly equip the advanced student in 'technical training with his personality unscathed.'[114] While White undoubtedly benefitted from this education he did not receive training in wood-engraving, later working out many of his problems by trial and error and developing his own style and decorative manner for which he became well known.

Pre-war White associated with British avant-garde artists and he and his future wife Betty were regularly to be found with other habitués at the Café Royal. Nina Hamnett painted the Bohemian couple's portrait c.1918 possibly at one of the many Fitzroy Street parties they attended. 'Bertie', as he was affectionately known strums his guitar, while Betty plays her banjo. Their renditions of folk songs, dances and flamenco were much in demand and remained so post-war. By this stage White was a member of the London Group and exhibiting with the New English Art Club. 'He was essentially a pastoralist, his artistic vision [being] rooted in his genuine delight in nature, in rustic charm and in the simple way of life of country people.'[115]

White's socialist and pacifist sympathies led him to register as a conscientious objector. Sent to a farm in Devon in 1916 to undertake (agricultural) 'work of national importance' he experienced the harsh realities of life on the land. Like other so-called 'conchies' White was subject to verbal abuse and vehement disapproval. His 'emotional turmoil was evident in the poetry he wrote [privately] at the time … on scraps of paper or in exercise books':

> *… And all mankind now turned to raging fools,*
> *Are trampled in each others bloody pools,*
> *Here in this barn, here in this straw,*
> *My vow I do confirm once more,*
> *Though hatreds spirits whirl in rage their wings,*
> *Ne'er will I raise my hand 'gainst living things.*[116]

During his period of enforced labour White was joined by Betty who stayed on the farm. In snatched moments White executed a series of tiny coloured drawings, some done on the back of cigarette packets including *The Artist's Wife at Her Dressing Table*, c.1916. The subject is almost certainly Betty, as he rarely drew or painted anyone else.[117] White's work was impacted by these experiences, most notably his figurative oil painting *Weariness*, c.1918 which reflects his sensitive understanding and sympathy for three exhausted workers and his small drypoint *The Digging Man*, which may be a self-portrait.

Post-war the Whites returned to Hampstead where he worked as painter, wood engraver, poster designer, book illustrator and commercial artist. His material for his work, which was much in demand, was frequently generated from his travels with Betty in a horse-driven gypsy caravan around southern England or overseas when they sought the warmth of the sun.

By 1940 with the collapse of the market for wood engravings White turned increasingly to watercolour and oil painting. They moved out of London away from the heavy bombing, staying in Amberley in West Sussex where they had a studio or in their house in Devon. Post-war they returned to London but White's work of predominantly rural scenes was no longer the height of fashion. From the 1950s only Oliver Brown's Leicester Galleries showed his work culminating with a solo show in 1971, the year before he died. ◆◆◆

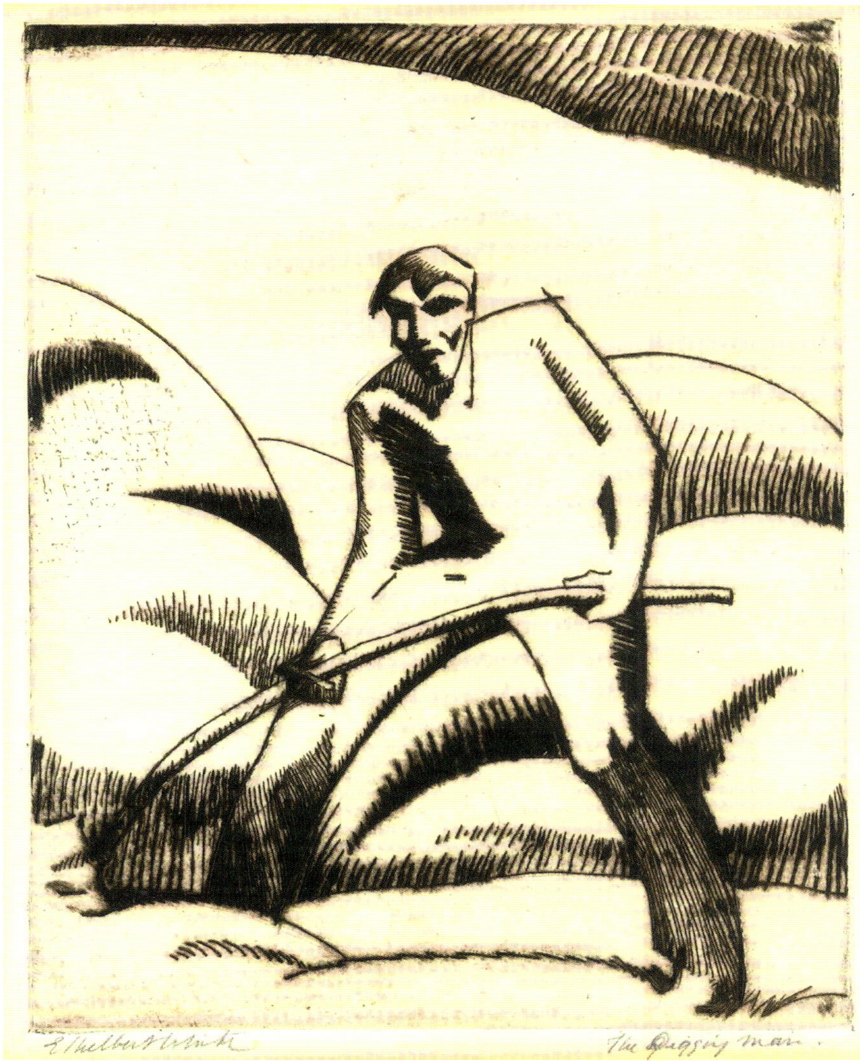

Ethelbert White | *The Digging Man* | Undated, Drypoint, 24.2 x 17.4 cm
Private Collection | © The Estate of the Artist

DONALD WOOD

(1889–1953)

Wood came from a Quaker family in Leeds. Little is know about his formal art training although he probably attended Leeds College of Art. A painter of landscapes, portraits and figures in oils and watercolours he exhibited extensively between 1919–46.

Wood attended Quaker meetings in Leeds before joining the Friends Ambulance Unit (FAU) agreeing to pay for his own uniform and training. He served initially with The Friends War Victims Relief Committee building huts in France in June 1915, and from September as an Orderly at the Queen Alexandra Hospital in Malo-les-Bains, Dunkirk. In his diary Wood recorded 'We had a peep into the wards & I got introduced to the Matron, a little dark woman, she told me she had worked in the Leeds Infirmary for three years.'[118] He also met his near neighbour from Leeds fellow Quaker William Roylance (b.1896)[119] and shared tea and bread and jam with him. This was followed by nearly four months service again as an Orderly but this time working for the Aide Civile Belge, at Parc St Georges, Poperinge in West Flanders some eight miles west of Ypres and nearer 'the action'. The Aide Civile Belge was based in Elizabeth Hospital in the town and had been established in the first weeks of 1915. It was a collaboration between the head nurses and the FAU. Wood described his experiences of the intense shelling:

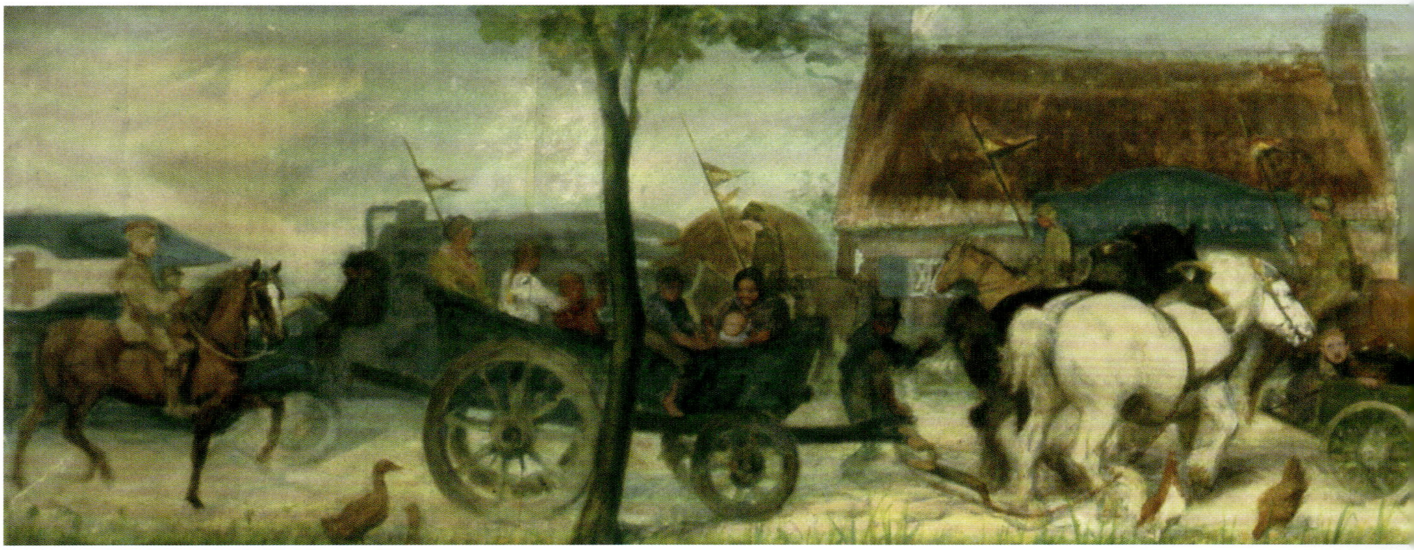

Donald Wood | *The Passers By on a Road near La Panne, Belgium* | 1916, Gouache, watercolour and pencil, 53.3 x 171.5 cm
Reproduced by permission of Edward Starkie Esq. / Leeds Quakers | © Religious Society of Friends (Quakers) in Britain

This day the 19th of Dec. 1915. I was awakened at 5a.m. from deep & delightful sleep by the sizzle & exploding of a shell in such close proximity [that] the mud, stones & small pieces of shell came pattering on the hut roof, we had hardly realized the fact when another & yet another came. The stupid lamp would not light some ass had turned the wick into the lamp too low. We got into our cloths [sic] as slick as pos. at the same time wondering where the next was coming.

Wood survived the bombardment and the following February was transferred to the Section Sanitaire Anglaise 14 (SSA 14), one of a number of motor ambulance convoys, which were assigned to French Army units. For the best part of three years Wood drove ambulances until he left the Unit on 30 January 1919. He served in various locations including periods at Coxyde and in Kursaal in Malo-les-Bains, before being stationed finally at Adinkerke from 13 August 1916. Wood was one of several members of SSA 14 to be awarded the Croix de Guerre in September 1918 for his service with the Convoy.

Throughout the war Wood drew sketches in his diary, but the most notable work that resulted from his experiences was *The Passers By on a Road near La Panne, Belgium*, 1916, part of a triptych.[120] Exhibited in Bradford in 1919 it is rich in detail, (a FAU ambulance can be glimpsed in

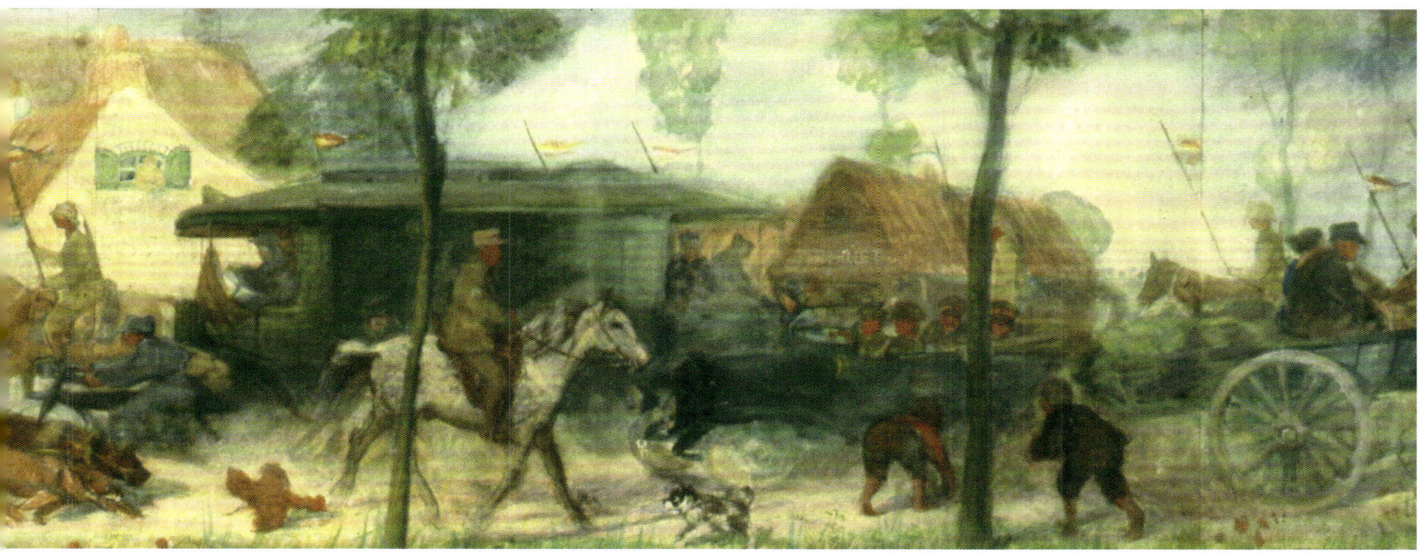

the left-hand corner) and shows the chaos of war and its impact. The *Yorkshire Post's* (1919) art critic thought it:

> *A work which is certain to attract much notice is a frieze in water colour by Mr Donald Wood, entitled* 'The Passers By' *which is based on the many types which were to be seen on a road near La Panne, Belgium, in 1916 not far from the fighting line. It is crowded with incidents, cleverly compiled, enriched by humour, and deftly drawn, and it should be worth reproduction on a much larger scale in a suitable environment.*

Wood continued to work as an artist exhibiting with a number of galleries and societies, including the prestigious Royal Academy and Royal Scottish Academy. The Arlington Gallery in Old Bond Street devoted several exhibitions to his work and between 1924–39 he showed over 100 works receiving mixed reviews in *The Times*. His sporting paintings were much in demand and in 1925 and 1927 he held two exhibitions devoted to 'Hunting, Portrait and Landscape paintings'. *The Times*' critic wryly commented 'Pictures of sporting subjects are always difficult to judge, because pictorial and sporting interest do not necessarily coincide, and it often happens that a bad picture is a good illustration – and the other way about: but the work of Mr Donald Wood … may be said to show an all-round competency.' Wood moved to London in 1931 where he also exhibited with the Batsford Gallery in one of its first exhibitions after the Second World War in June 1946. ◆◆◆

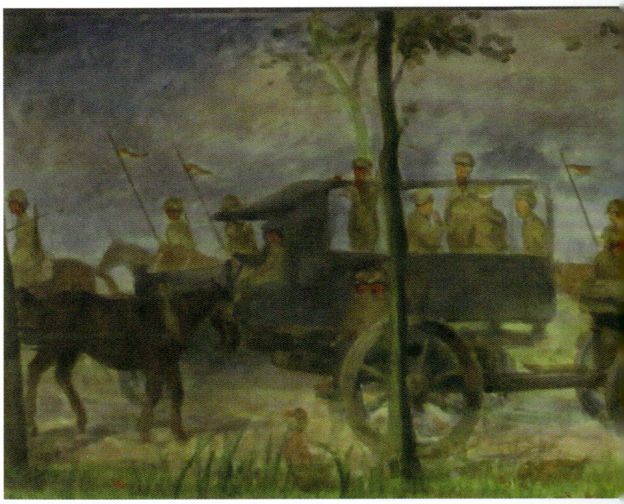

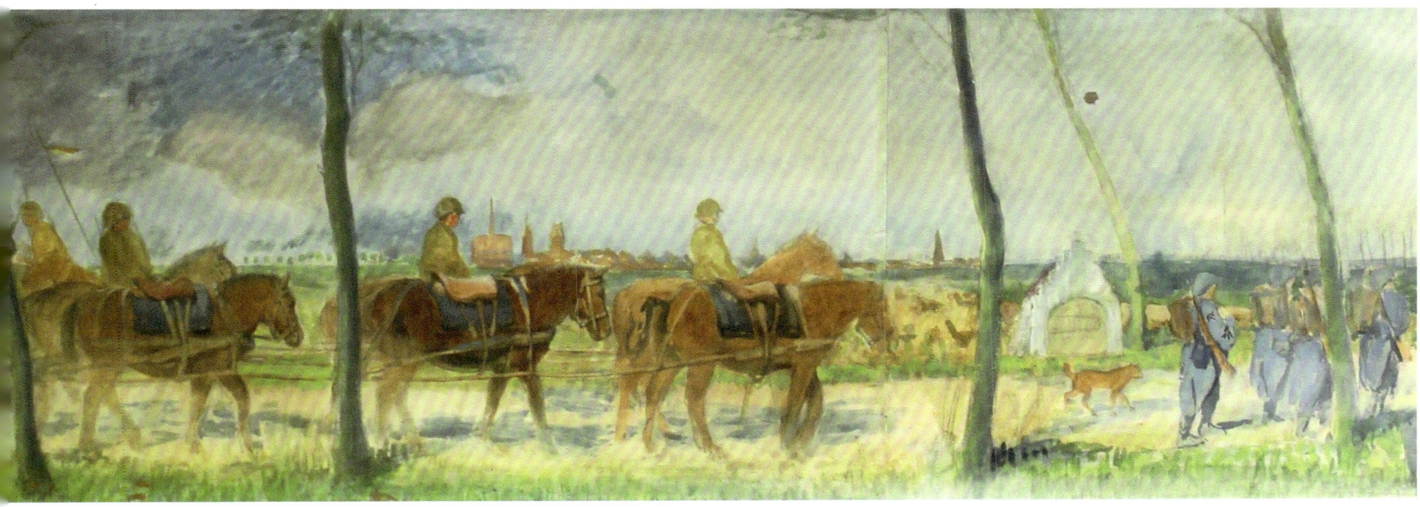

Donald Wood | *The Passers By on a Road near La Panne, Belgium* | 1916, Gouache, watercolour and pencil, 53.3 x 171.5 cm
Reproduced by permission of Edward Starkie Esq. / Leeds Quakers | © Religious Society of Friends (Quakers) in Britain

REFERENCES AND NOTES

1. See the entry for Adrian Allinson, accessed 10 February 2018, https://www.ltmuseum.co.uk/collections/collections-online/people
2. Cited in Skipwith, P. (1978) 'Adrian Allinson: A Restless Talent', *The Connoisseur*, 198, pp.264–73.
3. See Schwabe's Diary entry 8 February 1935 in Clarke, G. (Ed.) (2016) *The Diaries of Randolph Schwabe. British Art 1930–48*, Bristol: Sansom & Co.
4. Allinson won a 'New Ski-ing Race' in Muerren, Switzerland in 1925, see *The Manchester Guardian*, 3 February.
5. See Angier, C. (1987) Week-End in Gloucestershire: Jean Rhys, Adrian Allinson and 'Till September Petronella', *London Magazine*, 27, 3, June pp.32–46. T*he Blue Hour: A Portrait of Jean Rhys* by L. Pizzichini (2010) refers to Rhys's 'semi-demi love affair' with Allinson. Ella Rees Williams [*pseud.* Jean Rhys] (1890–1979) sat for Allinson when she was working in London.
6. Skipwith (1978) Op. cit. refers to Allinson's autobiography, p.103.
7. See Kirk, A. (2011) 'Beaumont Souvenirs' in J. Pritchard (Ed.) *Diaghilev and the Golden Age of the Ballets Russes 1909–1929*, p.184 and Clarke, G. (2012) *Randolph Schwabe*, Bristol: Sansom & Co.
8. Smedley founded the International Lyceum Clubs for Women Artists and Writers.
9. Brockington, G. (2004) Constance Smedley, *Oxford Dictionary of National Biography (ODNB)* entry.
10. Smedley, C. (1929) *Crusaders: the Reminiscences of Constance Smedley*, London: Duckworth, p.223.
11. Lee later explained that British responses to the sinking of the *Lusitania*, a passenger ship, in May 1915 by a German submarine and the intensifying of anti-German sentiment inspired the Ballet. See also Smedley (1929) Ibid., p.223, Brockington, G. (2010) in *Above the Battlefield: Modernism and the Peace Movement in Britain, 1900–1918*, London: Yale University Press points out that Armfield remembered this slightly differently writing that Lee made the first move but concurring that they both played a part in it becoming a book, see p.163.
12. Some accounts place their arrival in America in 1915 but Smedley states 1916.
13. See Armfield, M. (1925) *An Artist in America*, London: Methuen & Co.
14. Tate.
15. See Skipwith (2005) Joseph Southall, 1861–1944 in *Sixty works by Joseph Southall, 1861–1944 from the Fortunoff Collection Joseph Southall 1861–1944*, p.15 with essays by George Breeze, Peyton Skipwith & Abbie N. Sprague, London: Fine Art Society.
16. Campbell, K. (1999) *Moon Behind Clouds: An Introduction to the Life and Work of Sir Claude Francis Barry*, Jersey: Fine Art Productions Limited, p.17 & p.22.
17. Campbell (1999) Ibid., p.22.
18. Campbell (1999) Ibid., p.22 and see Tovey, D. (2003) *Creating a Splash: The St Ives Society of Artists. The First 25 Years (1927–1952)*, Tewkesbury: Wilson Books, pp.69–73.
19. Lawson, C. (2011) 'General Overview of Barry's Life', press release for the exhibition *Sir Claude Francis Barry, Bart. (1883–1970)* at the Royal Cornwall Museum.
20. Campbell (1999) Op. cit., p.29.
21. FAU Personnel Cards, Series 1: Details of Service. SSA 13 was formed of both British and French men who drove some 20 ambulances. Each section was normally staffed by 56 men, led by an officer in charge or 'Chef-Adjoint', a Sous-Chef and an assistant responsible for the administration of the convoy.
22. Kemplay, J. (1991) *The Two Companions the Story of two Scottish Artists, Eric Robertson and Cecile Walton*, Edinburgh: Ronald Crowhurst, p.55.
23. The IWM holds 27 works by Cotterell.
24. Rae, J. (1970) *Conscience & Politics. The British Government and the Conscientious Objector to Military Service 1916–19*, London: Oxford University Press, p.98 and see Kenefick, W. (1999/2014) *War Resisters and Anti-conscription in Scotland: An ILP in Scotland and The Great War* (Eds) C. M. M. MacDonald and E. W. McFarland.
25. See Starling, J & Lee, I. (2001) *No Labour, No Battle. Military Labour during the First World War*, Brimscombe Port Stroud: The History Press re the Formation of Agricultural companies and the differences in Scotland whereby a distribution centre was established at Tollcross School, Edinburgh to classify soldiers. Agricultural companies were normally formed from soldiers no longer fit enough for combat duties.
26. Oliver, C. (1980) *James Cowie*, Edinburgh: Edinburgh University Press, p.56 and p.58. *Evening Star* is in Aberdeen Art Gallery & Museums Collections.
27. Macmillan, D. (2016) *James Cowie. Enigmata*, The Scottish Gallery, p.5.
28. Dunlop, R. O. (1956) *Struggling with Paint*, p.12.
29. See Schwabe's diary entry for 8 July 1931, Clarke (Ed.) (2016) Op. cit.
30. Cannan's novel *Mendel* (1916) was based on Gertler's early life.
31. Gertler to Carrington, August 1914, italics in original, *Mark Gertler. Selected Letters* edited by N. Carrington (1965), London: Rupert Hart-Davis, p.75.
32. Hassall, C. (1959) *Edward Marsh: Patron of the Arts. A Biography*, London: Longmans, p.370 and Schwabe Op. cit. who states that March gave Gertler £12 a month and that Marsh was very hurt about the break-off.
33. See the catalogue for *Mark Gertler: Works 1912–28. A Tremendous Show of Vitality.* Exhibition curated by Sarah MacDougall (2012), Piano Nobile, Robert Travers (Works of Art) Limited, pp.38–39.
34. Levy, P. (Ed.) (2005) *The Letters of Lytton Strachey*, London: Penguin, p.307.
35. Brockington (2010) Op. cit., p.98.
36. Schwabe diary entry for 28 June 1933, Clarke (Ed.) (2016) Op. cit.
37. Gertler's parents who were 'technically Austrian, were forced to become Poles to escape the label "enemy alien."' See Dickson, R. and MacDougall S. (Eds) (2009) *Whitechapel at War: Isaac Rosenberg and his Circle*, p.73.
38. Schwabe diary entry for 26 June 1939, Clarke (Ed.) (2016) Op. cit.
39. See Reed's (2004) *Bloomsbury Rooms: Modernism, Subculture, and Domesticity*,

where he sheds new light on Vanessa Bell's agency vis-à-vis changing the men's attitudes to the war.
40. See Reed (2004) Ibid. for discussion re *Triple Alliance* and also Shone, R. (1999) *The Art of Bloomsbury: Roger Fry, Vanessa Bell and Duncan Grant*, London: Tate Gallery & Princeton University Press, p.124 and Spalding, F. (1997) *Duncan Grant*, London: Chatto & Windus, pp.150–51.
41. See Garnett's second of three volumes of autobiography *The Flowers of the Forest* (1955).
42. Morrell voted against conscription when it first was passing through the House of Commons. Summoned to Burnley to explain his action to the Liberal Association he informed the Association that he could not put party before principle. Still a solicitor he attended Tribunals of various young men all over the country giving evidence that they were genuine Conscientious Objectors. He went twice to Suffolk in support of Grant and Garnett and spoke for Lytton Strachey in Hampstead.
43. Cited in Knights, S. (2015) *Bloomsbury's Outsider: A Life of David Garnett*, London: Bloomsbury Reader, p.116.
44. Knights (2015) Ibid., p.119.
45. Bell appeared before a Military Service Tribunal in St Pancras in July 1916. His 'Work of National Importance' was at Garsington, the Oxfordshire home of the Morrells where he laboured for them half-heartedly on the farm.
46. Bell undated letter to Harvey. Library of the Friends of the Religious Society of Friends in Britain, London.
47. Spalding (1997) Op. cit. p.206.
48. Brockington (2010) Op. cit., p.27. Brockington makes a compelling case for viewing *Interior* as not necessarily expressing antipathy to the war, p.30.
49. Spalding (1997) Op. cit., p.373.
50. Clark, July 1941, IWM, War Artists Archive ART/WA2/3/68, 25.
51. Ginnett served from 1916 with the Royal Garrison Artillery in France. Although not an official war artist the Imperial War Museum hold several of his paintings including the large canvas *Ypres Salient, Dawn*.
52. Peace Pledge Union web site.
53. Richmond, a Quaker, died on 29 December 1916. His death was reported in *The Tribunal*, explaining that he had a severe heart condition, which rendered him rarely able to leave home. The point being that he could have secured exemption on the grounds of ill-health but his deeply held political beliefs precluded this and he was sent from Chichester to Northampton and the strain subsequently contributed to his death at home.
54. Calton Jail closed in 1925 and was demolished 5 years later.
55. Barnes, J. (1982) *Percy Horton: Artist and Absolutist 1897–1970*, Sheffield City Art Galleries, p.9. See also the papers of Ronald Horton re 'How the war affected our family … '. The Keep, Brighton, AMS6375/1/5.
56. Duncan, R. (2015) *Objectors & Resisters. Opposition to Conscription and War in Scotland 1914–18*, Berwick-on-Tweed: Common Print, p.98.
57. Morsberger, P. rev. Barnes, J. (2004) Percy Horton entry, *ODNB*, accessed 1 April 2018.
58. Werner, C. (1986) Left Review in A.Sullivan (Ed.) *British Literary Magazines. The Modern Age, 1914–1984*, London: Greenwood Press, p.217.
59. Hunter would have had to apply to a Local Tribunal for a Certificate of Exemption under the Military Service Act, 1916 before 2 March.
60. Honeyman (1937) refers to the painting as '*Kitchen Utensils*'.
61. See Smith, B. and Mariner, J. (2012) *Hunter Revisited: The Life and Art of Leslie Hunter*, Edinburgh: Atelier Books, p.68.
62. The term was not used until 1948.
63. See also *Les Peintres Ecossais* at the Galeries Georges Petit Paris in 1931, this additionally included work by Telfer Bear and R. O. Dunlop.
64. Janet Dunbar entry for Laura Knight. *ODNB*.
65. Later, artists were able to obtain special permits to work out of doors.
66. See Tovey (2003) Op. cit., pp.73–75.
67. Anon (1919) Digitised copy, p.89. Wellcome Library. RAMC/1081/1/11.
68. The IWM holds 24 works by Mackey and see the Wellcome Collection.
69. Baker, P. (2011) *Austin Osman Spare: The Life and Legend of London's Lost Artist*, London: Strange Attractor Press, p.124.
70. 'Painters of the R.A.M.C.' *Times* (London, England) 25 May 1920, p.8. *The Times* Digital Archive. Web. 30 Jan. 2018.
71. See Elliott, P. (1990) *William McCance 1894–1970*, National Galleries of Scotland, Broxburn: Alna Press, p.5.
72. They separated in 1955 and divorced in 1963.
73. See entry for Agnes Miller Parker in A. Strang (Ed.) (2017) *A New Era Scottish Modern Art 1900–1950*, National Galleries of Scotland.
74. Windsor in McCance's *ODNB* entry states 1919 or 1920. Dr Margaret McCance, (née Chislett) writes in a Biographical Note (1975) that he was in London from 1919. Chislett was a colleague at Reading University they married in 1963.
75. Anon (2016) 'Job Nixon in Lamorna', in *The Flagstaff*, The Lamorna Society Magazine, 37, Summer, p.15. See also Tovey (2003) Op. cit., pp.144–46.
76. See also Bertram, A. (1955) *Paul Nash: The Portrait of An Artist*, London: Faber and Faber, p.68.
77. Watkin co-founded the Catholic pacifist organisation Pax in 1936.
78. See Taouk, Y. (2008–09) The Guild of the Pope's Peace: A British Peace Movement in the First World War, *Recusant History*, 29, pp.252–71.
79. See Graham, J. W. (1922/1969) *Conscription and Conscience. A History 1916–1919*, London: Allen & Unwin, p.232.
80. Stevens, A. (1987) Introduction to *Claughton Pellew. Wood Engravings*, catalogue of an exhibition at the Eldon Gallery, Ashmolean Museum, Oxford, p.1.
81. Brockington (2010) argues that the Bloomsbury Group engaged in art as a form of pacifist resistance, p.121.
82. Fox, C. (1993) *Stanhope Forbes and the Newlyn School*, Newton Abbott: David &

Charles, p.71.

83. The ambulance convoys were eventually reduced to three, SSA 13, 14 & 19. Scottish artist Eric Robertson was assigned to SSA 13 from April 1917.
84. See the catalogue (1980) *Ernest Procter. Drawings from The Trenches*, Blond Fine Art Ltd., p.5.
85. James, A. (2007) *Dod Procter: A Singular Vision*, Bristol: Sansom & Co., p.55.
86. Procter's drawing and others illustrated the official record of *The FAU 1914–1919* (see p.184), the original is in the Papers of Laurence Cadbury, Cadbury Research Library: Special Collections, University of Birmingham.
87. Procter cited in James (2007) Op. cit., p.58.
88. The IWM holds an extensive collection of Procter's drawings of northern France and Flanders executed between 1917–18 together with other work from the period.
89. Republished in 2002 by Truran it also provides insights into Walke's pacifism in the First World War.
90. Kemplay (1991) Op. cit., p.27. Robertson's frank painting of a female nude was removed from the students' exhibition.
91. The large 6-foot painting is now in the collection of the Scottish National Portrait Gallery, Edinburgh.
92. Stapledon was an ambulance driver and later purchased several paintings by Robertson. He abandoned his pacifism and supported the Second World War effort.
93. Kemplay (1991) drew heavily on Robertson's war diaries to write his account.
94. I am grateful to Dr Helen Scott, Curator (Fine Art), City Art Centre, Edinburgh for drawing my attention to this portrait.
95. Cited in Strang (Ed.) (2017) Op. cit., p.111.
96. Nevinson came up with the title.
97. Founded in 1912 by Robertson and Cecile amongst others as an exhibiting collective. The exhibition in 1920 shocked sections of Edinburgh society.
98. *The Burlington Magazine for Connoisseurs*, 38, 219, June 1921, pp.261–62.
99. Breeze (2013) Joseph Southall entry, *ODNB*.
100. Martin Killeen, Cadbury Research Library, University of Birmingham, Joseph Southall and Pacifism, http://www.voicesofwarandpeace.org/portfolio/28/accessed 20/2/18.
101. Outhwaite's outspoken pacifist views contributed to him losing his Hanley seat in 1918.
102. Cited in 'Joseph Southall and the Pursuit of Peace' in *Joseph Southall 1861–1941. Artist-Craftsman*, 1980, Birmingham Museums & Art Gallery, p.49.
103. Southall (1915) available at The Library of the Religious Society of Friends in Britain, London.
104. For a nuanced analysis of this and the other papers given at Caxton Hall see Brockington (2010) Op. cit. and in particular her discussion re 'pacifist modernism'.
105. Southall 15 September 1916, The Library of the Religious Society of Friends in Britain, London.
106. A portrait of Spare's used to hang in Spradbery's studio at his home 'The Wilderness' in Buckhurst Hill, Essex. See Spradbery, J. (2010) *My Dear Jim: A Biography of Walter E. Spradbery*, Worthing: John Spradbery Publishing.
107. Sargeant, G. (2013) *Friends & Influences: The Memoirs of an Artist*, London: Jerusalem Press.
108. Private Papers of W. E. Spradbery (1914–15). Documents.11404, IWM, London.
109. Spradbery, W. (1914–15) Ibid., p.1.
110. Cited in Spradbery, J. (2010) Op. cit., p.33.
111. V. & A. Collections. Museum number: E.397–2008.
112. Spradbery also contributed *Mill House, Tilty* that appeared in *Recording Britain*, vol. II published in 1947 by Oxford University Press in association with The Pilgrim Trust.
113. Spradbery (no date) cited in Sargeant (2013) Op. cit., p.49.
114. See Eyre, A. M. (1913) *Saint John's Wood: Its History, its Houses, its Haunts and its Celebrities*, London: Chapman & Hall, p.267.
115. Chapman, H. (2003) *Ethelbert White 1891–1972 Painter Printmaker*, Bicester: Primrose Hill Press, p.19.
116. White quoted in Chapman (2003) Ibid., p.20. I am grateful to Hilary Chapman for her permission to use this extract and for her assistance re White.
117. See Liss Llewellyn Fine Art.
118. I am grateful to Edward Starkie, descendant of Donald Wood for permission to quote from Wood's diary and Leeds Quakers for their research assistance and in particular Susan Robson, Robert Keeble, Veronica O'Mara and Pat Gerwat.
119. Roylance was awarded the Croix de Guerre in 1918 for his work driving an ambulance repeatedly through heavy fire at the Somme.
120. The location of the third panel is unknown. See also Wood's painting *A Song in the Mess*, 1917 in the RAF Museum, Hendon, London which is possibly a Recreation Room in Dunkirk.

SECOND WORLD WAR

CONSCRIPTION AND CONSCIENCE

DISSENTING VOICES, PACIFIST ARTISTS

AN INTRODUCTION

At 11.15a.m. on 3 September 1939 Prime Minister Neville Chamberlain, in a radio broadcast to the Nation, announced that a state of war existed between Britain and Germany. On the same day Parliament passed The National Service (Armed Forces) [NSA] Act, which imposed conscription on all men aged between 18–41. Provision was made for Conscientious Objectors (COs) to apply to be placed on a Register of Conscientious Objectors and be provisionally registered. The explanatory notes made it clear that a CO should within 14 days, apply to the local Tribunal (of which there were 17 in Great Britain) to have their case considered. By the end of July 1940 51,000 men had registered as COs. Following the introduction of conscription of women who were aged between 20–30 and unmarried or childless widows in December 1941 they were also given the right to register as COs. At the same time the age range for men conscripted was raised from 41 to 51. By the end of the war some 62,000 had applied to register as COs, of these over 1,000 were women.

Tribunals were administered by the Ministry of Labour and National Service; members were more carefully selected and were in general regarded as being more fair-minded and tolerant than those of the First World War. The artists who appeared before the London Tribunal were questioned by 'a lawyer, a professor, an alderman, a trade unionist, a woman J.P. and the headmistress of a girls' school'[1] under the chairmanship of Judge Hargreaves. If the Tribunal was not satisfied by the claim the applicant's name was removed from the Register and they were liable for call up to the armed forces. There was a right of appeal to an Appellate Tribunal within 21 days 'by any applicant aggrieved by the determination of a local Tribunal.'[2] 'Chairmen' were nominated by the Lord Chancellor; in Scotland it was the Lord President of the Court of Session who appointed the well regarded 'Lord Elphinstone, a courteous aristocrat, who allowed full latitude to claimants.'[3]

If the Tribunal was satisfied that the ground on which the application was made was established, then they were required to direct either:

> *A) that the applicant be finally registered without conditions …* [the absolutist position and most difficult to obtain]
>
> *B) that the applicant be conditionally registered … until the end of the present emergency, the condition being that he … undertake work specified by the Tribunal of a civil character and under civilian control, and … undergo training … to fit him for such work …*
>
> *C) that the applicant's name be removed from the Register of Conscientious Objectors, and that he be registered as … liable under the Act to be called up for service, but to be employed in non-combatant duties only.*

The Non-Combatant Corps (NCC) was reformed in August 1940 to receive category C objectors, of whom some 6,750 served. Gordon Scott and Keith Vaughan were among their number. John Minton served for a time with the Pioneer Corps. The Friends Ambulance Unit (FAU) was reformed by former members, including Paul Cadbury and Arthur Rowntree, to provide medical aid to civilian and military casualties; some 1,300 men and nearly 100 women served. Hugo Powell did so from 1939 having established his CO status at a Tribunal.

The majority of COs were assigned to category B and directed to a variety of work, including forestry, coal mining, hospital and ambulance services and agriculture. The latter received the largest numbers of COs, and by April 1942 there were over 7,000 working on the land. Within this small group of artists the following were engaged in such work for various periods during the war: Sven Berlin, Roland Collins, Patrick Heron, John Petts and Peter Reddick. In addition, Robert Adams made agricultural machinery, while elsewhere fellow sculptor Reg Butler repaired it. Bryan Wynter initially undertook land drainage and Jonah Jones worked in forestry. (Jones and Petts later transferred to the 224 Parachute Field Ambulance, Royal Army Medical Corps. and Wynter worked in a laboratory.) Finding agricultural work was at times problematic as farmers were reluctant to employ COs, although a labour shortage in certain regions in 1941, led to farmers being more inclined to employ them.

Public attitudes, which during the phoney war had been notably tolerant, shifted and became more overtly hostile in 1940–41 in the face of rumour and speculation about possible invasion as German troops swept through continental Europe. While John Tunnard was not subject to hostility as an auxiliary coastguard from 1940 having met the qualifications being 'over the age of 40, with good eyesight and hearing, long residence on the coast, and good knowledge of ships and shipping'[4] he was well aware of the anxieties about invasion. Following the evacuation of Dunkirk the *Sunday Pictorial* published a blistering article condemning pacifists headlined 'Pacifists and Pansies'.[5] Many private employers sacked COs, and barely a month later, over a hundred local authorities had dismissed all COs in their employment or suspended them.[6] This climate of hysteria and scare mongering led Winston Churchill to comment in the House of Commons 'anything in the nature of persecutions, victimisation or man-hunting is odious to the British people.'[7]

Towards the end of March 1941 COs found themselves being drafted to Civil Defence services as a result of the recently amended National Service Act which was in response to the shortage of full-time workers therein, particularly given the impact of the Blitz. Newly called up John Bridgeman elected to serve with the Civil Defence Heavy Rescue Service. Most, however, were drafted to the Auxiliary Fire Service where the need was greatest.[8]

As the war continued and the horrors of Nazism emerged many pacifists and indeed COs faced a moral dilemma. Bernard Meadows reconsidered his decision midway through 1941 and served with the RAF in the air-sea rescue service; Sven Berlin enlisted in December 1942. For those artists who were COs in First World War similar challenges had to be faced albeit their age precluded call-up, Duncan Grant and Percy Horton for instance revised their stance.

Lawrence Gowing, George Kennethson and Arthur Wragg all registered as conscientious objectors and convinced their respective Tribunals that they should be allowed to continue to paint. 'It was not a consciously selfish attitude, for these men and women were convinced their real contribution to world betterment lay through their art and in no other way.'[9] Similar sentiments were expressed in the influential literary magazine *Horizon: A Review of Literature and Art* which began publication in January 1940 and continued for a further ten years. Founder and editor Cyril Connolly (1903–74) referred to it as a 'child of war'; in his regular Comment he wrote in May 1940:

> *The war is the enemy of creative activity, and writers and painters are wise and right to ignore it and to concentrate their talent on other subjects. ... But they must also realize that their liberty and security are altogether threatened, that Fascism is against them ... They must celebrate by creating more culture as fast as they can ...*[10]

Gowing and Wragg were particularly aware of the threats posed by Fascism. Pre-war Gowing was active in the radical Artists International Association (AIA) whose aims were to fight for peace against Fascism and graphic artist Wragg in the Peace Pledge Union whose drawings enlarged on anti-war posters caused public wrath. Victor Pasmore, also an active AIA member, failed in his efforts to register as a CO but following an appeal in September 1942 he too was allowed to paint full-time, being described as 'one of half a dozen men in England whose art is important for the future.'[11] Kenneth Clark, chairman of the War Artists' Advisory Committee, supported his appeal and was instrumental in enabling Quaker and CO objector Kenneth Rowntree to undertake commissions that did not conflict with his pacifist views.

Arnold Machin was not so fortunate and despite powerful support when he appealed received a twelve-month prison sentence. Nonetheless, the number of COs imprisoned in the Second World War was significantly lower with only about three per cent, as opposed to thirty per cent in the First World War and their treatment was generally more lenient.

After the war some COs found their old jobs no longer open to them and many continued to be subject to social disapproval and found it difficult to find sympathetic employers. However, this group of artists were eventually able to resume and/or develop their careers, which for some were markedly affected by their war experiences and reflected in the work they later produced.

REFERENCES AND NOTES

1. Ministry of Information (1944) *Manpower: The Story of Britain's Mobilisation for War*, London: HMSO, p.51.
2. See The National Service (Armed Forces) Act, 1939, Explanatory Note.
3. Marwick, W.H. (1972) 'Conscientious Objection in Scotland in the First World War', *Scottish Journal of Science*, 1, 3, p.158.
4. HMSO (1939) *National Service: A Guide to the Ways in which the People of this Country may give Service – With a message from the Prime Minister*, p.25.
5. Rose, S.O. (2003) *Which People's War: National Identity and Citizenship in Wartime Britain 1939–1945*, Oxford: Oxford University Press, p.175.
6. Calder, A. (1986) *The People's War: Britain 1939–45*, London: Granada, p.496.
7. Kennedy, T. (1973) 'Public Opinion and the Conscientious Objector, 1915–19', *Journal of British Studies*, 12, May, p.119.
8. See Barker, R. (1982) *Conscience, Government and War. Conscientious Objection in Great Britain 1939–45*, London: Routledge & Kegan Paul.
9. Hayes, Denis (1949) *Challenge of Conscience: The Story of Conscientious Objectors of 1939–1949*, London: Allen & Unwin, p.45. To date I have not identified any women artists who were officially registered as COs in the Second World War.
10. Connolly, C. (1940) Comment, *Horizon*, 1, 5, p.314. His views were challenged by Goronwy Rees, a writer in uniform, who pointed out that war should not be ignored. Connolly published Rees' objection in the issue that followed and in his response modified his aesthetic position.
11. Cited in Hayes (1949) Op. cit., p.45.

ROBERT ADAMS

(1917–84)

Adams left school aged fourteen and later studied life drawing and painting part-time at evening classes at Northampton School of Art between c.1937–46 becoming an accomplished draughtsman. As there were no sculpture classes the various manual jobs which Adams undertook and where he learned to use wood and metal working tools, enabled him to become a skilled carpenter and wood carver, important attributes as he was largely self taught as a sculptor.

During the Second World War, Adams, a conscientious objector worked variously in a printing shop, a timber yard and for Cooch and Sons, a long established Northampton firm making agricultural machinery. Cooch and Sons specialised in elevators and potato sorters and Adams' sketchbook contains drawings of the wooden frames of elevators some of which were developed into watercolours (c.1944). These drawings were exhibited with his early sculptures at one of the Civil Defence Artists group shows at the Cooling Galleries in New Bond Street during 1944. He first exhibited with members of the Red Cross, police, ambulance, V.A.D., National Fire Service and the like in 1942. Adams' sketchbook also contains studies 'of men working belt-driven machines such as lathes, of the machines themselves, and of sawn wood seasoning in stacks. All the studies have a matter-of-fact quality. They are records of what caught his eye in his everyday life. ... there are two pages ... [which] show studies for sculpture;'[1] whether Adams made them is not known. In the evenings Adams undertook voluntary duties as fire warden in Civil Defence.

Two years after the ending of the war Adams held a one-man show of sculpture at the Gimpel Fils Gallery in Duke Street, it was to be the first of many with the Gallery. Charles Gimpel (and his brother Peter) was a particularly sympathetic and understanding art dealer showing faith in Adams' work from the outset. He held his eighth exhibition with Gimpel Fils in 1962: *The Times* art critic noted that over that period Adams had 'moved from wood and stone to metal, and from the chunkiest of solid forms to aerial arrangements of spars and bronzed steel plates, [and] pursued his abstract ideal with relentless integrity. He was abstract before it was fashionable ...'.[2]

From 1949–61 Adams taught at the Department of Industrial Design and Sculpture at the Central School of Art and Design in London. There he came into contact with Victor Pasmore and other staff and experimented with styles, mediums and scale, [most of his work in the 50s was small scale], moving from the wooden figurative forms of the 1940s, to his later bronze works which combine fluidity and asymmetrical shapes to create smooth clean lines.'[3] The school provided facilities for welding.

In 1951 Adams was commissioned by the Arts Council alongside eleven other young sculptors to contribute to the Festival of Britain. The following year he received early recognition internationally as one of Britain's foremost abstract sculptors when his work was included in the Venice Biennale alongside Reg Butler and Bernard Meadows (also COs) and others. Adams' work was also shown in the British Pavilion at the XXXI Biennale in 1962 and in 1964 in the section arte d'oggi nei musei (art today in museums). He continued to exhibit worldwide and to receive numerous private and public commissions both at home and abroad and execute large-scale architectural works, returning in the 70s to carving, which he cast in bronze. ♦♦♦

SVEN BERLIN

(1911–99)

Berlin enrolled at Beckenham School of Art but stayed only for six weeks becoming instead a professional adagio dancer appearing on the stage throughout the 1930s. He abandoned this to pursue his lifelong ambition to be an artist and returned to Cornwall and attended Redruth and Camborne School of Art. Berlin met the resident artists of St Ives and soon became one of their number; seeing paintings by Wallis he started to research and write his biography *Alfred Wallis, Primitive* which was published in 1949.

On the outbreak of war Berlin applied to be placed on the Register of Conscientious Objectors, as he did not want his name on the Military Service Register and thus eligible for call up. At the time he was working as a boilerman in the Milk Marketing Board factory in Treswithian. The workforce were increasingly hostile to his pacifist stance and threatened to throw him down a mine shaft, Berlin persuaded them that he believed in God and that the sacredness of life was more important than destroying it and the threat was temporarily averted. Appearing before the South-Western Tribunal in Bristol under Judge Wethered to explain why he should be exempt Berlin convinced the board his artistic work was of 'national significance' and his pacifism and moral convictions genuine. Berlin's forebears on his mother's side were Quakers in Yorkshire and 'their simplicity and lack of flourish'[4] appealed to him. He recalled in his autobiography *The Coat of Many Colours* (1994) that the Quakers he stayed with the night before his Tribunal heckled the Judge and panel members who questioned him. Granted exemption, Berlin was required to undertake work on the land. His hearing was reported locally and headlined 'Pacifist faces Boomerang Argument'. From then on Berlin noted that public opinion turned against him and rumours abounded that he was a spy. He was later arrested in Redruth for drawing in the street and in a churchyard which was also used as the Local Defence Unit's HQ and for signalling to German submarines from the North Cliffs but not charged.[5]

Berlin together with his first wife Helga and baby son Paul joined a pacifist commune in Ashburton, Devon established by Deryck Bazalgette (1913–2010), through the Society of Friends. When not working as a 'coalheaver' he made portrait sketches of fellow commune members Max Chapman, a painter and art critic, and Oswell Blakeston, a painter and film maker. Berlin then secured work as a gardener at Greylands, Ashburton a small private girls' boarding school, before moving to work as gardener and art-teacher at an evacuated Rudolph Steiner school in Carbis Bay, just outside St Ives and the growing art colony. He also worked nearby on the influential art critic Adrian Stokes' market garden where amongst other artists he met Stokes' wife Margaret Mellis, Wilhelmina Barns-Graham, Ben Nicholson, Barbara Hepworth and Russian refugee Naum Gabo, the pioneering sculptor. Berlin's *Construction by the Sea*, series of drawings in ink, pencil and crayon executed in 1941–42 show the influence of 'the more industrial early constructivist works of Gabo.'[6] This influence was not reflected in other work of the period such as his sketches of agricultural workers *Dung Skating*, *Broccoli Picking* and *Hedging*. Versatile throughout his life Berlin resisted efforts to be allied to any specific art movement working from the heart and viewing his writing as always part of his work.

In 1941 Berlin met Patrick and Delia Heron and became close friends with Bernard Leach with whom he shared an interest in 'Oriental Art' and his son, David. At the pottery he supplemented his income rebuilding clay dryers after a German landmine hit it whilst taking the opportunity to learn to throw pots. Berlin later sketched Leach drawing at Hellesvean and Heron amongst other St Ives personalities ably capturing their likenesses. Leach, like Berlin, had been subject to suspicion by local people and following a bombing raid he was accused of signalling to the German planes with his furnace. Heavy bombing raids in March and April devastated Plymouth and killed many civilians, events that greatly troubled Berlin who was working on land near

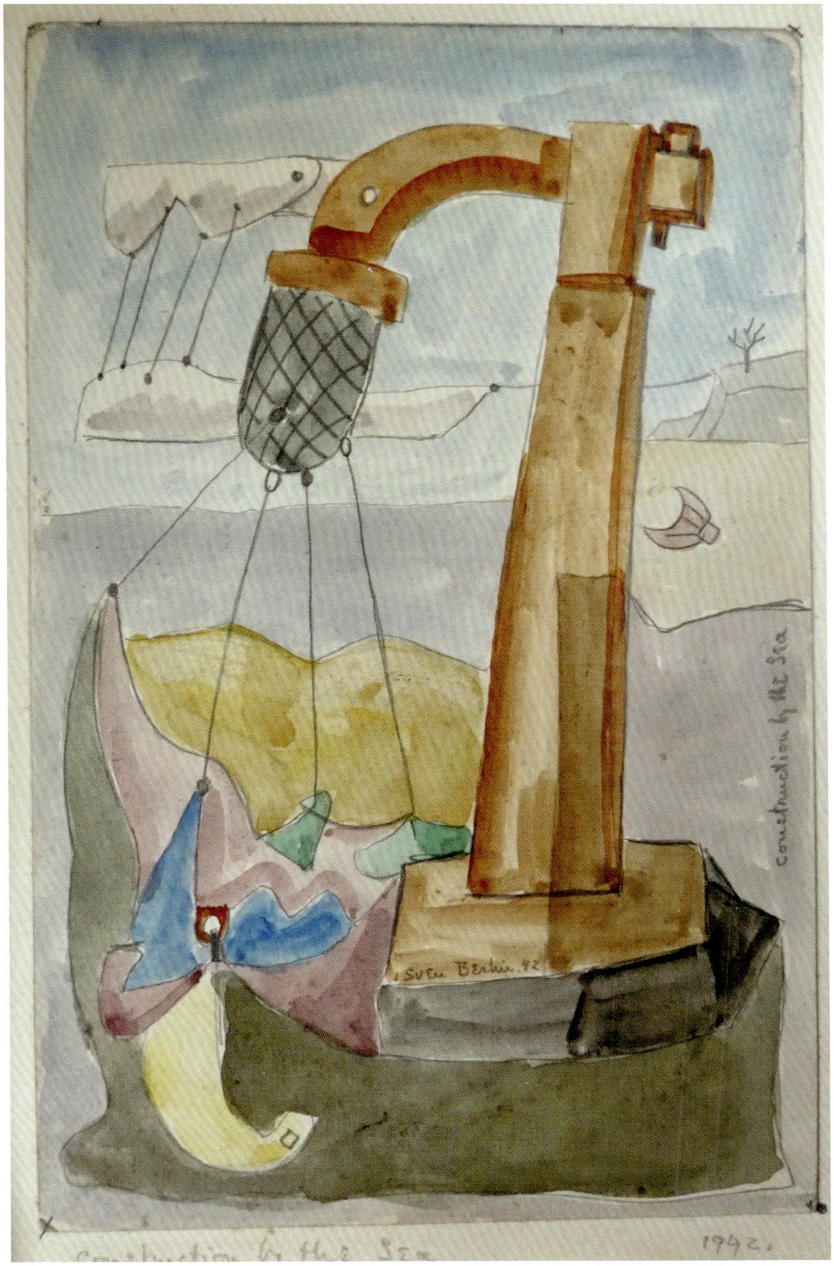

Sven Berlin | *Construction by the Sea* | 1942,Watercolour, 37.5 x 31.3 cm | © Julia Berlin

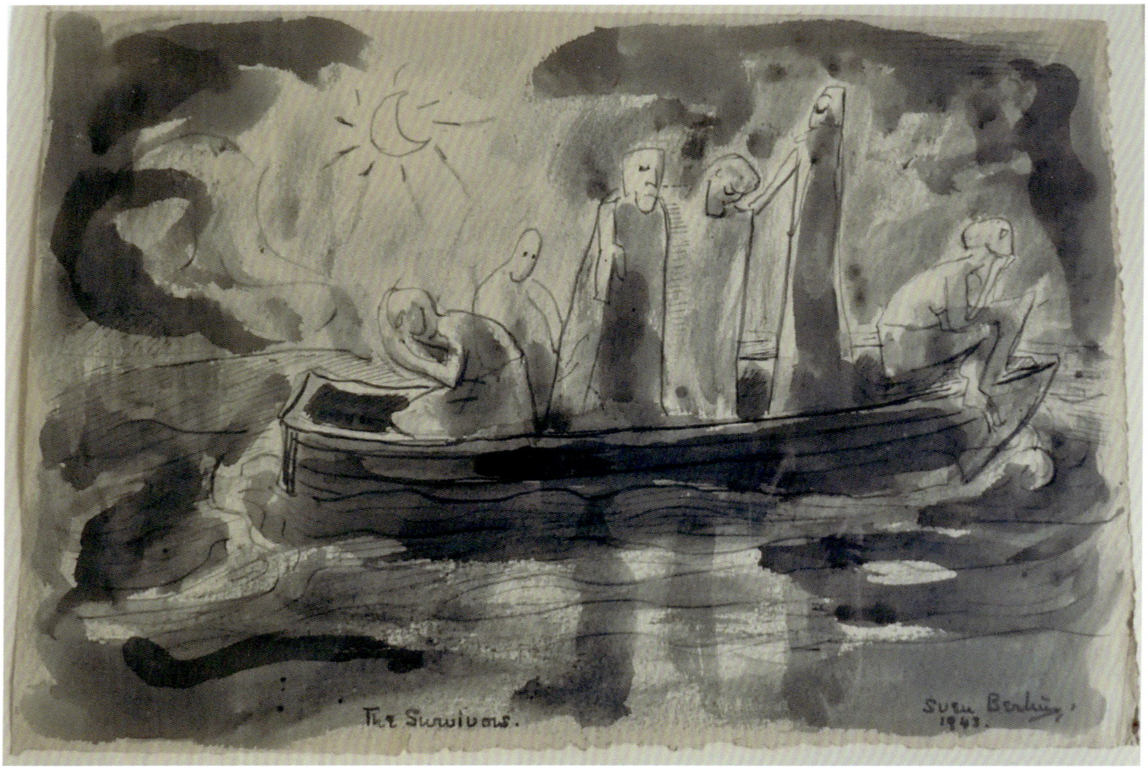

Sven Berlin | *The Survivors* | 1943, Pen and wash, 19 x 28 cm | © Julia Berlin

Zennor where he now lived. Returning late from a visit to friends of Alfred Wallis he witnessed a German attack on a British convoy in the Atlantic and wrote:

> *I ... realised the destructive force of war and that I could not become a complete artist until I had experienced its full horror. I decided to join up. A complete reorientation took place.*[7]

Berlin enlisted on 3 December 1942 and took part in the invasion of France as Forward Observer for the Royal Artillery landing on K-Beach (Juno) on 24 June 1944.[8] He went on to record his experiences not only in France but also Belgium and Holland. *I am Lazarus* (1961), Berlin's well-received account of a front-line soldier's life under fire, drew on his records and drawings and correspondence with Stokes. Whilst training Berlin also received books on art from Nicholson and completed the first draft of *Alfred Wallis, Primitive*. By the end of 1944 he was back in 'Blighty' suffering from jaundice and deep depression dreading the prospect of returning to the hell of war. Berlin was transferred to a military psychiatric hospital in Birmingham and discharged from the Army on 8 May, 1945, VE (Victory in Europe) Day.

Post-war Berlin became one of the most active and colourful members of the St Ives community, painting and writing prolifically and carving the local granite. In 1946 he formed with John Wells, Peter Lanyon and Bryan Wynter the Crypt Group. A gifted draughtsman he also helped to form the Penwith Society in 1949 and through Heron met sculptor Reg Butler. In 1952 he worked on an entry for the internal competition for a monument for 'The Unknown Political Prisoner' that Butler later won. The following year bitterly disillusioned with the emphasis on modernist art and its elitism he left St Ives with his second wife Juanita, for the New Forest in a horse-drawn wagon to live for the next 10 years or so with gypsies near Lyndhurst an 'exile' from which an intensely creative period ensued. In 1962 he published *The Dark Monarch*, a novel based on his life in St Ives; controversy and legal action by several of those depicted followed and it was withdrawn. Following libel suits he and his third wife Julia whom he had married in 1963 moved to the Isle of Wight returning to rural Dorset in 1975 where they remained for the rest of his life, writing and drawing to the end. ◆◆◆

JOHN BRIDGEMAN

(1916–2004)

Bridgeman's aptitude for drawing was noted by Sir Alfred Munnings, a close neighbour, who advised sending-him to Colchester School of Art. Bridgeman studied under sculptor and designer (Herbert) Barry Hart (1894–1954) and newly appointed Edward Morss (1906–94), who had recently completed his studies at the Royal College of Art (RCA). 'They were enlightened teachers ... Hart introduced a nude-life-class, attracting London models ... and an awareness of modern art'.[9] Bridgeman won an Essex Major Scholarship to study painting and engraving at the RCA in 1938. He studied under Gilbert Spencer (1892–1979) and Malcolm Osborne (1880–1963) but the war interrupted his studies.

Bridgeman 'was an agnostic with a very strong sense of morality and ethics.'[10] A conscientious objector, he served full-time with the Civil Defence Heavy Rescue Service from 1941–45 in Fulham, rescuing the injured and recovering dead bodies from the rubble and debris of damaged buildings particularly during the London Blitz. Bridgeman worked alongside civil engineers, carpenters, bricklayers and plumbers who were first on the scene to assess if the damaged building was safe for members of the emergency services to enter. They used their pre-war experience often in dangerous situations to work out the safest and quickest way to reach the injured and safely demolish collapsing buildings. 'This experience left a deep scar on Bridgeman and later found expression in his sculpture which reflected his profound understanding of and compassion for the human condition.'[11] Aside from his rescue work Bridgeman exhibited with the Civil Defence Artists at the Cooling Galleries in July 1942, *The Times* critic commenting that his was 'good work.' He sketched bombed buildings, stretcher-beds used to carry the dead and wounded, and sleeping members of his team at the Fulham depot. This ceased late in 1942, when the wartime censor refused his request for a permit to paint and sketch such subjects.[12] Bridgeman returned to sketching and painting less sensitive topics. He 'became aware of the horrors of the Nazi concentration camps before the British public through his wife's [Irene Dancyger] work at the BBC during the war, and his convictions as a conscientious objector were severely tested by this information.'[13]

In 1946 Bridgeman was awarded the Sigismund Goetz Scholarship for painting. He returned to the RCA in September 1947 to study sculpture with Frank Dobson (1886–1963) and John Skeaping (1901–80), graduating in July 1949. He turned down a prestigious Rome Scholarship, due to family commitments: in 1941 he had married Irene Dancyger, a writer and journalist, and they now had two small children. He remained at the RCA teaching sculpture part-time and exhibiting paintings with major London galleries. In 1951 he worked for Misha Black's Design Research Unit, and created large panels of marine life for 'The Sea' in the Dome of Discovery at the Festival of Britain. Bridgeman was appointed Head of Sculpture at Carlisle School of Art in 1951, and in 1956 succeeded William Bloye (1890–1975) as Head of Sculpture at Birmingham School of Art where he remained until retiring in 1981.

Working in stone, concrete, ciment fondu and bronze and always experimenting with new materials and forms, he contributed greatly to the regeneration of Birmingham after the war with for example his large-scale innovative 'play sculptures' for children in playgrounds in the 1960s. His many commissions included the *Mater Dolorosa* (1970) in the Lady Chapel of Coventry Cathedral. In 1974 he co-wrote with Irene Dancyger *Clay Models and Stone Carving*, his philosophy of art and interest in methods and materials are embodied in the book. Bridgeman's *The Torture Wall* (Leamington Spa Art Gallery & Museum) an unfinished exploration of the brutality of war, and its impact upon the defenceless and vulnerable is perhaps his most forceful work. Bridgeman admired Goya's *The Disasters of War* (1810–20). His own work was begun in the aftermath of war and resulted in an installation in ciment fondu made up of approximately 20 figures 'with distorted heads some devil-like and others suggesting a mutant form of humanity'.[14] He reworked some of the figures as late as 2000. ◆◆◆

REG BUTLER

(1913–81)

Butler trained as an architect from 1933–36 at Regent Street Polytechnic before becoming a tutor at the Architectural Association School in London. From 1939 he practised as an architect as Cotterell Butler in partnership with Oscar A. Bayne and during the war he wrote a series of articles on pre-fabricated buildings. He was for four years Technical Editor of the *Architect's Journal*.

Rosemary Butler, (b.1930, née Young) who trained at Camberwell and Wimbledon Schools of Art and the Slade School of Fine Art (1949–53) recalled him telling her how the war completely affected his life because he knew he was not going to go, as he was a pacifist. (She was his assistant from 1952). Previously, when a member of the Officer Training Corps at Hertford Grammar School he turned down the offer of a scholarship to Sandhurst.[15] Butler voluntarily attended his army medical and on passing was assigned to the Parachute Regiment. Butler believed that killing and maiming and fighting was no answer and moreover he had seen the wastage of life as a result of the First World War and could see it happening all over again.

Butler registered as a conscientious objector, a decision he gave great thought and care to and one that did not come easily despite his pacifist beliefs. At his local tribunal, Butler, who had sought advice from Ambrose Appelbee a solicitor who had advised a number of COs, presented his case for exemption from military service. The panel granted him exemption on the grounds that he did alternative civilian service, a decision Butler never understood, as they had appeared to reject his arguments. The Butlers moved to Iping, a small village near Midhurst in West Sussex where they lived in a caravan on the land of Esmé and Richard Strachey. They set up a small business[16] and for the remainder of the war Butler repaired farm machinery and travelled around the county, for which he received a petrol allowance, mending tractors, milking machines, combined harvesters and making spare parts where necessary. As Rosemary Butler said 'it wasn't blacksmithing as such', he had no formal training in making the most precise instruments on his lathe, 'he just learnt it all himself'.

After the war the Butlers rented a property in Hatfield and although still practising as an architect he started to make small sculptures c.1947–48 having already experimented with casting lead. During the war he had begun to carve smooth, polished bone forms in wood and paint watercolours. Butler gradually realised he wanted to be a sculptor, in spring 1948 he worked briefly as an assistant to near neighbour sculptor Henry Moore (1898–1986). He had his first one-man show at the Hanover Gallery, London, in July 1949. The work was forged after which he started to weld. Rosemary Butler recollected that he called it 'knitting in metal'; and that he began to feel the need to move away from the iron. The following year Butler became the first recipient of a Gregory Fellowship in sculpture at Leeds University. This awarded him a three-year bursary to extend his work without conditions. He continued to live in Hatfield travelling to Leeds as necessary. Butler commenced teaching one day a week at the Slade in 1951 and working in clay producing more solid sculpture. In the same year he participated in the Festival of Britain.

The following year Butler was chosen as one of nine sculptors to exhibit in *New Aspects of British Sculpture* in the Britain Pavilion at the XXVI Venice Biennale. The others were Robert Adams, Kenneth Armitage (who succeeded him as Gregory Fellow), Lynn Chadwick, Geoffrey Clarke, Bernard Meadows, Eduardo Paolozzi and William Turnbull. Butler's work was starting to receive critical acclaim and attract widespread interest and he commenced work on his entry for the international sculpture competition for a monument to the 'Unknown Political Prisoner' making detailed preparatory drawings of the heads of three women who stand on the rock base. The idea was that the work would commemorate those who had given their lives or liberty to the cause of human freedom. Sponsored by the Institute of Contemporary Arts, London, whose president

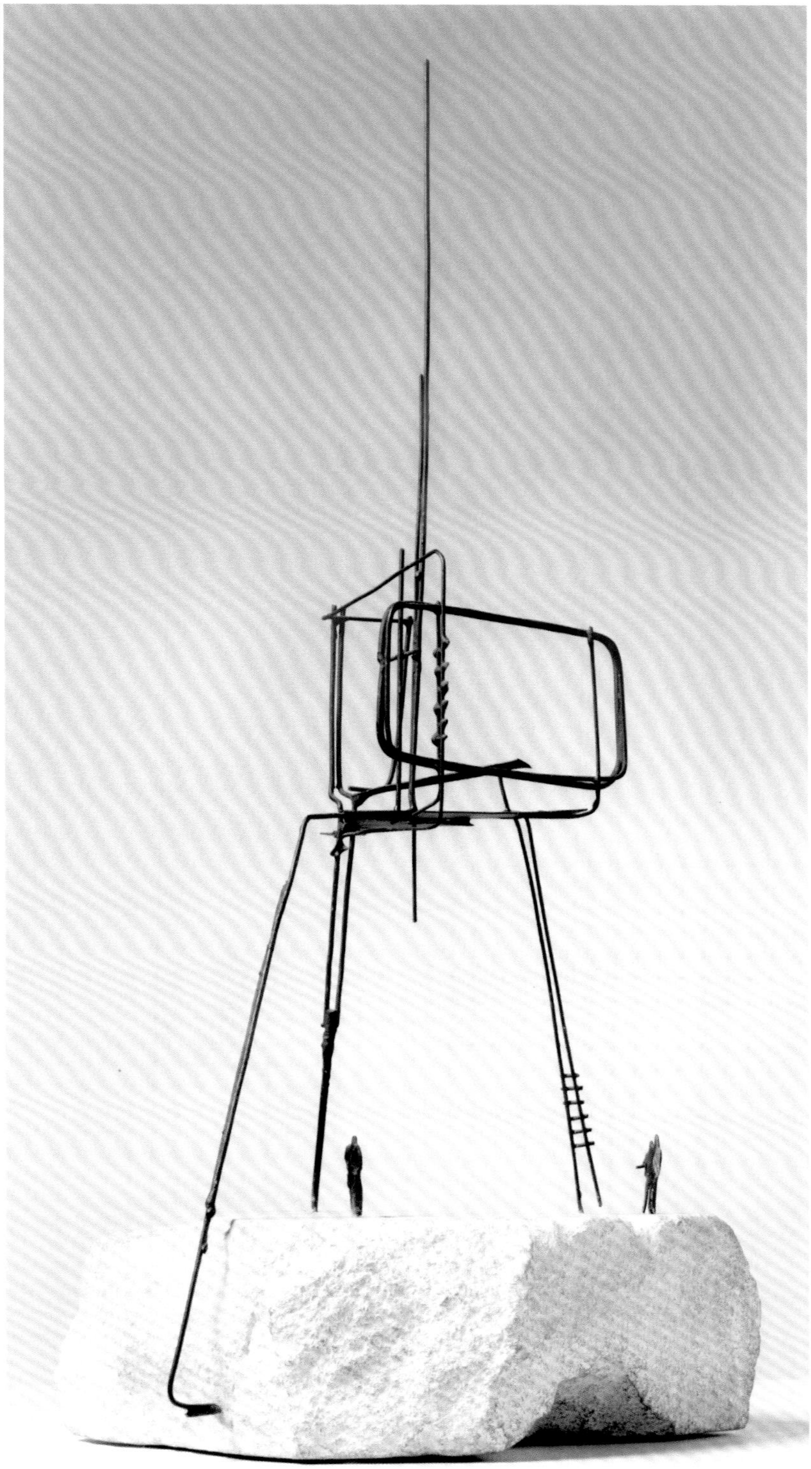

Reg Butler | *Final Maquette for 'The Unknown Political Prisoner', 1951–2*
© The Estate of Reg Butler/Photograph: © Tate London 2018

was Herbert Read, over 50 countries held preliminary competitions (there were *c.*2,500 entries) before sending their quota of winners to be judged in London. The sculpture winning the grand prize was to be installed on a site of international importance to be determined after the award was made. In March 1953 Butler gained international fame winning the competition, which said much about his pacifist beliefs, his sculpture being a part of who he was and a projection of himself.

He received £4,500, which enabled him to buy a substantial property near Berkhamsted, complete with outbuildings suitable for a forge, where he lived for the rest of his life. Barbara Hepworth and Naum Gabo were two of the runners-up. Butler's work, and indeed the competition's subject, caused controversy and Butler's maquette was smashed when it was on public display in the Tate. According to *The Times* this act of malicious damage was by an artist, formerly a Hungarian national, and now a stateless person who was affronted by it. Butler attended the subsequent court proceedings at Bow Street Court. The art dealer and co-founder of Gimpel Fils, Charles Gimpel (1913–73), who had been a member of the French resistance and tortured and sent to Auschwitz, attended the court and spoke in support of Butler about his Political Prisoner entry and what it meant to him.

Butler spoke at length about his entry some years later in an arts documentary television programme devoted to his work and practice, as part of the series *The Artist Speaks*, produced for the BBC in 1958 by John Read, the son of Herbert Read, the art critic. He expressed his regret that his sculpture composed of wire and stone seemed widely misunderstood, *The Times* had described it as 'like an iron cage on a stick.' Butler explained how he saw it:

> *... it's a tower standing on a rock against the open sky and on this rock stand three figures gazing up into the heights of the tower and remembering the political prisoners that died in the concentration camps.*
>
> *... people thought it was inhuman and there is an inhuman element in it expressed by the tower, but the really human part of it is the three women that stand and gaze from their position on the rock. It's a kind of stage set high up overlooking the world around.*

To Butler's bitter regret the sculpture, which was due to be built overlooking the east-west frontier in Berlin, was never built despite his trips to Berlin to meet Willy Brandt, and other political figures.

In 1960 Butler became a member of the British anti-war group the Committee of 100 set up with a hundred public signatories by Bertrand Russell and others; Russell resigned from the presidency of the Campaign for Nuclear Disarmament (CND) to do so. Butler had been active in the disarmament campaign as an Aldermaston marcher.[17] After 1963 Butler made little sculpture and rarely exhibited, 'his own modelled bronze figures were beginning to look dated ... and the explicit sexuality of Butler's painted bronze women [with a sugar-almond surface ran the risk of proving] uncomfortable to some.'[18] Nonetheless, his work continued to be well-regarded in particular in Europe and America. A memorial exhibition was held at the Tate Gallery in 1983 two years after his death. ◆◆◆

ROLAND COLLINS

(1918–2015)

Collins won a London County Council grant to attend St Martin's School of Art for two years where he studied life drawing, design and lettering. In 1936 he worked for the advertising agency London Press Exchange in the design department. The following year he showed a small landscape drawing *Chiswick* for the first time in the Royal Academy's Summer Exhibition.

At the outbreak of the war Collins registered as a conscientious objector. As a schoolboy 'he had deserted classes to hold protest meetings in the basement against Hitler, Mussolini, Franco and the Baldwin-inspired abdication of Edward VIII.'[19] He was exempted from military service on the grounds he undertake light agricultural work. Collins was briefly at Dartington Hall in Devon but as he had:

> *… a doubtful lung so nothing much materialised out of it. Back in London, I was doing a painting of the Nash terraces in Regent's Park when a policeman came along and I was taken back to the station for questioning. I discovered that there were military people based in those terraces and they wanted to know why I was interested in it.*[20]

Post-war Collins had a studio in Percy Street in Fitzrovia, London in the same building as the office of designer and publisher Noel Carrington. Collins produced a set of lithographs for Carrington's book *Colour and Pattern in the Home* while working freelance as an illustrator and designer. It was not until his nineties that Collins, whose colourful, bold landscapes have been overlooked for decades, received the attention his distinctive work warranted. 'A topographer in the mould of Ravilious, Piper and Bawden, Collins is an expert on forgotten histories, adept at evoking the spirit of the past through architectural detail.'[21] ◆◆◆

LAWRENCE GOWING

(1918–91)

Gowing was first inspired to paint when a pupil at The Downs, a preparatory Quaker school for boys in Colwall, near Great Malvern. The Downs'[22] headmaster Geoffrey Hoyland, a conscientious objector in the First World War who served with the FAU, placed great emphasis on the arts appointing the influential teacher, and Slade-trained artist Maurice Feild (1905–88). Feild's open-air teaching methods based on direct observation impacted on Gowing and Kenneth Rowntree and many other painters of national standing between 1928–55 before he returned to the Slade to teach (at the invitation of William Coldstream). From 1932–35 Gowing attended Leighton Park School, Reading, which The Downs 'fed'. He subsequently became a private pupil of Coldstream's before joining the Euston Road School where 'he closely identified with [his] penchant for discrete paint strokes.'[23] Gowing was introduced to Coldstream by poet W.H. Auden, a friend of Feild's, who had also taught at The Downs.

A member of the Artists International Association (AIA), Gowing in February 1939 was involved with other members painting illustrated slogans onto advertising hoardings calling for support for the campaign to send food to Spain. Around this time he was also briefly a member of the Hogarth Group of communist painters that was loosely allied to the AIA; Gowing only had a Party card for some three months. The group was named after Hogarth as he was regarded as being a socially conscious British artist. Gowing produced the banners with Graham Bell, Victor Pasmore and Rodrigo Moynihan and others from their circle for the 'Arms for Spain' demonstration in Trafalgar Square on 12 February, taking motifs (or paraphrases as Coldstream and Pasmore described them) from Goya's *The Disasters of War* (1810–20). However, according to Pasmore the painters had intended that the banners be used for anti-war propaganda. Gowing and Coldstream in a joint interview explained that the 6' x 4' cloth banners:

> *... were lettered on the back with the inscription 'Hitler, Mussolini, Daladier, Chamberlain did this to Spain'. It did not impress the Essex Home Guard. They were taken to Monkesbury in Essex to be stored during the War in Rodrigo Moynihan's garage and they were confiscated by the Home Guard in a spy scare in 1940 and no one ever found out what happened to them.*[24]

More finished paintings from the same source were shown at the AIA's *Art for the People* (the theme was Unity of Artists for Peace, Democracy and Cultural Development) exhibition at the Whitechapel Gallery in 1939; Gowing exhibited his oil painting *Non-Combatant 5th May (after Goya)*, which had been made at the Euston Road School.

Gowing listened to Prime Minister Neville Chamberlain's radio broadcast to the nation, solemnly declaring 'that this country is at War with Germany' at Rodrigo Moynihan's on 3 September 1939 and where he painted for several weeks after. They and other artists over the previous 10 days had helped remove all the National Gallery paintings amid fears of widespread bombing of London. Gowing was a conscientious objector, a stance that probably grew out of his Quaker schooling, Bloomsbury connections and varied socialist political activities. At some stage in 1940 he appeared before a Military Tribunal and was exempted from service on condition that he continue painting. He moved to the Wiltshire village Chilton Foliat, gradually adjusted to the solitariness of the landscape and painted along the River Kennet, becoming friends with Paul Nash. *Apples II* was painted in his studio above the mill-race, it was the second of a series of fourteen paintings that he produced over the next five years. The apples were the first pickings of cooking ones. 'The bright green was a kind of inheritance from Graham Bell. He had used it with enviable richness in Suffolk before he went to the Air Force.'[25] After working on the painting it occurred to Gowing that

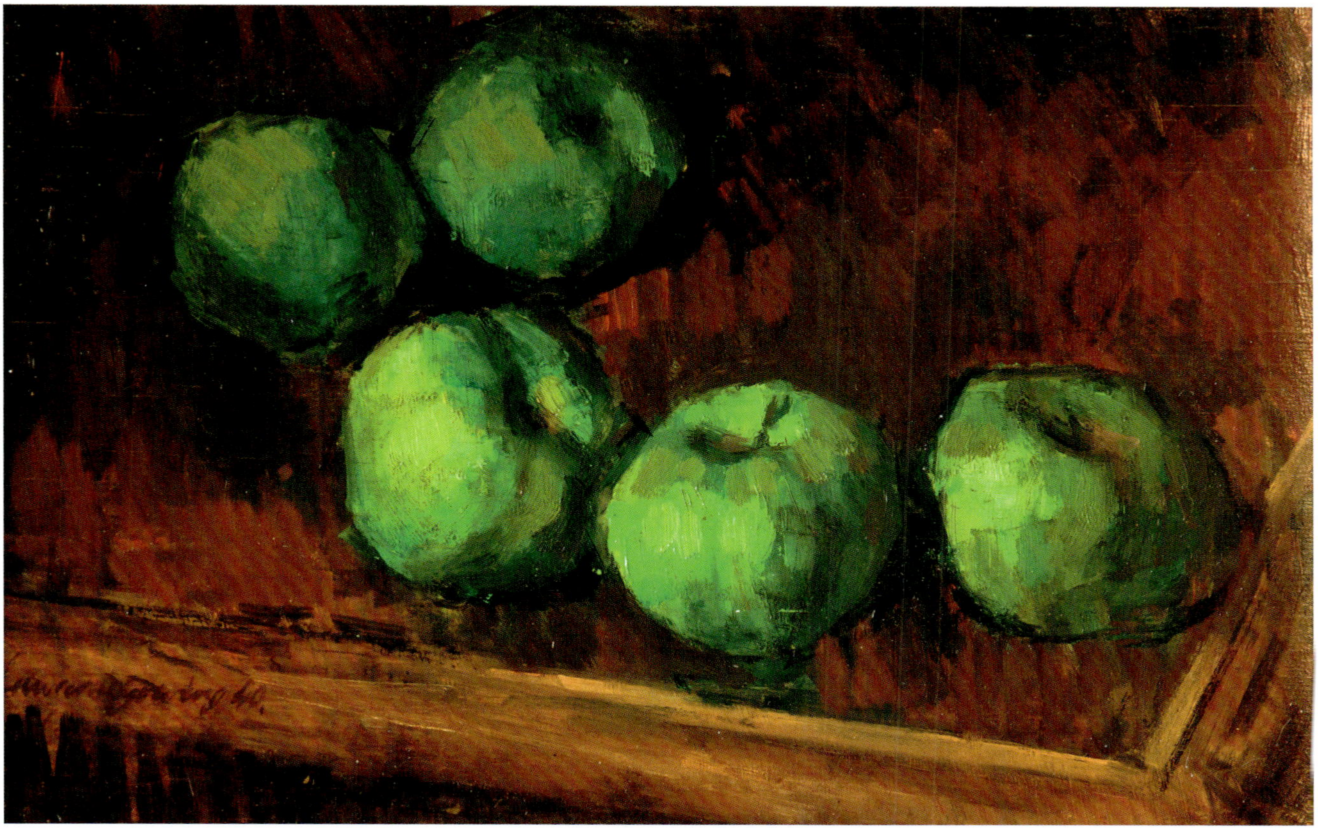

Lawrence Gowing | *Apples II* | 1940, Oil on canvas, 18 x 28 cm | Swindon Museum and Art Gallery 'the mutual examination of painter and subject was a theme of some drama and he began writing a dialogue between a painter and an apple, which takes him to task, to his private delight.'[26] At the same time he was wrestling with completing a portrait he brought with him from his London studio of Alfie Bass (1921–87), a talented young actor whom he met at the influential left-wing amateur Unity Theatre, Kings Cross. Gowing provided the set designs for the London première of *The Star Turns Red* by Sean O'Casey on 12 March 1940.

In 1943 Gowing settled in Chelsea and the following year commenced a brief spell of teaching at Camberwell School of Art. He received his first portrait commission in 1945 from Balliol College, University of Oxford to paint Lord Lindsay, Master of the College since 1924. Gowing spent the following two summers painting landscapes in Sutton, near Petworth, West Sussex. A succession of academic and other appointments followed including Professor of Fine Art, King's College, University of Durham, 1948–58 and from 1975–85 Slade Professor of Fine Art. The latter period marked a change in his painting style, moving away from the Euston Road tradition and using his own body as a kind of template to be covered in paint with feet and arms outspread by his students or studio assistants in the manner of Leonardo da Vinci's famous drawings of the Vitruvian proportions of a man's body.

Gowing received forty guineas from Ruth Borchard for his self-portrait for her collection; it was the highest figure paid. Gowing also wrote a number of well-received monographs including *Renoir* (1947), *Vermeer* (1952) and *Lucian Freud* (1982). Gowing was knighted in 1982 and made a Royal Academician in 1989. ◆◆◆

PATRICK HERON

(1920–99)

Heron spent part of his early childhood in St Ives before moving in 1929 to Welwyn Garden City where his father set up Cresta Silks and he attended St George's co-educational boarding school in Harpenden. He was greatly influenced by his art master Ludwig van der Straeten (1892–c.1985) who, while Heron was a pupil, completed three fine portraits of the headmaster, his wife and the chairman of the Trustees, (commissioned by the School Governors). Heron, excused from the compulsory afternoon games session because of his asthma, spent the time painting in an art hut; on one occasion Van der Straeten drove him some 30 miles to the National Gallery and led him to Cézanne's *Mont Sainte Victoire*. Although Van der Straeten simply pointed at it, the impact was immediate and Heron, enthralled, recalled going straight back and painting in the manner of Cézanne. Reflecting on his schooldays Heron recognised that in his youth French painting was exclusively his personal ideal.

Heron studied briefly at the Slade between 1937–39, attending only two days a week as he found it of little value and steadfastly refused to take any course. With the outbreak of war he registered as a conscientious objector. His decision was likely influenced by his parents who were deeply important to him: his father was a pacifist and Fabian and his mother's brother had been imprisoned during the First World War for his beliefs and their father a pacifist Unitarian minister. At his Tribunal Heron was directed to undertake agricultural work for the Cambridgeshire War Agricultural Executive Committee. He worked on the land alongside Czechs and Poles, and other refugees for three years digging ditches in the Fens, earning 18s 6d a week.

In 1943 when not working Heron would 'escape' to London to repeatedly visit the Redfern Gallery's basement room to gaze at Matisse's *The Red Studio* (*L'Atelier Rouge*, 1911), one of his largest canvases, painted at Issy-les-Moulineaux, which was on extended loan, 'to absorb, in every detail, the revelations of this great masterpiece. It was ... by far and away the most influential single painting in my entire career.'[27] The war put 'rather a stopper' on Heron's painting but he did produce a number of very small pictures, keeping barely a dozen of them. The oil painting *The Piano: 1943* which began as 'a pencil drawing, and was then filled in with area-shapes – a method which survived until the 1970s in [his] work'[28] was painted in his parents' house in Welwyn. In April Heron gave the painting of the grand piano before an open window to Delia Reiss as a present, they married in 1945. Heron made a screen print of *The Piano* in 1978, and in his second E. William Doty Lecture in Fine Art at the College of Fine Arts, University of Texas at Austin, entitled 'Brushwork is Spatial' he explained that he had come with hindsight:

> *... (and by hindsight I literally mean thirty years) to recognise that this picture marks the greatest step forward in my whole life, in the sense that it is visibly related, in shape after shape and colour after colour, to works typical of my production at point after point in time from the Fifties on.*[29]

Labouring on the land often in appalling conditions prompted Heron to get a job working in a large mass-production chicken farm closer to his parents' home in Welwyn. He cycled daily from Welwyn the five miles to the village of Codicote to the farm but the feathers severely affected his asthma and led to his health collapsing. (He had not declared his asthma at his medical as highly principled he knew it would have exempted him from military service).[30] Heron fortuitously received an invitation in 1944 from Bernard Leach, a friend of his parents since the mid-1920s in St Ives, who had persuaded the authorities to allow him to employ conscientious objectors to help in his Pottery with the production of 'utility ware'. Leach at that time was a member of the Home Guard with sculptor Denis Mitchell and landscape painter Borlase Smart. Heron had to make a swift decision with regard to the offer of an approved work placement in view of the Government plan to make the south coast and the Cornwall, Devon peninsula out of

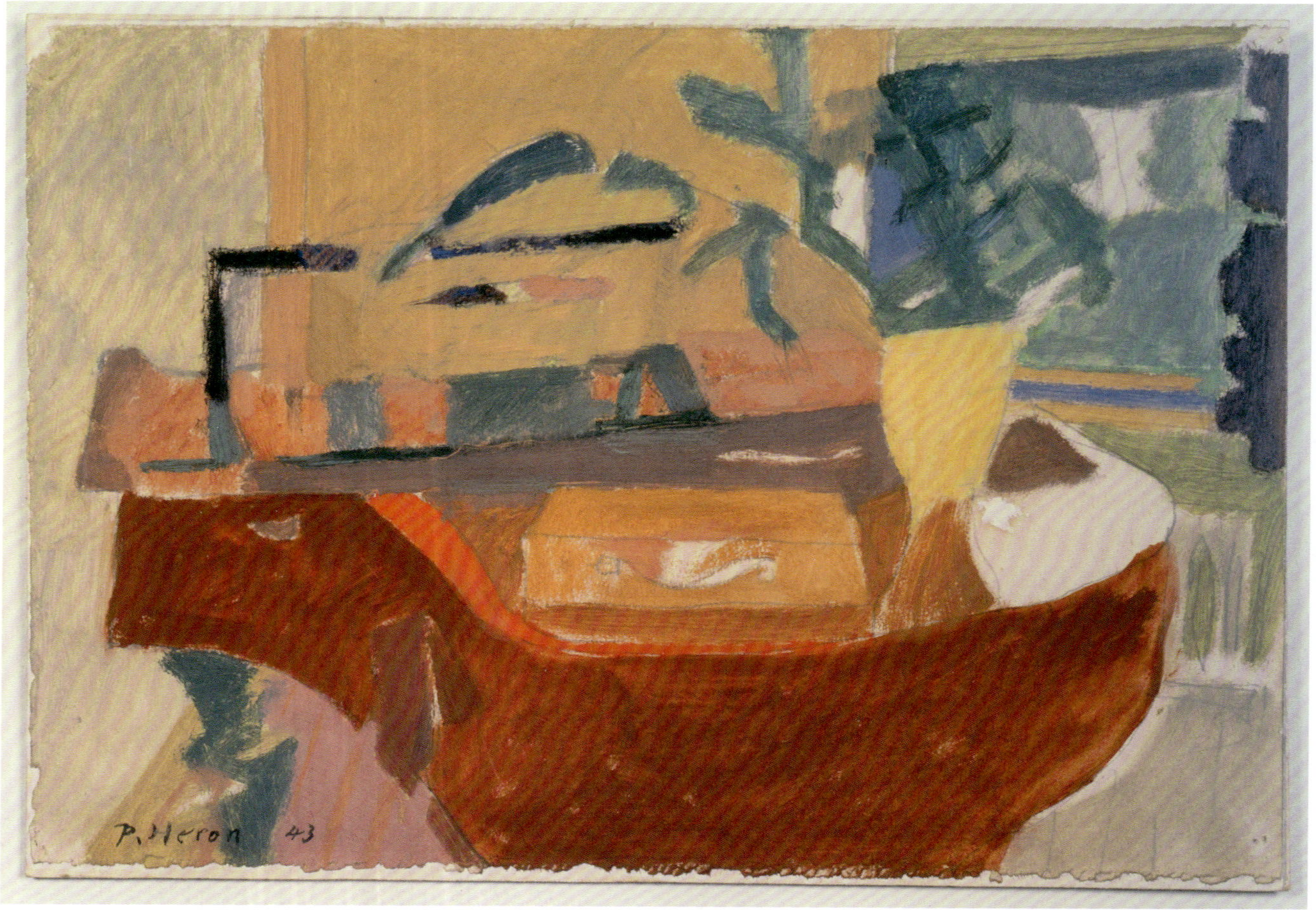

Patrick Heron | THE PIANO : 1943 | Oil on paper, 19 x 27.3 cm | Photograph: David Ward bounds prior to the pending D-Day invasion. American troops were already stationed there. Heron accepted and within a few days joined Leach where he spent the final fourteen months of the war assisting with meeting the demand for domestic pots making specifically mustard and jam-pots. His wartime return to Cornwall, working in the Pottery was a moving experience. This together with the light and landscape, which had left a lasting impression from his formative years, impacted on his artistic development, alongside meeting many leading artists including Naum Gabo, Barbara Hepworth and Ben Nicholson whose studio in Porthmeor he took over in 1958.

From 1945–58 Heron worked as an art critic, including from 1945–47 for the prestigious *The New English Weekly* where some of his most influential articles appeared. The Redfern Gallery in 1947 hosted his first one-man exhibition and in the same year he gave a series of talks on contemporary art on BBC Radio. From 1953–56 Heron taught at the Central School of Arts and Crafts, London. In the mid-50s he began to paint abstract works, moving away from his earlier figurative work, influenced particularly by Matisse and Braque (whose Paris studio he visited in 1949). In April 1956 he moved to Cornwall with his young family to 'Eagles Nest' in Zennor, on the moors above the sea where he had stayed as a child.

Heron, a lifelong pacifist and socialist was a supporter of the Campaign for Nuclear Disarmament (CND) from its founding meeting in 1958. He also actively campaigned to protect and preserve the ancient landscape of West Penwith and was involved with other campaigns through to the 1970s, which occasionally took him away from painting. Heron received many awards and accolades over his career exhibiting extensively nationally and internationally but he staunchly refused a knighthood from Conservative Prime Minister Margaret Thatcher. In the last decade of his life he completed a number of large scale, bright paintings and a highly acclaimed retrospective at the Tate Gallery was held the year before he died in 1998. ◆◆◆

JONAH JONES

(1919–2004)

Jones came from a family of miners in Tyneside; he excelled in art at Jarrow County Secondary School winning a scholarship to study at the King Edward School of Art in Newcastle. Lack of finance prevented this and although he later attended evening classes, his main priority was to find a job, no easy matter given chronic unemployment in the north-east in the mid-1930s. His political consciousness was fast developing against the backdrop of economic hardship, the rise of Fascism and the Spanish Civil War. Jones attended Labour and the Independent Labour Party rallies and began to attend Quaker meetings. He joined the Peace Pledge Union (PPU), selling copies of *Peace News* (which was first published in June 1936) and determined never to take up arms.

Jones appeared before the Northumberland and Durham Tribunal to make his case as a conscientious objector to Judge Richardson. He was granted exemption from military service on the condition that he undertake agricultural work. Directed to work in forestry he spent the next four years working in various locations including Kirkcudbrightshire, Scotland; Wensleydale in Yorkshire and Exmoor in Devon. Detail is scant but it is known that Jones arrived in Exmoor around August 1940 and worked with other COs.[31] While working in Wensleydale he met the landscape painter Fred Lawson (1888–1968) who lived in the village of Castle Bolton. Lawson, a CO in the First World War had established a studio with his close friend and fellow painter, George Graham (1882–1949), which inspired an artists' group. Jones benefitted from such company extending his knowledge about the arts and watercolours in particular.

Jones, like Sven Berlin and John Petts reassessed his stance as a CO and made the difficult decision to join the Non-Combatant Corps. On 8 February 1944 he was posted to Buxton, for a month's training with the Pioneer Corps (probably just before Petts arrived), where he was given the nickname 'Jonah'.[32] Stationed later in Warwickshire he took opportunities to travel to London where those in 'khaki' could spend their leave drawing at the Central School of Arts and Crafts and where he was warmly welcomed by wood engraver John Farleigh (1900–65), who had taught there since 1925.[33] Finding life in the Pioneer Corps unsatisfactory Jones applied for transfer to the Royal Army Medical Corps. (RAMC) prompted by seeing an illustration by Petts in *The Listener* of one of Dylan Thomas's stories, and whom he discovered was serving with the 224 Parachute Field Ambulance (PFA), RAMC. Jones met Petts, who was to be influential both on his artistic career and beliefs, at 'the [parachute] training centre at Ringway, where, together with John Ryder, the typographer, they set up a primitive press, printing instructional material for trainee parachutists on purloined paper.'[34] Jones, like Petts, was assigned to the 224 PFA, RAMC and was involved in Operation Varsity although he supported the 1st Canadian Parachute battalion. He also celebrated VE Day in Wismar returning to England before his final posting with the 224 PFA, RAMC to the Middle East where he was involved in peacekeeping in Palestine. Reluctantly he too agreed to a transfer to the Royal Army Education Corps and was promoted to sergeant joining the staff at Carmel College, Haifia where he lectured on literature and art and ran the library and later at the army education college at Genifa, near Suez. He was demobbed in 1947 and returned to Tyneside.

Jones and his wife, the writer Judith Maro, whom he had met and married in the Middle East, later moved to North Wales having agreed with Petts while in Palestine to help with the revival of The Caseg Press. He received £16 a month from Petts for setting the type and working the press but resigned in 1949 determined to become a sculptor. Jones won a York Trust scholarship to Eric Gill's workshops (Gill had died in 1940) at Pigotts in Buckinghamshire where Laurence Cribb taught him how to cut letters in stone. Public and private commissions followed and his main patron in the 1950s was architect Clough Williams-Ellis for whom he did work at Portmeirion and whose biography he wrote in 1996 (he also did a portrait bust of him). In the 1960s Jones embraced the approach and philosophy of Romanian sculptor Brancusi.

Looking back on his life in the late 90s he saw his career as having taken three paths, those of sculptor, educationalist (he spent 17 years teaching in Rome at the British School; and in Belfast and Dublin), and writer. Jones remained committed to his role as artist-craftsman and its transforming power and his pacifist beliefs, believing that it 'is the soft rain that gradually wears down the hard rock.'[35] ◆◆◆

GEORGE KENNETHSON

(1910–94)

Kennethson studied at St John's Wood School of Art, under Patrick (Pat) Millard (1902–77), a renowned draughtsman, for a year before attending the Royal Academy Schools to study painting from 1929–32 where he was greatly influenced by the work and approach of Cézanne. In his final year Kennethson met painting student Eileen Guthrie who had just started her studies: they married in 1938.

In 1936 Kennethson, who had a studio in St John's Wood, began to experiment with sculpture making small terracotta models for future stone carvings and sculptures. The commercial galleries in London offered Kennethson the opportunity to attend a wide range of exhibitions, which were significant in his development as a sculptor and in particular those showing non-European art. Of these, the Zwemmer Gallery, near Charing Cross, which was establishing itself as a centre for modernism, would most likely have been a draw. In July 1937 they held an exhibition of Nigerian wood-carvings, terracottas and watercolours, such was the response, the *Morning Post* described it as being 'of extraordinary interest', that it was extended. The young artists, similar in age to Kennethson, were selected by Kenneth Murray, Superintendent of Art Training in Nigeria, and included the gifted Ben Enwonwu, who later studied at the Slade and went on to become a leading figure in African modernism. Enwonwu showed watercolours and a number of carvings including *The Bending Man* in afzelia africana; *Head of a Chief* in abura wood and *Walking Man* in iroko wood. For Kennethson 'Tribal wood carvings from Africa and stone sculpture from India'[36] were to be a key influence. In the same year Kennethson and Eileen visited Paris to see Picasso's painting *Guernica* (1937), which was created in response to the bombing of the town in April by Nazi Germany, 'which moved them profoundly, both artistically and politically.'[37]

A committed pacifist, Kennethson did not want to see a repeat of the horrors of the First World War that he had heard so much about, and as a consequence of his political and philosophical views on the outbreak of the Second World War, he sought exemption from military service. He appeared before two military tribunals in Oxfordshire (he was now based in Uffington) to make his case on the grounds of conscience before it was finally granted.

Kennethson's work over some five decades was inspired amongst others by Epstein and Gaudier-Brzeska, mostly modest in size, and carved directly, it drew on his detailed sketch books and experiences of places and stone such as from the Isle of Purbeck in Dorset where he regularly holidayed. His subjects were 'the sea, birds, plants, the land, sky even and humanity, motifs common in the world of painting in which [he] was trained and which [he'd] always been deeply interested [in].'[38] His oeuvre also contains 'many fine images of young women of a "blockiness" which recalls Eric Gill, Frank Dobson and Henry Moore, though these figures often have a light-heartedness and a relish for their subject which is entirely his own.'[39]

In 1954 Kennethson moved to Oundle, in Northamptonshire where he taught art at the public school until 1969, having been recommended to apply for the post by his Uffington neighbour and friend the poet John Betjeman. Kennethson accepted only on condition that one day a week was set aside for his personal work. In 1958, he carved *The Serpent of Knowledge* (Emblem of Aesculapius) on the wall of the Palmer Science Block (now located on the exterior of Scitec).[40] Kennethson also carved the Crest of the Grocer's Company situated above the cloisters by the Art Department where he taught until 1969.

In 1959, Kennethson converted a disused brewery in Oundle into a living space complete with a sculpture workshop and painting studio. He exhibited infrequently preferring to concentrate on his sculpting, which was of paramount importance, rather than being dictated to by a dealer. Jim Ede who created Kettle's Yard, Cambridge, in 1957, was a great supporter of Kennethson, buying two of his more abstract pieces for the gallery. Kennethson nonetheless held a number of solo exhibitions and two retrospectives were held the year before he died in 1993. ◆◆◆

ARNOLD MACHIN

(1911–99)

Machin started his career as an apprentice at the Minton China Factory in Stoke-on-Trent, before moving to Derby to work for the Old Derby China Works. He studied variously at Stoke and Derby Schools of Art and in 1937 was awarded a scholarship by the Royal College of Art (RCA). Machin studied under Richard Garbe (1876–1957), a skilled stone and woodworker and developed his skills in working with terracotta. In his final year he won the Silver Medal for the best sculpture student and a Travelling Scholarship, but was unable to take advantage of it owing to wartime conditions.

In 1940 Machin, a conscientious objector (CO) returned to the Potteries. In the summer he was offered the position of Head of Stoke Art School, which he accepted after some anguish as his friends were being drafted into the military. However, soon afterwards his CO status was reported to Gordon Forsyth (1879–1952), Superintendent of Art Instruction for Stoke-on-Trent City Art Schools who asked him to resign. Forsyth contacted Josiah Wedgwood & Sons as Machin had previously done some work for them. Wedgwood was sympathetic and directed Machin to Victor Skellern (1909–66). Wedgwood's first professionally trained Art Director, Skellern appointed Machin as a designer and also commissioned Eric Ravilious (1903–42) and other freelance designers. Machin spent his spare time, 'modelling a series of tortured figures of Christ' in terracotta in a studio provided by Tom Wedgwood.[41]

Machin returned to London feeling that he should do something for the war effort, and joined the International Voluntary Service for Peace (IVSP), which had been formed in 1920. The first international voluntary project in Britain was set up in Wales in 1931. One of Machin's jobs was to erect Anderson shelters in back gardens in the East End and provide hot soup for those 'sleeping rough' who would take shelter at Charing Cross. The so-called 'Hungerford Club', was a little known segregated shelter for the homeless under Charing Cross Bridge established by COs from the Anglican Pacifist Fellowship. Writer and CO Ronald Fuller (1904–74) who served as an ambulanceman drew the shelter in June 1943.[42]

Machin received his call up papers on 5 November 1942 and instructions to attend for a medical examination. He refused, strongly believing that fighting was wrong and futile. He attributed this in part to the stories he heard from his elder brothers about the 1914–18 war. As a consequence of his refusal Machin was summoned to appear before the Court of Summary Jurisdiction sitting at the Police Court, West Ham Lane, Stratford on 19 January 1943. Josiah Wedgwood (1872–1943), who the previous year had been granted the title Baron Wedgwood of Barlaston by Winston Churchill, and who in the First World War had spoken in Parliament in defence of the rights of conscientious objectors, attended his appeal but despite Wedgwood's support it was turned down. Machin received a twelve months prison sentence in Wormwood Scrubs where he spent much of the time stitching mailbags and packaging white bandages and red flannel to send to the troops. The monotony was somewhat relieved by Sunday evening visits from a prison visitor who showed films with religious themes and by visits to the prison library. Machin was one of a number of COs who produced a monthly magazine surreptitiously passed around fellow CO inmates lampooning the warders. The composer Michael Tippett (1905–98) also a conscientious objector was imprisoned at 'The Scrubs' for three months from June 1943 for refusing to do full-time civil defence work when directed. He and Machin became good friends. Tippett later invited him to attend the performance of his secular oratorio *A Child of Our Time* when it was first performed at the Adelphi Theatre, London, on 19 March 1944. Machin, like Tippett, was released early for good behaviour.

Wedgwood welcomed Machin back on his release and he created more than twenty figures during the 1940s. The trustees of the Tate Gallery bought his terracotta bust *St John the Baptist* and two terracotta figures *The Annunciation* through the Knapping Fund. *The Times*

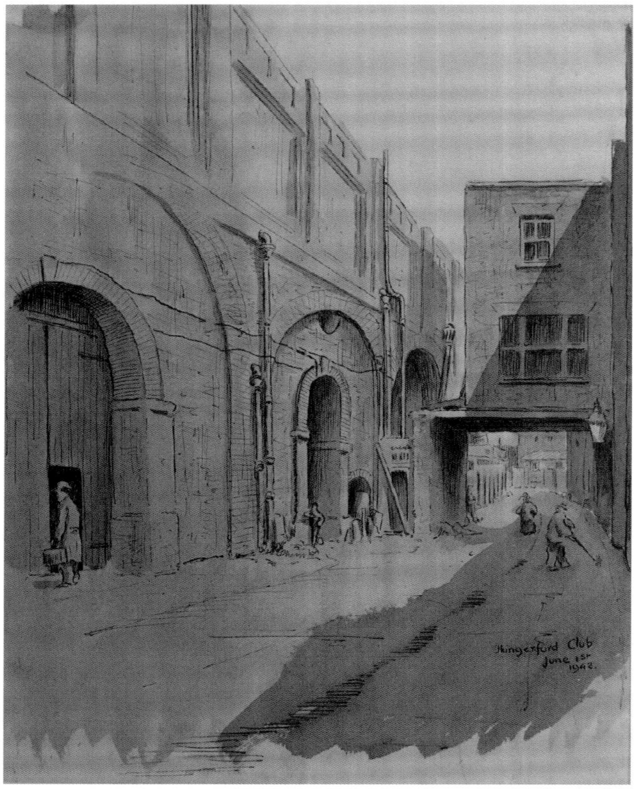

Ronald Fuller | *The Hungerford Club* | 1943, Pen and wash, 26 x 23 cm | Private Collection | Courtesy Sim Fine Art

on 3 February 1944 announced the purchase from the young and little known sculptor pointing out 'both are remarkable for subdued tenderness of feeling and grace of handling.' John Rothenstein, Director of the Tate had earlier visited the Wedgwood factory and been impressed with Machin's work and terracottas.

In 1951 Machin became a part-time tutor at the RCA in the Ceramic School, eight years later he was appointed Master of Sculpture at the Royal Academy Schools. He had been made a full RA in 1956. In 1963 he won a competition to model Her Majesty the Queen for decimal coinage and in 1966 to design the new definitive postage stamp, which was issued the following year. ◆◆◆

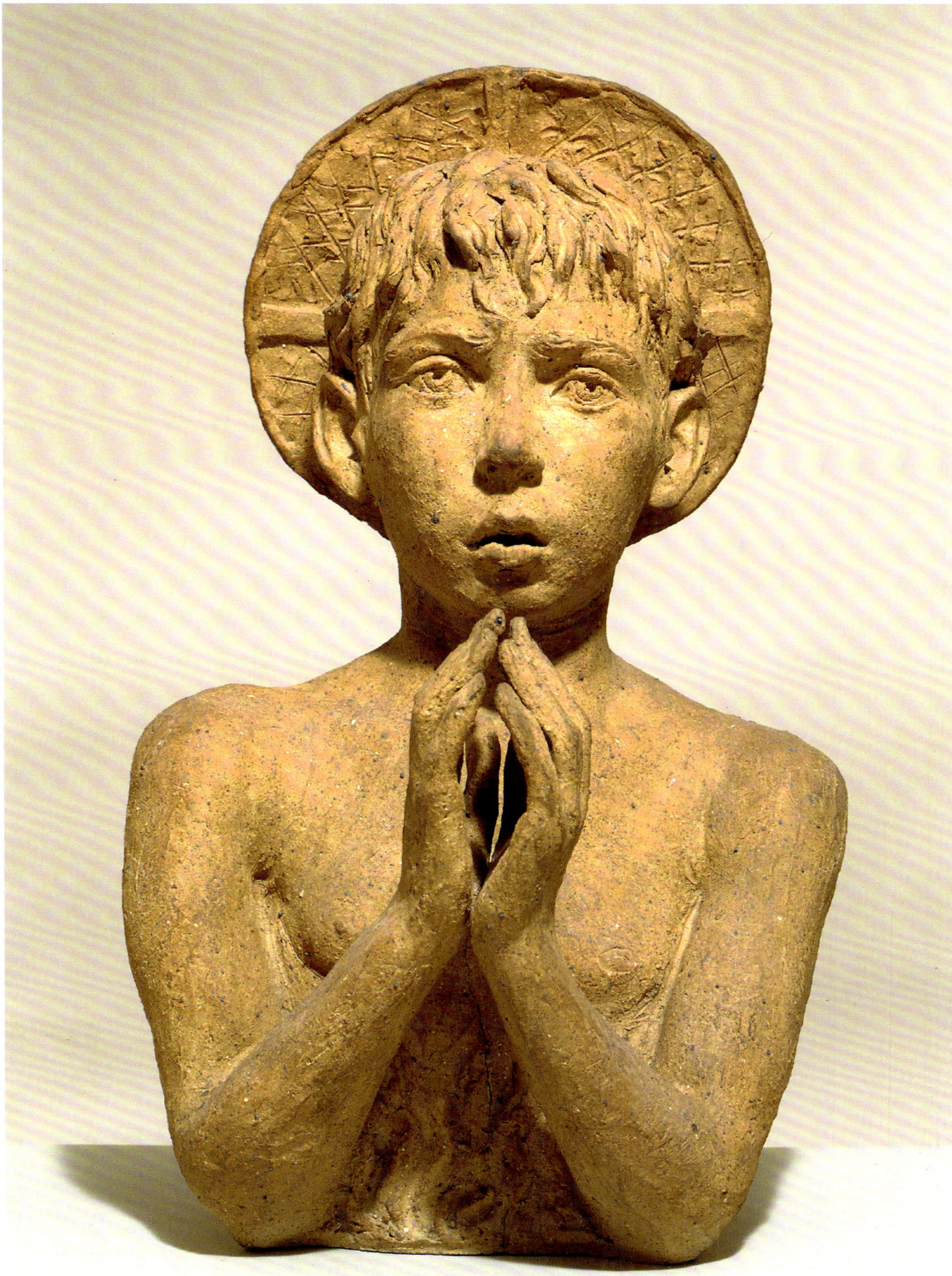

Arnold Machin | *St John the Baptist* | c.1944, Terracotta, 52.1 x 31.1 x 29.2 cm

BERNARD MEADOWS

(1915–2005)

Meadows first studied art in his home town of Norwich from 1934–37, becoming Henry Moore's assistant in 1936 following a visit with two other students from the School of Art. Meadows showed Moore an enlarged copy of a flint he had carved out of beechwood, and received an invitation the following day to work with him; which he did for the next eighteen months during his vacations from Norwich. 'It was to be by far [Moore's] most enduring relationship with another artist, lasting with only a few gaps for the rest of his life. … Generally Moore allowed Meadows to carve down to within a quarter of an inch of the final surface …'.[43] It was 'a matchless education' for Meadows as they discussed work and politics, (Moore was an early supporter of the Campaign for Nuclear Disarmament), over the three years, and on occasions he joined Moore's modelling classes at Chelsea School of Art, London. Meadows was a member of the Communist party for a period in the 1930s. In 1938 he gained a place at the Royal College of Art (RCA) and in the same year assisted Moore with his *Recumbent Figure* (1938) and the following year *Reclining Figure* (1939).

On being called up Meadows registered as a conscientious objector; 'his attitude to the war was at first a questioning one, on both moral and political grounds.'[44] He briefly taught at a secondary school in Dagenham but with the invasion of the Soviet Union by Nazi Germany on June 22, 1941 he reconsidered his stance. Less than two weeks later he volunteered for service with the Royal Air Force (RAF), in the air-sea rescue service. Based initially in Dover, Meadows found it quite exciting, especially the rescue boats, which were mostly torpedo boats stripped down with powerful engines rather 'like having a high-powered motorbike.'[45] In 1943 he was posted to India and was horrified by the poisonous black widow spiders that he would see in the woven palm-fronds hut walls and then they would disappear and he didn't know where they had gone. Such experiences of fear and vulnerability were to be the basis for much of his later work. From Bombay he sailed down the coast to Cochin (Kochi), then to Colombo, and finally to the Cocos Islands (later also known as Keeling Islands), a small archipelago approximately midway between Australia and Sri Lanka (formerly Ceylon). There was a mutiny on the small coral atoll over demobilisation in 1946. Meadows, in charge of the base (he held the rank of Flight Lieutenant), had to address the assembled company asking them what they were going to do as they were on strike, telling them that they would not get any dinner and the toilets would not get cleaned and nothing would happen. He recalled that it was all very amicable and they saw the sense of what he was saying and decided that perhaps they would not go on strike. Meadows saw little action and found it 'very boring', occupying himself by painting.

After five years in the RAF Meadows was demobilised and returned to his studies at the RCA, on occasion assisting Moore in his studio where Meadows carved most of the left-hand figure of Moore's *Three Standing Figures* (1947–48). Reg Butler who lived near Moore also helped to finish off the right-hand figure. On leaving the RCA Meadows took Moore's old job at Chelsea in 1948, joining Willi Soukop and becoming Head of the Sculpture Department in 1950.

Meadows contributed the imposing *Standing Figure* in elmwood to the exhibition associated with the Festival of Britain in 1951. He began to experiment with animal forms in bronze looking to get away from the influence of Moore, not wanting 'to be so identified with him as to be thought of as being a sort of second-hand Moore'. In fact Meadows thought he was nearer to Picasso than he ever was to Moore. He said 'it's all about the human condition. The crabs, and the birds, and the armed figures, the pointing figures, … it's a certain sort of threat, it's a certain sort of fear …'.[46] In the Cocos Islands Meadows had been fascinated by the large land crabs he witnessed foraging, wildly waving their claws and scurrying to their burrows at the first hint of danger. At one stage of his observations he tied one to the table leg in his room, but during the night it cut through it and escaped. Meadows saw startled birds as reflected in the 'hysteria' of chickens 'as a vehicle for people ... that same sort of hysteria

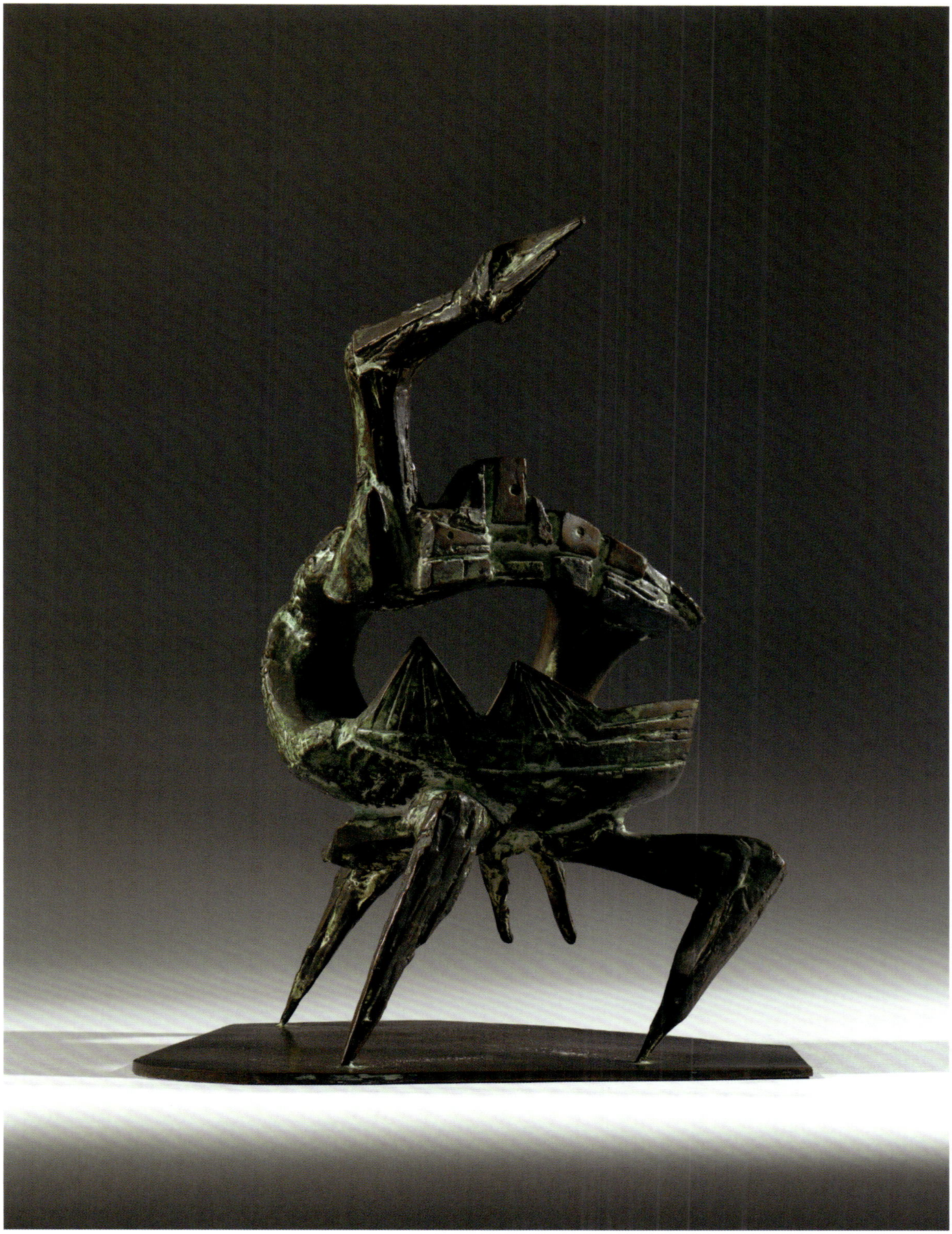

Bernard Meadows | *Large 'Jesus' Crab (Larger Jesus Crab)* | 1952, Bronze, 32.7 × 20.6 × 17.4 cm
Private Collection © The Estate of the Artist / Image Courtesy of Osborne Samuel Gallery

which people get when life gets on top of [them] ... all these birds, all these figures have got things which human beings have ... '.[47] Meadows' selection for the 1952 Venice Biennale gave him the opportunity to exhibit for the first time two Cocks and two Crab sculptures and three studies in pencil and wash, which attracted considerable international attention. Writing about the British sculptors Herbert Read coined the now much used phrase 'the geometry of fear' as embodying the work of the young sculptors, in the case of Meadows it was particularly apposite reflecting the trauma of the war years.[48] In 1957 Meadows had his first of six one-man exhibitions at the Gimpel Fils gallery in London. The following year he completed his large bronze sculpture *Spirit of Trade Unionism* situated at the entrance to the Trades Union Congress Building on London's Great Russell Street. It depicts a worker aiding his fallen comrade and represents the spirit of trade unionism with the strong helping the weak.

In 1960 Meadows became Professor of Sculpture at the RCA, remaining until retiring in 1980 and where he was remembered as an influential and inspirational teacher. Following a visit to the Italian city of Florence and seeing the Renaissance sculptures he returned to the human figure and 'embarked on a new "awkward" subject, which he designated alternatively as "Armed Figures", "Directors" or "Tycoons" ... far from pleasing or attractive ...'.[49] These figures were bullies; Meadows in his later work changed to employing a highly polished finish. He was 'a wry observer of humanity and created an enduring set of sculptural images to express the often discomforting truths he felt about the world and man's place in it.'[50] ◆◆◆

JOHN MINTON

(1917–57)

Minton attended the well-respected, independent St John's Wood Art School, known as 'The Wood', from 1935–38 under co-principals Patrick Millard (1902–77) and Ernest Perry (1908–76). These enlightened principals ended the segregation of male and female students in life drawing classes on their appointment in 1933 and introduced a monthly sketch club inviting well-known artists to criticise students' work. Minton, a prodigiously talented student, won three prizes for his work, which were presented by Bloomsbury artist Vanessa Bell. He subsequently visited Charleston at her invitation. Minton first met Michael Ayrton (1921–75) at The Wood, where they became lifelong friends; travelling together to Paris in 1938 where they spent eight months.

On 23 October 1939 shortly after the outbreak of the war Minton registered as a conscientious objector (CO). His pacifism stemmed from his school days in Reading where he had 'written an essay abhorring the indiscriminate killing which modern warfare entailed.'[51] His tribunal took place in February 1940 but his explanation as to why he should be exempt from military service was rejected. His objections were deemed "intellectual" and not "conscience".[52] COs who objected on political or ethical grounds tended to be treated less favourably than those who objected on religious grounds.[53] Given Minton's failure to satisfy the tribunal, the panel directed his name be removed from the Register of Conscientious Objectors rendering him liable to call up for service in the armed forces. Minton dissatisfied with the verdict exercised his right to appeal within 21 days although this was unsuccessful.

In 1941 Minton produced a number of works of the devastation following heavy bombing raids in the East End of London including Wapping, Poplar and Rotherhithe where he made many visits meeting young men as he explored his sexual identity at a time when homosexuality was illegal. The solitary young man in *Blitzed City with Self-Portrait* (1941), is deep in thought, his gaze troubled, behind him stand ruined buildings with a river and bridges across, there is a an ominous feeling of tension and desolation. In October 1941 he was called up. On 10 December Minton left to join the Pioneer Corps (formerly the Auxiliary Military Pioneer Corps). The Corps specialised in heavy manual work and built camps, airfields and fortifications, cleared rubble and demolished roadblocks, and undertook a myriad of other jobs. Minton was initially stationed at Ilfracombe, Devon, like Vaughan some months earlier. He wrote to Ayrton explaining that he 'lack[ed] the purpose and firmness of conviction' to remain a conscientious objector his appeal having failed and moreover he could not face the thought of not being a free man.[54] Minton was at the time collaborating with Ayrton designing sets and costumes for John Gielgud's production of *Macbeth* at the Piccadilly Theatre.

By October 1942 Minton's thinking had developed and he was attending a pre- Officer Cadet Training Unit as an infantry candidate having expressed a wish to transfer from the Pioneer Corps. The training lasted for four months; Minton was posted to Barmouth, Wales in late December and received his commission the following year but the demanding training had a deleterious effect on his health both physically and mentally, which also impacted on his painting. Minton transferred to the Oxfordshire and Buckinghamshire Light Infantry, stationed in Little Missenden and was later admitted to Shenley Hospital, a psychiatric hospital, some twenty miles from central London in Hertfordshire. With the advent of war the hospital had discharged many of its patients so that half of the site could become a Military Hospital. Minton was eventually discharged in June 1943 on health grounds although his homosexuality appears to have been a major factor in this.[55] The following year his younger brother was killed in action north of Antwerp, Minton vowed never again to have anything to do with war or the government's prosecution of conflicts.

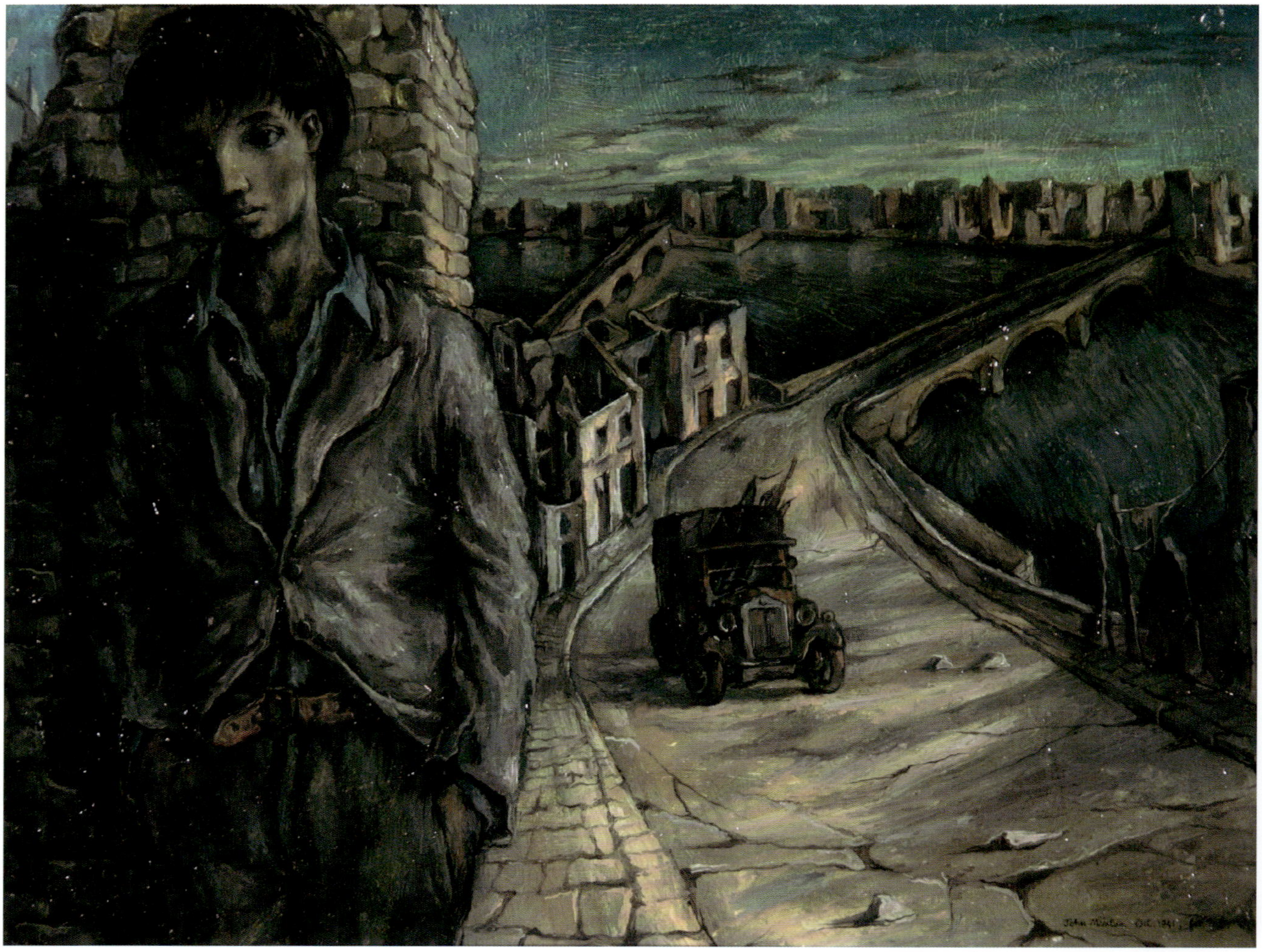

John Minton | *Blitzed City with Self-Portrait* | 1941, Oil on board, 30.5 x 40 cm | © Imperial War Museum Art.IWMART LD16739

In autumn 1943 Minton obtained a teaching post at Camberwell School of Art under principal William Johnstone who was responsible for employing younger artists as teachers. He had previously employed Ayrton who had been invalided out of the RAF in 1942. Minton was a popular, charismatic teacher who exerted much influence over his students passing on his skills in draughtsmanship. During his tenure he held his first one-man show at the Redfern Gallery in 1945, he was at that time sharing a studio with the two Roberts, MacBryde and Colquhoun. From 1946–52 Minton shared a flat with Keith Vaughan having moved with Johnstone to the Central School where he taught drawing and illustration. His talents were well used and over the next decade he illustrated numerous books and magazines and his ability to produce relevant, complementary and imaginative images was much in demand. Minton moved to the Royal College of Art in 1948 where he taught painting, a move that heralded a shift away from his graphic work.[56]

Minton exhibited widely and in 1949 he was one of thirteen new members elected to the London Group, the greatest number in a single year, including Edward Burra, Julian Trevelyan, Keith Vaughan and William Scott. His passion for travel led to visits to Corsica, Paris, Spain, Jamaica and other countries, and this was reflected in many of his densely patterned and richly coloured landscapes. Minton, part of the British Neo-Romantic group of artists, felt increasingly side-lined in the 1950s and out of touch with the move towards abstraction. His struggles with self-doubt and self-destruction contributed to his taking his own life, at the age of 39. ◆◆◆

VICTOR PASMORE

(1908–98)

Kenneth Clark (1977) a great admirer of Pasmore, revealed in *The Other Half: A Self-Portrait*, his sequel to his autobiography, that he believed Pasmore was one of the most talented English painters of the twentieth century. Pasmore's early interest in painting was fostered at Harrow School, but his aspirations to paint professionally were thwarted with the early death of his father. Moving to London in 1927 he worked as a clerk for London County Council (LCC) painting at weekends and studying at evening classes under A. S. Hartrick at the Central School of Arts and Crafts until 1931. The following year he was elected to the London Artists' Association (LAA), and in 1933 under their auspices had his first solo exhibition at the Cooling Galleries.

Pasmore together with William Coldstream and Claude Rogers (who knew each other from the Slade) established a private art school in 1937 to teach solely drawing and painting. In early 1938 the school, which had quickly gained a reputation for being progressive, moved to Euston Road taking its name from its new location. Lawrence Gowing became its most celebrated student and progressed to giving lessons in the life class. The outbreak of the Second World forced its closure.

Pasmore's application to register as a conscientious objector to the war was rejected. The painter William Townsend (1909–73) in his journals recalled meeting him and his fiancée the painter Wendy Blood and their discussion in March 1940 noting:

> *he is against taking any interest in the war, politics, etc ... [sic] Against state patronage, official war artist appointments; and as usual vehemently. ... The war has made little if any difference to him. Outside events never did trouble him much and he doesn't propose they shall now.*[57]

The war ultimately made a difference to Pasmore and on 25 March 1941 he wrote to painter and art critic Graham Bell (1910–43) who had shared a studio with Coldstream, and who was training to be a navigator in the RAF:

> *... I expect you have heard about me, it is all very painful. I am not given to thinking much, but I had to do a lot of thinking over this. All things like Nazism, Fascism, Communism, Democracy, Empires and other organisations mean very little to me; they seem to have very little to do with real life. However, other people seem to think they do and it is very difficult to know what to do. So bewildered was I, that at the first hearing; I was unable to convince the tribunal of my sincerity. However I have been at great pains to write a statement which clearly expresses my feelings and hope to be more successful at the appeal ...*[58]

In July Pasmore wrote to Bell to praise his work in the exhibition *Paintings by Members of the Euston Road Group* that had opened in May at the Ashmolean Museum, Oxford and to update him with regard to his CO status:

> *I realise now how much the Euston Road owes you. I know very little of your association with Bill [Coldstream] and how much his great genius has been influenced by you. ...*
>
> *All my efforts to be registered as a conscientious objector have failed. I do not feel that going to prison to prove my point is very constructive, so I shall probably just accept what comes to me now. Wendy is shortly to be a mother and prison is not a helpful place for a father to be!*[59]

Pasmore also contacted Clark who had funded the first prospectus for the Euston Road Group and who had supported him via a Trust he had established to help artists, including Bell and Coldstream. The £15 he received each month had enabled Pasmore to leave his job at the LCC and

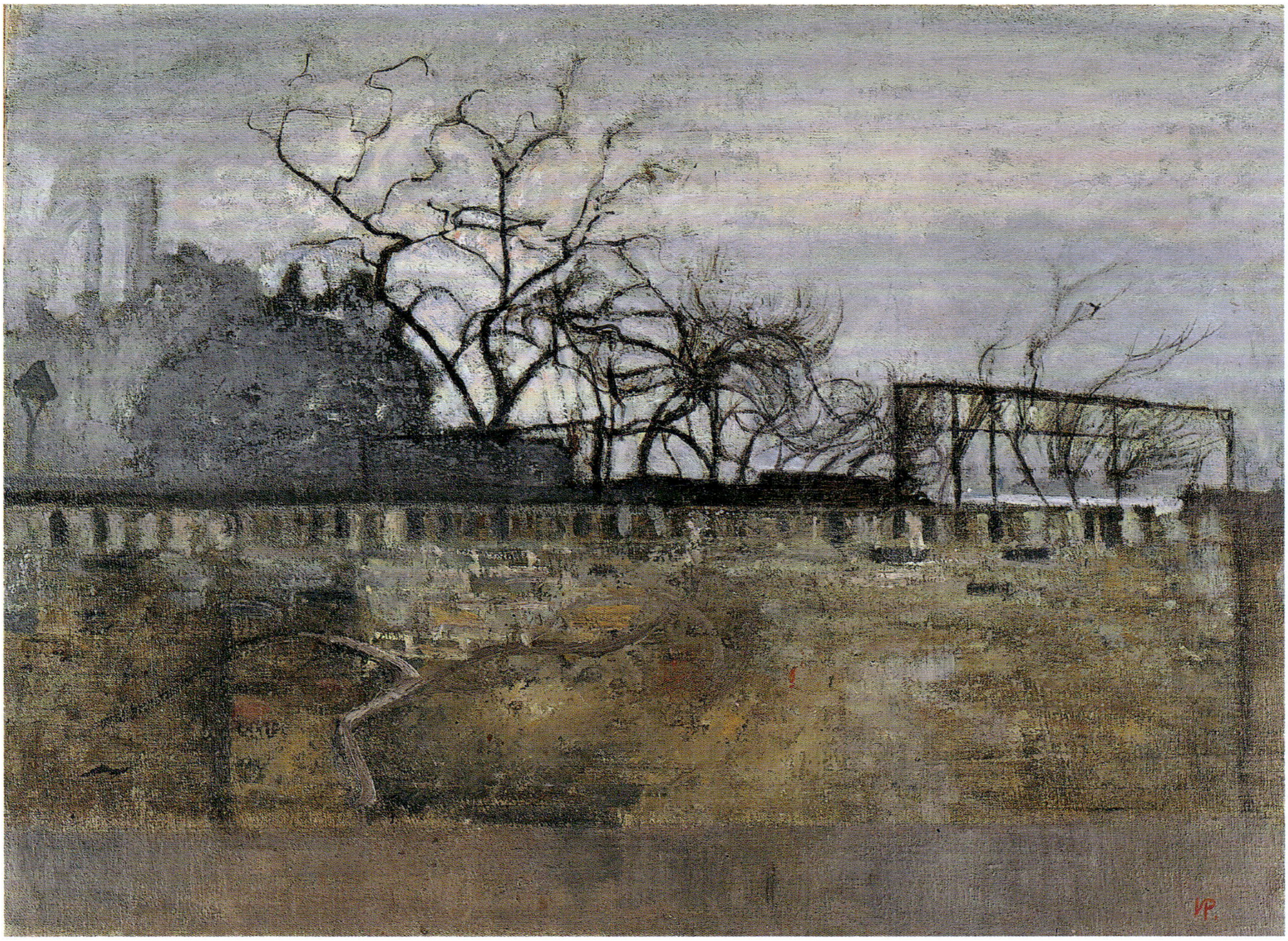

Victor Pasmore | *Riverside Gardens, Hammersmith* | c.1944, Oil on canvas, 45.7 x 61 cm |

become a professional artist.[60] He told Clark on 23 July 'I am still at large and am painting as much as I can until the arm of conscription descends upon me once more.'

The arm of conscription finally descended on Pasmore who was sent to Redford Barracks in Edinburgh in autumn 1941 having been undertaking River Patrol duty. The following summer he was recommended for officer training at Sandhurst, which on completion would have enabled him to join a camouflage unit, but after three weeks he was ordered to go to India. He refused and resigned from the course and was instructed to return to Edinburgh. On leave in London he absconded.[61] During his 20-day absence Pasmore visited Clark at the National Gallery, where he was Director. He advised him to give himself up immediately or run the risk of being shot. According to Clark they went to the nearest police station where Pasmore was well treated. On being formally questioned Pasmore said that he didn't mind joining the army but he was not going to kill anyone. He received a brief prison sentence, gaining permission to fresco the walls of the prison corridor in Scotland. He appealed and received letters of support from Clive Bell, Augustus John and Clark who expressed the view that Pasmore's first duty to society was to paint. The appeal was upheld and on 30 September 1942 he was released and exempted from military service. 'This suited Pasmore for his sole passion and purpose in life was to make art, not only for his own fulfilment but for the redemption of others.'[62] The following year he was appointed as a part-time teacher at Camberwell School of Arts and Crafts where he reassumed his acquaintance with Gowing.

Pasmore who had moved to Hammersmith began a major series of paintings of riverscapes and parks and gardens of west London in 1943, his studio in Ebury Street having been repeatedly bombed. These paintings were to occupy him for the next four years and included the misty, atmospheric *Riverside Gardens, Hammersmith*, c.1944 which demonstrates his perception and feeling for the natural world (which continues in spite of the conflict) and invites comparison with Whistler's paintings of the Thames in the 1870s. Further, 'while realistic in its conception, [it] bears many of the hallmarks of an increasing preoccupation with pattern over representation, [and] reduction over detail.'[63]

Post-war Pasmore continued his in-depth study of Post-Impressionist theories and in December 1945 visited the Picasso and Matisse exhibition at the Victoria and Albert Museum. Their work influenced his move to abstraction and abandonment of naturalism and working in unconventional materials such as household paint, cement and glass fibre. In 1947 Pasmore moved to Blackheath, on the other side of London, which remained his base in England although in 1966, he bought a house and studio in Gudja, Malta being much attracted to the bright Mediterranean light. He died there in 1998.

In 1948, at the London Group's exhibition in May, Pasmore exhibited two of his first abstract paintings and the following year he became a visiting teacher at the Central School of Arts and Crafts remaining until 1953. During that period he designed murals for the Regatta Restaurant at the Festival of Britain (1951) and helped organise exhibitions devoted to abstract art in London including at the Artists International Association, Lisle Street and produced his first abstract reliefs. In 1954 Pasmore was appointed Master of Painting at Durham University and introduced an abstract Foundation Course, 'The Developing Process'. His approach and that of his colleagues had a major impact on art education. He returned to full time painting in 1961 and four years later the Tate Gallery, London gave him a major retrospective. Pasmore's work was wide-ranging, he 'never ceased to experiment and push beyond the boundaries of his art, and this was his lasting strength.'[64] ◆◆◆

JOHN PETTS

(1914–91)

Petts studied wood engraving from 1930 under Norman Janes (1892–1980) at Hornsey School of Arts and Crafts in London and from 1934 at the Central School of Arts and Crafts under William Palmer Robins (1882–1959), author of *Etching Craft* (1923). Petts held a studentship at the Royal Academy Schools, London and became a British Institution Scholar but left to live in north Wales. Here he and Brenda Chamberlain, whom he met at the RA Schools and married in 1935, established The Caseg Press in 1937 at LLanllechid, in Gwynedd, North Wales. The press produced Christmas cards and bookplates, together with illustrations for *The Welsh Review*, a monthly literary periodical from their own wood-engravings which were also produced for numerous private and corporate commissions. During the period 1941–42 The Caseg Broadsheets were produced in collaboration with the poet Alun Lewis. Wood-engravings were juxtaposed with poems by Alun Lewis, Lynette Roberts, Brenda Chamberlain, Dylan Thomas, Glyn Jones and translations of traditional Welsh poems by H. Idris Bell.[65]

Petts who grew up in north London during the First World War had vivid memories as a small child picking up shrapnel, these fragments were faceted like the planes of rocks, which influenced so much of his later work. He could trace his pacifism and hatred of war with 'men smashing each other to pieces' back to his contact with family members who 'were half destroyed'[66] by the conflict including an uncle who was blinded and lost a leg. Petts held a deep conviction that 'he could not and would not go' to war and registered as a conscientious objector. His tribunal was held in Caernarvon in 1941, to his surprise he was well treated, the Judge, Sir Thomas Artemus Jones (1871–1943), Chairman of the North Wales Conscientious Objectors' Tribunal even allowed him to hold a card rather than the Bible when he swore that the evidence he would give would be the truth and nothing but the truth. Petts, who did not believe in opting out totally, spent the next three years working on the land, a period he described as the toughest of his life. He obtained his first position 'as a horseman and teamsman on farm in Derbyshire' following answering an advertisement in the newspaper. The 'daily slog' involved carting and tractor ploughing. While Petts did not experience the brutality many COs were subjected to in the First World War he found people distanced themselves and viewed him as an outcast and coward, but he accepted it as a 'load to wear'. Petts found the isolation difficult and was able to join a friend (Betsan Ouston, fellow RA student) working on a diary farm in Headley, Epsom where he looked after nineteen pedigree Guernsey cows (all named after flowers beginning with the letter C). Following a vacancy he saw in *Farmer's Weekly* he then took a job on an Uplands farm in Wales where he learned to plough and where his skills as an artist stood him in good stead as he needed to 'have an eye for the curve of the hill' and his ability to draw a straight line was reflected in the furrows. These experiences influenced his work and while on the farm he did a pen drawing of himself ploughing and recalled the young Samuel Palmer meeting the elderly William Blake who said 'Do you work with fear and trembling?'[67]

The break-up of Petts' marriage in 1943 led him to reconsider his position, as he was now free to go anywhere. He requested a change in registration, but not his CO stance, and a transfer to the Royal Army Medical Corps (RAMC) where he might help save lives. However, he was called up to join the Pioneer Corps and sent to Buxton in spring 1944. For Petts this largely involved loading supplies for the war effort, tasks that did not sit comfortably with his pacifism. He persisted in seeking a transfer to the RAMC but the only way to get in at that stage in the war was to volunteer for parachute duties. Following parachute training involving jumping from a balloon and aircraft at RAF Ringway, Manchester, Petts qualified for his parachute wings. He then undertook medical training at Bulford, Salisbury Plain where he found that he was good at blood transfusions being skilled inserting needles into collapsed veins. Petts attributed this to the exactness of engraving and his familiarity with handling the steel tools. This training for foreign operations as medical orderlies to battalions on the ground also required them dropping onto Salisbury Plain with containers strapped to a leg and apparatus for carrying casualities. Assigned to a Resuscitation Unit he also had to train with glass pint blood bottles strapped across his stomach. The 224 Parachute Field Ambulance (PFA), RAMC was attached to the 3rd Parachute Brigade of the elite 6th Airborne Division with whom Petts saw service in North West Europe in the Ardennes at the end of December 1944 where deep snow blanketed out the horror of war before moving to the more dangerous situation in south Holland on the western side of the Maas river. Here Petts was confronted by not only starving Dutch civilians to whom they were forbidden to give food but also his first real experience of conflict and the 'dreadful smashing of bodies', which confirmed his pacifist beliefs. He returned to Bulford in early spring 1945 where he trained to be dropped into Germany. On 24 March Petts was dropped in daylight over the Rhine as part of Operation Varsity and was subject to German ground fire for the first time and recalled the 'nasty sound' as it hit the plane and feeling like he was in a tin can. Petts was fortunate and landed in young larch trees which afforded some protection, however they were swiftly in action ferrying the wounded on stretchers to dressing stations whilst avoiding other gliders. He described it as a nightmare situation. Petts then moved with the 6th Airborne Division to Wismar on the Baltic tending the wounded from both sides on the 300-mile plus journey across Germany and where he spent VE Day. He returned to England and was subsequently posted to Palestine with the 224 PFA, RAMC.

While Petts was serving in the Negev Desert, south of Gaza in Israel, he was commissioned by Christopher Sandford to illustrate the novel *The Green Island* by Gwyn Jones published by The Golden Cockerel Press in 1946. 'He engraved a set of eleven blocks, crouched over a card table in a tent in the desert. … [he believed his parachuting experiences] 'gave him an unusual point of view of most things and of people.'[68] He eventually transferred to the Royal Army Education Corps, in order to do so he was obliged to request his name be withdrawn from the official register of COs, as it carried the minimum rank of sergeant. He did not have to abandon his pacifist stance. The new National Service Act simplified the process whereby COs could give up whole or part their exemption. Petts ran art courses at the Educational College in Cairo, Egypt and produced sets for a production of *King Lear*. He was also the visual editor for all the military educational publications in the Middle East having block makers and printers at his disposal. Petts was finally demobbed some six years after he first registered as a CO.

Adjusting to post-war life and employment was not easy for Petts given the horrors he had witnessed. In 1947 he married Kusha Miller and together they took up the opportunity of setting up and running the Lloyd George museum in Llanystumdwy, north Wales. The Caseg Press was restarted at this time (with the help of a loan from James Bramwell, writer and academic, fellow CO and member of 224 PFA, RAMC) with the assistance of Kusha and Jonah Jones (also fellow CO and member of 224 PFA, RAMC) and ran until 1951. Two years later he was elected to the Society of Wood Engravers and in 1957 an Associate of the Royal Society of Painter-Etchers and Engravers.

In 1951 Petts took up the post of Assistant Director at the Welsh Committee of the Arts Council with the remit to sponsor the creative work of original artists and to stimulate a wider public interest in the visual arts in Wales. He undertook many lecture tours and organized several exhibitions including the first retrospective of the work of David Jones.

After resigning his post at the Arts Council, in 1957 he accepted a lectureship in design and crafts at Carmarthen School of Art, moving to Llansteffan in west Wales, it was here that Petts began to explore the art of stained glass design producing many fine stained glass windows for places of worship in Wales and beyond (71 in total).

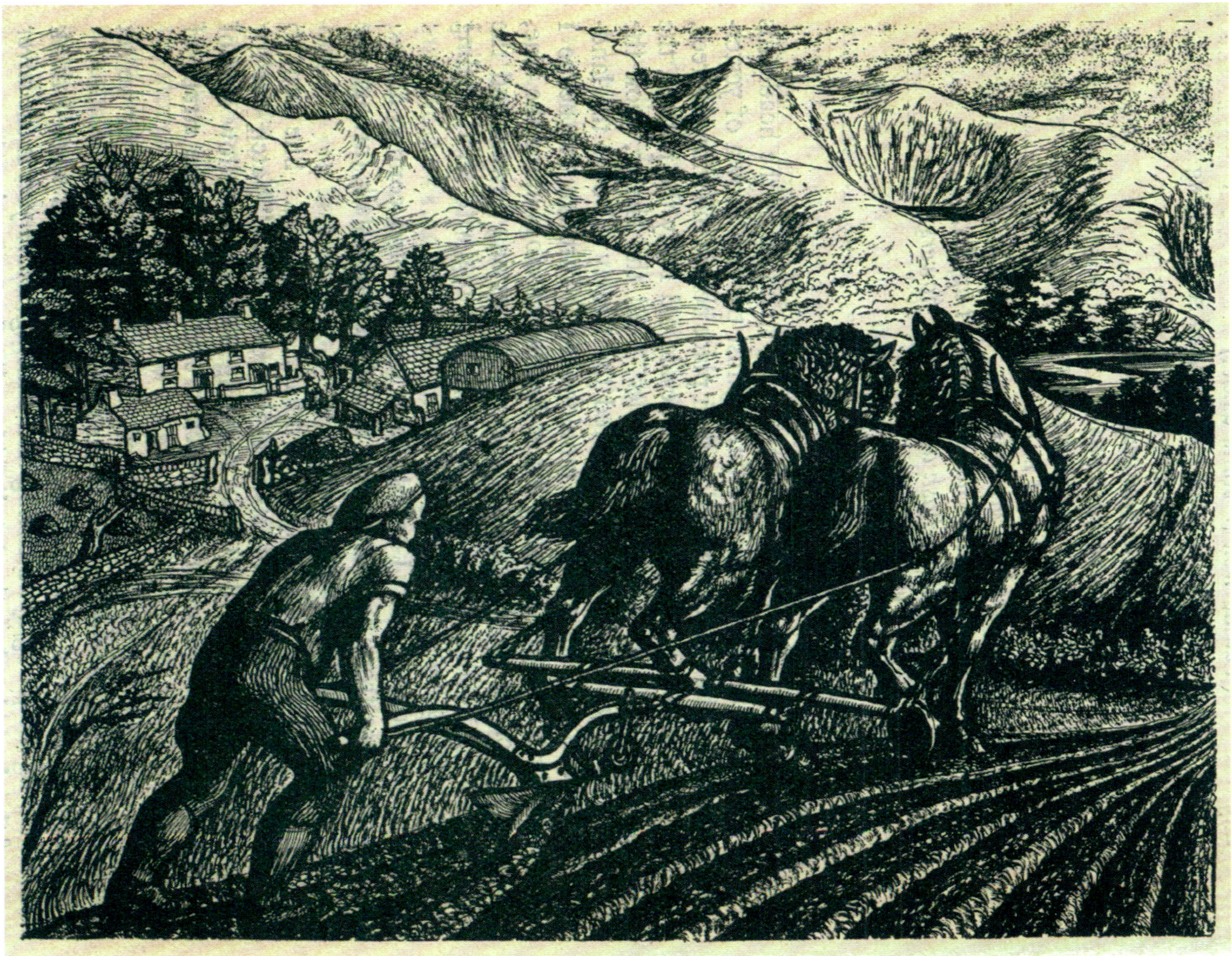

John Petts | *The Upland Team* | 1944, Pen and ink drawing, 11.2 x 13.7 cm | © Anna and Mick Petts

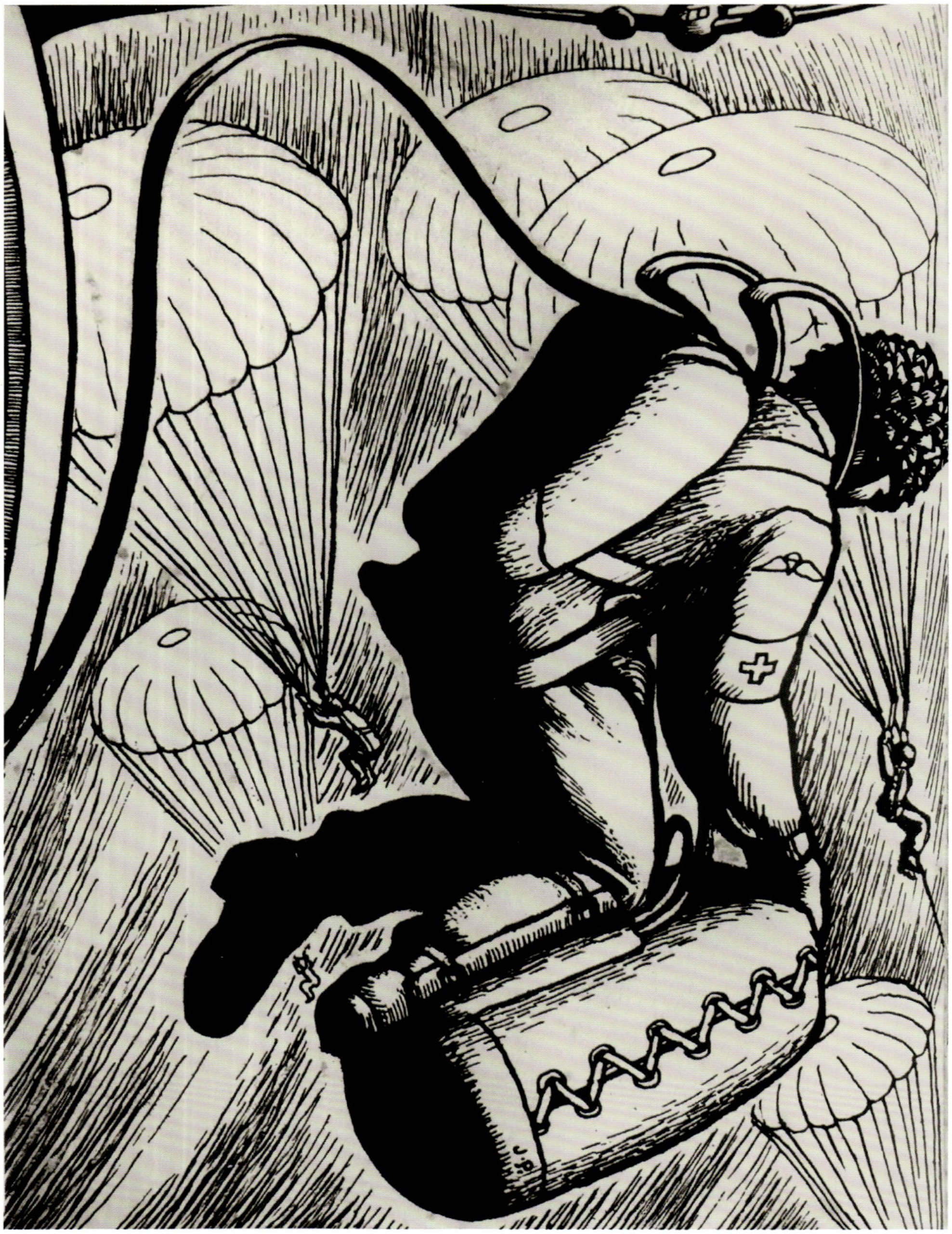

John Petts | *Operation Varsity, the Rhine, March 1945*
Pen and ink drawing, 7.5 x 6.2 cm | © Anna and Mick Petts

Of these the 'Alabama Window' he designed between 1963–65 is one of his most acclaimed designs arising out of his anger and indignation at the racially motivated bombing of the 16th Street Baptist Church in Birmingham, Alabama, in the United States of America, where four young black girls who were attending Sunday School were killed in 1963. On hearing the news Petts had felt compelled to do something as a gesture of fellowship and goodwill. He telephoned his friend David Cole who edited the *Western Mail* and they launched a fund for the replacement of the church's stained glass windows. Subscribers could contribute no more than 2s 6d and in a very short time £900 was raised. Petts' bold window showed a black Christ in front of a rainbow of racial unity, his right arm pushing away hatred and injustice, the left offering forgiveness, below which an inscription reads 'YOU DO IT TO ME'. Within the design were included the jets of water cannons used on civil rights protestors and the bullets of the Sharpville massacre in South Africa. It was installed and dedicated in 1965 with the words: 'Given by the people of Wales' and according to The National Library of Wales it has become 'an iconic symbol of the American civil rights movement.'[69]

Petts also notably designed a set of 40-foot stained glass windows for the Brighton and Hove New Synagogue (now known as the Reform Synagogue) to commemorate Holocaust victims. The commission had initially been offered to Chagall but he declined on the grounds of age.

Petts re-married in 1985 and moved to Abergavenny, his third wife Anna assisted him with his work up to his death in 1991. ◆◆◆

HUGO POWELL

(1919–2014)

Powell attended Leighton Park School near Reading, where Maxwell Armfield had been a pupil some decades earlier. The foundations of Powell's pacifism were laid at Leighton Park, (a Quaker school), under E.B. (Edgar Bradshaw) Castle (1897–1973),[70] headmaster from 1928–47. Powell while not a Quaker, related to their ideas and beliefs about peace and war and joined the school's Pacifist Society.

On leaving school Powell attended Hornsey School of Arts and Crafts, a purpose-built private school of art, established in 1882 by artist and teacher Charles Swinstead. The curriculum post-First World War had expanded to include lithography, etching and fashion drawing and the County Council now held financial responsibility for it. Powell attended in the late 1930s when the headmaster was painter and etcher John Charles Moody (1884–1962). Powell joined the Peace Pledge Union while a student. A key influence on him was his tutor the distinguished sculptor Harold James Youngman (1886–1968), who he recalled was 'a stickler for realism'.[71] Powell who met Henry Moore at the Leicester Galleries in London however 'developed an interest in "revolutionary, under-the-counter sculpture", including a passionate admiration for Henri Gaudier-Brzeska.'[72] As a teenager Powell had been inspired following visiting sculptor Eric Gill[73] in his studio, and also Eric Kennington while he was working on a sculptural commission in Dorset.

In June 1939 Powell followed his conscience albeit not an easy decision and completed his 'Application to Local Tribunal for Registration in the Register of Conscientious Objectors' as a requirement of the Military Training Act, 1939. Prior to this he read '*How Shall I Serve*' a short pamphlet E.B. Castle had written on 22 May 1939 to outline the choices to be made with regard to conscription. Castle concluded 'We shall not all decide to act in the same way; but we shall have obeyed the best we know.' Powell later wrote to thank Castle for his help and advice and aware of 'what a terrible thing war was'; his father had been a surgeon and restored damaged faces and throats post-First World War.[74] In his statement in support of his application he outlined his beliefs:

> *That a standard of humane & tolerant conduct is vital among men & that human life should be respected above all things. A man is firstly a member of humanity & secondly a member of his nation. That injustice cannot be removed by unjust means, & that therefore one should have faith in the common decency of other men & try to meet injustice with reason & good actions. …*
>
> *I believe war to be crime against humanity because it involves the indiscriminate slaughter of the innocent & guilty by the cruellest means; & because it is unjust it can not really solve the problems it is meant to.*
>
> *I therefore conscientiously object to war and regard it to be in the best interest of everyone that I should refuse to fight, to prepare or to assist others to prepare for war.*
>
> *I do not however, deny the right of the state to demand that every citizen between the ages 20–21 shall do some work for Peace compatible with his conscience. I am perfectly willing to do now a period of any work of social value irrespective of war needs so long as I am not debarred from the rights of free speech and pacifist activities.*

Powell joined the Friends Ambulance Unit (FAU) and was sent to Manor Farm in Northfield, Birmingham which was owned by Dame Elizabeth Cadbury, to attend the 'Friends Ambulance Camp for Social War work'. During his six weeks training his appeal to Register as a Conscientious Objector (CO) came before the Midland Local Tribunal on 27 November 1939. Powell attended and made it clear that he had 'held his pacifist views since he was at school' and that he 'Would not undertake any work under Military Control.' He was conditionally registered as a CO subject to his continuing 'in the kind of Ambulance work you are now engaged upon.' Powell continued and additionally attended courses of 'Instruction in Home Nursing' and 'First Aid to the Injured' under the auspices of The St John Ambulance Association in December 1939.

Between 1939–41 Powell's FAU work comprised hospital work in Gloucester and in London's East End hospitals during the Blitz. He adapted well to the change from Art School finding that he 'seemed to be good at coping with damaged people.'[75] From 1941–45 he was attached to the Hadfield Spears Unit (HSU)[76] and 1st Free French Division serving in Palestine, Syria, North Africa, Italy and France. He described it as having 'a delightful surreal quality' and commented:

> *It was perhaps one of the most extraordinary units that existed anywhere in the war. To have such marvellous cooperation between perhaps the most chauvinistic collection of Frenchmen imaginable and pacifists, many of them Quakers, was truly astonishing – let alone the bizarre mix of people making up the hospital…*[77]

Powell produced a number of memorable pen-and-ink sketches of wounded soldiers in Field Hospitals. He also carved a memorial stone for the first HSU casualty James Tonks that was placed in the Friends' burial ground at Brummana, east of Beirut overlooking the city and the Mediterranean.

After being demobbed and 'a year's preliminary dithering' Powell decided to make sculpture his life work rather than go into art teaching like many of his contemporaries.[78]

> *Before [he] could start modelling & carving [he] had to spend nearly four months making [his] own equipment & turning an old coach-house into a studio. Tools and materials were a shocking problem. [He] had to make all [his] benches turntables etc out of salvaged timber from bomb damaged houses – a lengthy & tedious performance, whilst tools were a matter of constantly searching through second-hand shops. …*[79]

Powell later produced commissions for many public buildings and churches. One early commission was to make 'two monumental plaques, later known as "The Olympic Roll of Honour" … to commemorate the names of the gold medal winners [from the XIV Olympiad, London 1948].'[80] The process included making an original font for the lead letters within the glazed ceramic tiles forming the plaques, which measured approximately 3.11 metres in height and 1.95 metres in width. These were set within the concrete walls to either side of the Royal Tunnel entrance at Wembley Stadium. 'Powell never considered the plaques to be a significant element of his oeuvre, but rather as an essential commission to tide his family over a difficult period.[81]

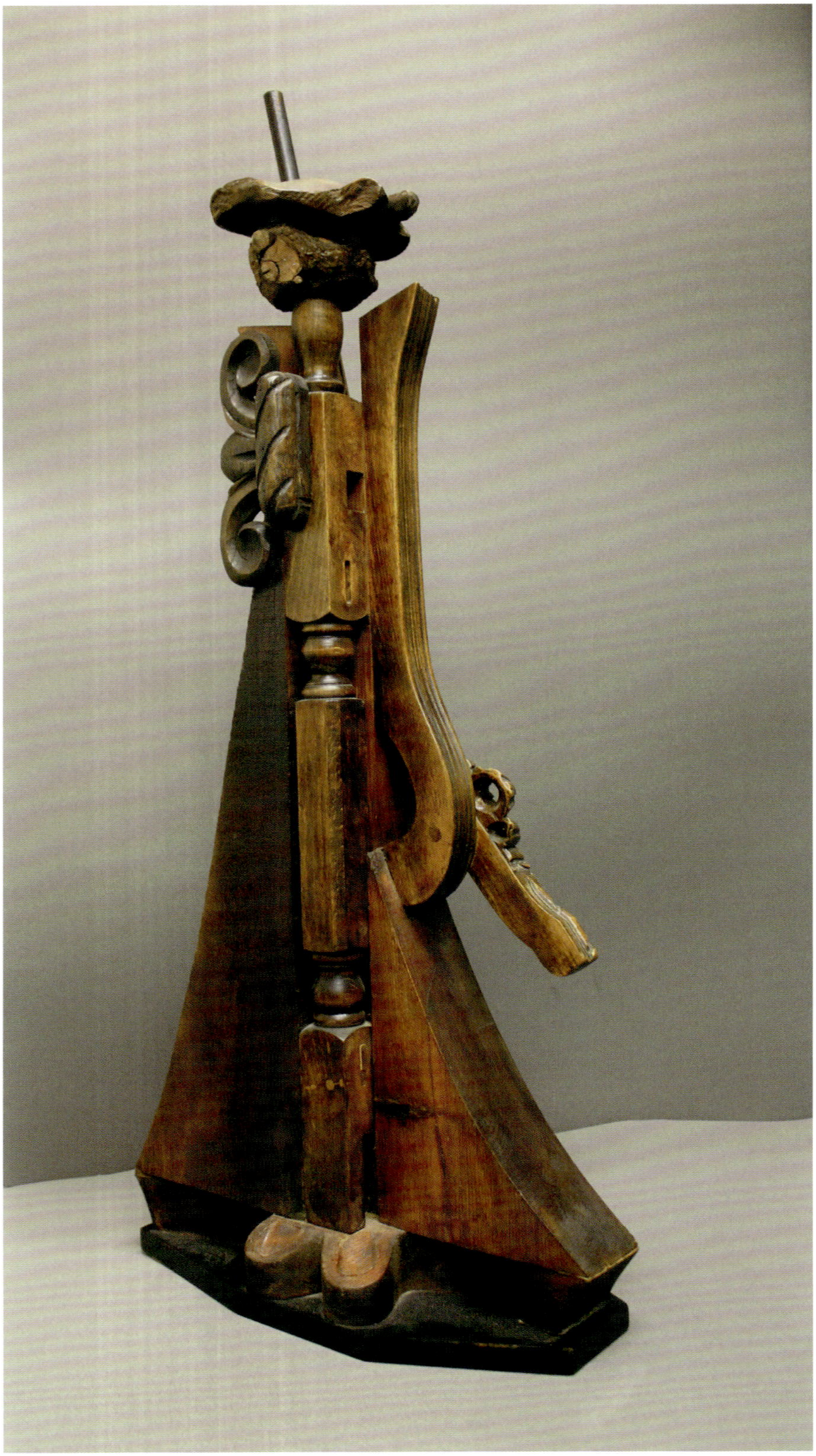

Hugo Powell | *The Sentinel* | 1986, Wooden assemblage, 98 x 35 cm

In the mid-1950s Ruth Borchard (1910–2000) asked Powell to contribute a self-portrait for her collection of British artists' self-portraits. Their friendship dated from just after the Second World War and Powell later rented a studio from her in Redhill near his home in Reigate, Surrey. The self-portrait took the form of a relief sculpture. Borchard purchased *The Light Seeker*, one of his many abstract woodcarvings in about 1950.

Powell moved to Oxford in 1969 and set up a studio in which he worked for the next 45 years and gave up conventional work. This change of direction was influenced by a number of artists and texts including Paul Klee's *Pedagogic Notebooks* (about two dimensional work and colour). Powell (1994) explained in the catalogue note for his exhibition 'Shapes and Meanings' that Klee gave him the clue to what he was really looking for: an approach to three dimensions that was rigorous, analytical and at the same time genuinely liberating and poetic.

The wooden assemblage *The Sentinel* (1986) is one of Powell's most emotive and profoundly poetic works and perhaps the closest he came to capturing some of the horror of his war experiences with any satisfaction. *The Sentinel,* which he affectionately referred to as 'that little statue of the French sentinel', emerged one evening after he had finished working on another piece and was playing around with old bits of wood in his studio and seeing what emerged. He recalled that 'suddenly a cloak, and suddenly a beret, and suddenly the rifle and it connected at once with a period in Italy when I spent a night looking for camp'. Powell had become separated from his unit near the Front and had difficulty locating their camp in the dark. He remembered approaching a French sentinel and swiftly making himself known as he did not want 'to get blanked full of lead'. Powell was taken back as the assemblage later emerged and found himself thrown back into the memory of searching all night for his unit and approaching the sentries standing in the dark with their cloaks and rifles. He said of *The Sentinel* 'it's not a great bronze memorial of an official kind – it's just a friendly sort of reminder of the people that I once knew under these circumstances but all the pain and suffering that one remembers so excruciatingly afterwards I've never really wanted to put it into a great work…'. The theme of the phoenix was explored in Powell's final series of works, a bronze cast of his last piece, *The Dancing Phoenix* (2014), was delivered to his studio two weeks before his death. ◆◆◆

PETER REDDICK

(1924–2010)

Reddick, a Quaker, spent a year at South East Essex Technical College and School of Art Dagenham before registering as a conscientious objector in 1942. Sent to the Quaker Relief Training Centre for conscientious objectors at Spiceland in the Uffculme area of mid-Devon he followed an intensive practical skills course, including farm work, cooking, building repairs, laundry and first aid. After three months COs were moved on to various projects, some run by Friends and by the end of the war 400 had passed through the Centre. Reddick first worked as a gardener in Northamptonshire where he taught himself wood engraving having found a length of felled box tree, and then in Lincolnshire as an agricultural labourer before being demobilised in 1946.

Reddick studied in Cardiff for a year and in 1948 enrolled at the Slade School of Fine Art to study engraving under Norman Janes and John Buckland-Wright receiving his diploma in Fine Art in 1951. He was elected a member of the Society of Wood Engravers in 1953. Unable to make a living as a book illustrator he worked as a visiting tutor in lithography, lettering, calligraphy, and later typography at the Regent Street Polytechnic between c.1951–57. He was later an assistant to Willy De Majo (1917–93) founder of the International Council of Graphic Design Associations.

Reddick contracted polio in 1958 and the following year studied at London School of Printing and Graphic Arts, finding engraving easier to undertake than painting at an easel. In 1960 he went to Ghana to lecture in commercial design at Kumasi College of Science and Technology before returning in 1962. From 1963–67 he worked at Glasgow School of Art. Harry Jefferson Barnes (1915–82), Director from 1964 later wrote a detailed introduction and appreciation for Reddick's exhibition of watercolours and wood engravings in 1981 following his year-long Gregynog Fellowship. Reddick retired in 1989 having taught illustration in the Department of Graphic Design at the West of England School of Art in Bristol since 1967.

Reddick described his early work as 'romantic ruralist',[82] his four years of rural life and his experiences gained working on the land left a lasting impression and continued to inspire him. His Quaker principles and pacifism permeated his life and work. Reddick 'was one of the first wood engravers to exploit the portrait, but most of his subjects [were] historical.'[83] During his long and distinguished career he provided over five hundred wood engravings for the Folio Society, 'including 18 volumes of the novels and stories of Thomas Hardy. No other artist has achieved a complete Hardy, and, as the illustrators of the first serialisations of the books were various, Reddick's Hardy has become definitive.'[84] ◆◆◆

KENNETH ROWNTREE

(1915–97)

Rowntree came from a Quaker family, and attended The Downs School, Colwall, where he first met Lawrence Gowing who was to become a lifelong friend. Like Gowing he was encouraged to paint by art master Maurice Feild. From 1929–32 Rowntree attended Bootham School, York. Rowntree again benefitted from a good art teacher and was given his own studio before leaving to study at The Ruskin Drawing School, Oxford, where he won Prizes for Life Drawing and Life Painting and was influenced by Albert Rutherston. In 1935, Rowntree attended the Slade School of Art part-time but felt he was unprepared for the 'conventional academics and huge studios,'[85] which were not to his liking. He gradually 'went less and less' but owing to an allowance from his father was able to continue painting.

Rowntree embraced Quaker values and beliefs and, like his father in the First World War, registered as a conscientious objector. His father served with the Friends' War Victims Relief Service in Holland driving ambulances. In November 1939 Kenneth Clark, who was keen to find artists employment following the outbreak of war, asked Rowntree for his curriculum vitae with a view to his contributing topographical watercolours 'of places and buildings of characteristic national interest, particularly those exposed to the danger of destruction by the operations of war'[86] in what came to be called 'Recording the Changing Face of Britain'. Funded by the Pilgrim Trust, it ran until 1943, and was intended to boost national morale and reaffirm what Britain was fighting for. Over 1500 works were eventually produced by some of the country's finest watercolour painters including Stanley Badmin, Sir William Russell Flint, Thomas Hennell, Charles Knight and John Piper. Rowntree contributed twenty-three drawings and paintings, including a number from his native Yorkshire and Essex, where from 1941 he lived in Great Bardfield. Tirzah Garwood and Eric Ravilious, who taught him briefly at the Ruskin, helped him find his cottage. Rowntree was well suited to topographical recording and took great pleasure focusing on those places he had personal knowledge of and attachment to, often favouring a frontal view to his compositions. For Rowntree the quiet and solitude experienced in chapels and churchyards afforded him opportunities for contemplation as well as fostering his fascination with lettering and signage. Accordingly he was able to painstakingly record the inscriptions on gravestones and monuments in his own individual way such that his lively wit is often reflected in his work.

On 28 March 1940 Rowntree received a letter from the secretary of the War Artists' Advisory Committee (WAAC), E. M. O'Rourke Dickey, asking him to undertake work on their behalf. Clark, appointed chairman the previous year saw the two schemes (*Recording Britain* and *War Artists*) operating in tandem. Rowntree expressed an interest in undertaking pictures of training camps at home, but was concerned there might be objections owing to the fact that, as a Quaker, he was a conscientious objector. Coote of the War Office while not objecting thought it might be rather difficult for Rowntree and suggested he tackle different subjects. Rowntree's first choice was for ports 'and the way in which war has changed their character … and all subjects connected to them, transport, warehousing, the manifestations of coastal defences' or secondly 'Railways in war-time, transport of war materials.'[87] He also expressed an interest in the changes to England and English people caused by the war such as interiors in the black out, digging for victory, but he found this subject rather difficult to define.

Rowntree's initial commission, for two pictures for 50 guineas, was deferred until June 1940, when he was sent to the north-east coast near Whitby. Although he was carrying Admiralty identification, Rowntree's fears were confirmed when he and his wife were arrested at Flamborough Head and taken to the police station in case they were spies. Over the next five years he completed a number of oil and watercolour paintings including those of a polo ground in war-time which had been converted to allotments; a canteen concert under the auspices of the

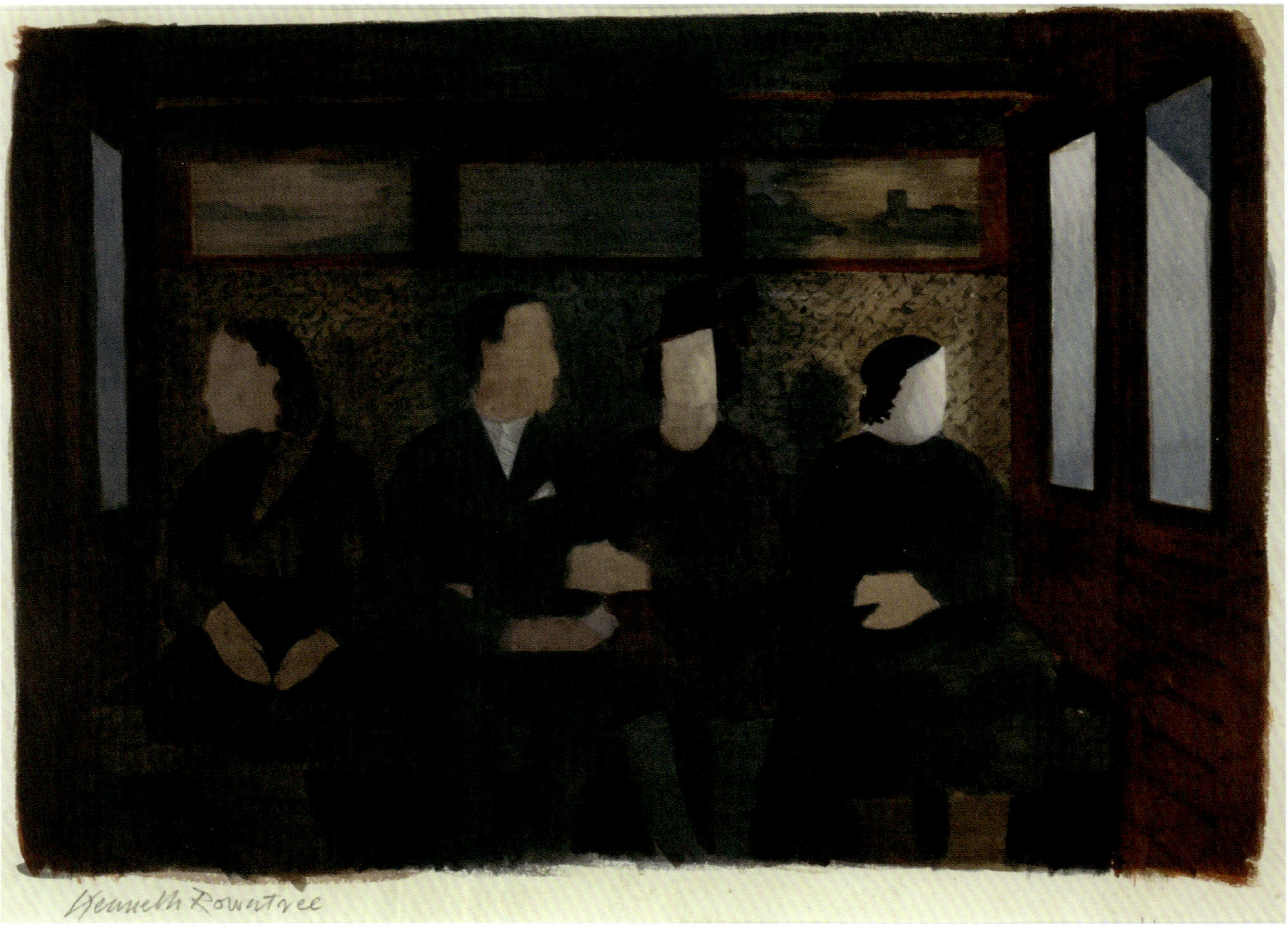

Kenneth Rowntree | *The Railway Carriage – Blackout* | c.1942, Watercolour on paper, 30.2 x 42.7 cm

Council for the Encouragement of Music and the Arts Committee and members of the Women's Institute making jam. *Experimental Establishment, Shoeburyness* was one of two pictures of production at Shoeburyness commissioned in February 1945, for 35 guineas the pair. The painting also known as *The Government Ordnance Establishment* shows rows of shells and explosives neatly stacked on the railway siding which appears at odds with Rowntree's pacifist sentiments as expressed in 1940 to the WAAC.

Rowntree was one of thirty-five artists including Barbara Jones, A.S. Hartrick, Mona Moore and Randolph Schwabe who contributed to The Londoners' England Scheme, which was designed to continue, in a modified way the work of the Recording Britain Scheme. Established in 1944 it resulted in 164 drawings and watercolours of London scenes and places of beauty and historic interest in the Home Counties. Rowntree contributed a number of works including *The Signwriter's Shop* and *Anchor Brewery, Southwark*.[88]

Rowntree held his first one-man show in 1946 at the Leicester Galleries, much of the work depicted aspects of his domestic life in Essex. In the late 1940s he undertook various design commissions and book jackets most notably *A Prospect for Wales* (1948), one of The King Penguin Book series, edited by Pevsner. The cover took the form of a portfolio, Clough Williams Ellis was asked to write the text but refused, as he did not agree with Rowntree's paintings, and Gwyn Jones took over the task. There was no disagreement over Rowntree's contribution to the first series of School Prints, his Essex *Tractor* was one of the most successful

Rowntree's skill as a mural artist was recognised by his appointment as head of the mural painting department at the Royal College of Art from 1949, a post he held until 1958. During this period he contributed a mural to the Lion and Unicorn Pavilion at the Festival of Britain in 1951. His next teaching post was to Newcastle as Professor of Fine Art at the University of Durham's progressive art school, as successor to Gowing. His contact with colleagues such as Victor Pasmore and Richard Hamilton influenced his work and 'he became receptive to various modernist idioms, incorporating them in his own work.'[89] Rowntree retired in 1980 but continued to paint and exhibit. ◆◆◆

GORDON SCOTT

(1914–2006)

Scott studied at Croydon School of Art and at the Royal College of Art (RCA) from 1934–38 under Gilbert Spencer (1892–1979), Alan Sorrell (1904–77) and Charles Mahoney (1903–68). In his final year he was awarded a Travelling Scholarship for painting.

A reserved and highly principled man Scott registered as conscientious objector (CO) and was directed to be employed in non-combatant duties. He joined the Non-Combatant Corps (NCC) and was stationed at Bulford Camp on Salisbury Plain. Little is known about the precise tasks he undertook or where else he was posted. However, during his time at Bulford Camp he produced a number of sketches and striking portraits of fellow COs who passed through the camp.

After the war Scott taught part-time at Camberwell School of Arts and Crafts where he remained until his retirement in 1980. 'He played an important part in introducing Foundation and Textiles students to the buildings of London.'[90]

Scott considered himself as one of the generation and persuasion of the Euston Road School of painting and drawing, though he never studied or taught with them.[91] He painted throughout his life, continuing to work direct from nature, buildings always fascinated him, 'sensitive to place and season, catching the characteristic light of Clapham, southern Greece or wherever it might be with his gentle palette and beautiful tones.'[92] He exhibited widely including with the London Group, Royal Society of British Artists, Royal Academy and at the Highgate Gallery in 2006. ◆◆◆

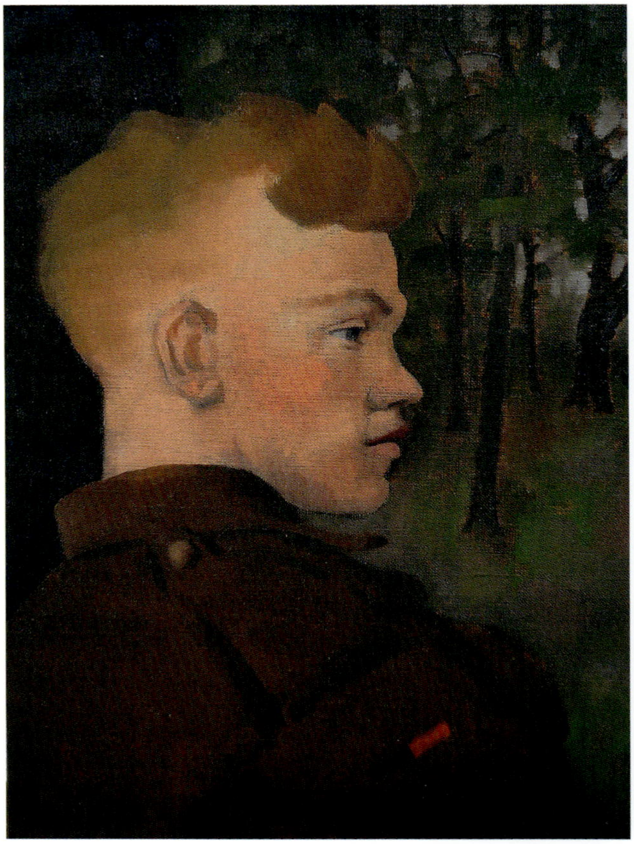

Gordon Scott | *Portrait of a Conscientious Objector*
Undated, Oil on canvas, 47 x 37 cm | © Darnley Fine Art

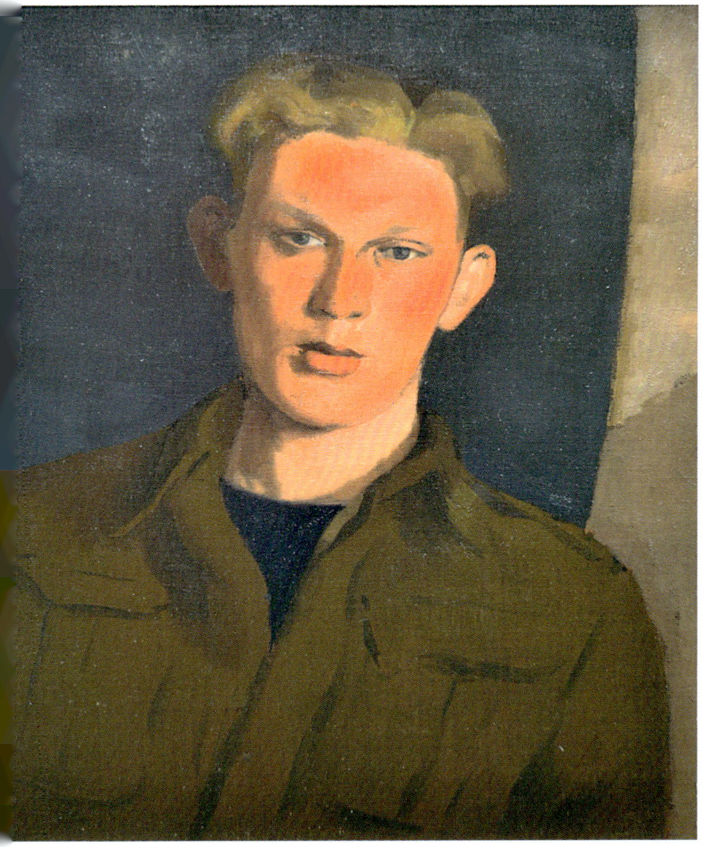

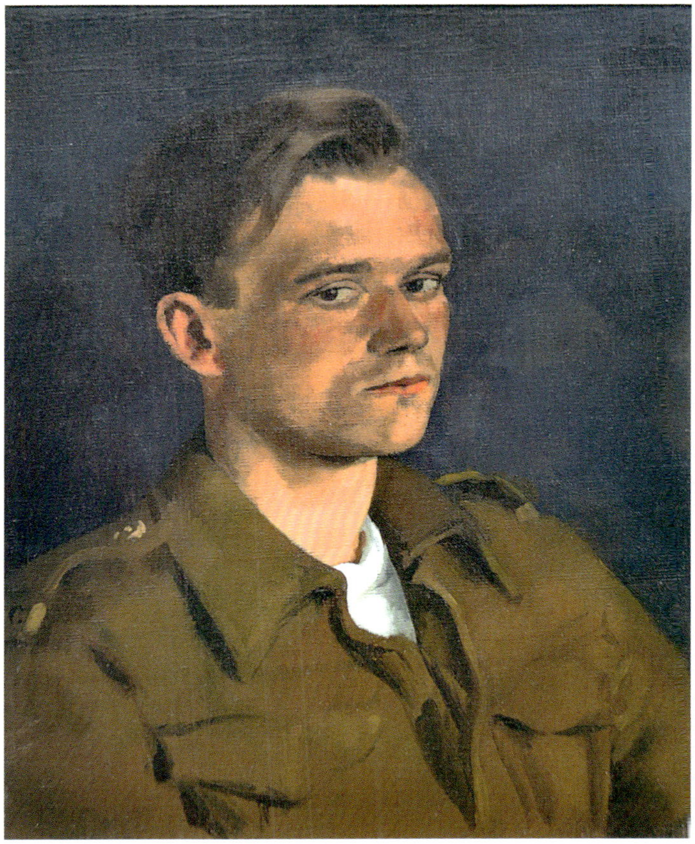

Gordon Scott | *Portrait of a Conscientious Objector*
Undated, Oil on canvas, 61 x 51 cm | © Darnley Fine Art

Gordon Scott | *Portrait of a Conscientious Objector*
Undated, Oil on canvas, 58 x 38 cm | © Darnley Fine Art

JOHN TUNNARD

(1900–71)

Tunnard graduated from the Royal College of Art (RCA) with a Diploma in Design in 1921 and after a short spell lecturing at the Central School of Arts and Crafts became a designer for Tootal, Broadhurst and Lee who manufactured textiles in Manchester. By 1928 he was working in London as a selector for woven and printed fabrics for John Lewis & Co. but left the following year to work freelance.

The relative isolation of west Cornwall with its cliffs and wild coastal scenery attracted Tunnard and his wife Mary (known as 'Bob'), a fellow artist at the RCA, whom he married in 1926. They first visited in 1930 camping for five months. He exhibited for the first time with the London Group and showed three works at the Royal Academy (RA) summer show in 1931. Two years later the Tunnards moved to Cadgwith, a small fishing village on the eastern side of the Lizard peninsula. His work was evolving from romantic landscapes into a highly inventive and individual non-representational style, combining the stylistic influences of surrealism and abstraction. In 1937 he showed work in the Surrealist section of the left-wing Artists International Association's (AIA) exhibition in Grosvenor Square, London. Surrealist was a term he never used of himself eschewing being closely aligned with any art movement while remaining interested in artistic developments. Tunnard's compositions showed echoes of work by Joan Miró (1893–1983) and Yves Tanguy (1900–55). The AIA exhibition was linked to the First British Artists Congress and was titled *For Peace, For Democracy, For Cultural Progress*. Sentiments that resonated strongly with Tunnard's politics.

Tunnard's friend and fellow artist Julian Trevelyan[93] wrote the introduction to his one-man exhibition *Paintings and Watercolours*, Tunnard's first non-representational show, which collector Peggy Guggenheim organised at her influential gallery Guggenheim Jeune in London, in March 1939. Trevelyan's light-hearted and perceptive introduction captured Tunnard's interest in the natural world[94] and technological progress. He provocatively asked:

> *Who is John Tunnard?*
>
> *... Don't tell me you haven't heard him. [sic] The man who is always talking about shipwrecks and pirates. ...*
> *But what does he do?*
>
> *... Don't believe them when they tell you he paints. ...*
> *It's all done for him by an army of insects. Five hundred spiders, twenty ship-worms, seventy five beetles, quite a few exotic caterpillars, a hard-worked slug, and a Bol-Weevil. ...*
>
> *First Tunnard walks along the seashore till he spots an old ship's timber, a cast-off ironing board, a washed-up chart, an unfinished lavatory seat. To see him returning from one of these expeditions is to mistake him for a submarine junk-shop. Next he turns his spiders to work on them. Delicate webs are spun, while the slug ambles round leaving his silvery trail behind him. .... Finally, it all goes into a sort of glass box on the wall. ...*[95]

The show with its synthesis of Constructivism and Surrealism did much to enhance Tunnard's reputation both at home and internationally.

In 1940 Tunnard after briefly working as a fisherman served as an Auxiliary Coastguard at Cadgwith, which enabled him, as a conscientious objector, to avoid directly helping the war effort. Badly paid, he felt morally obliged to make some contribution, although he would have

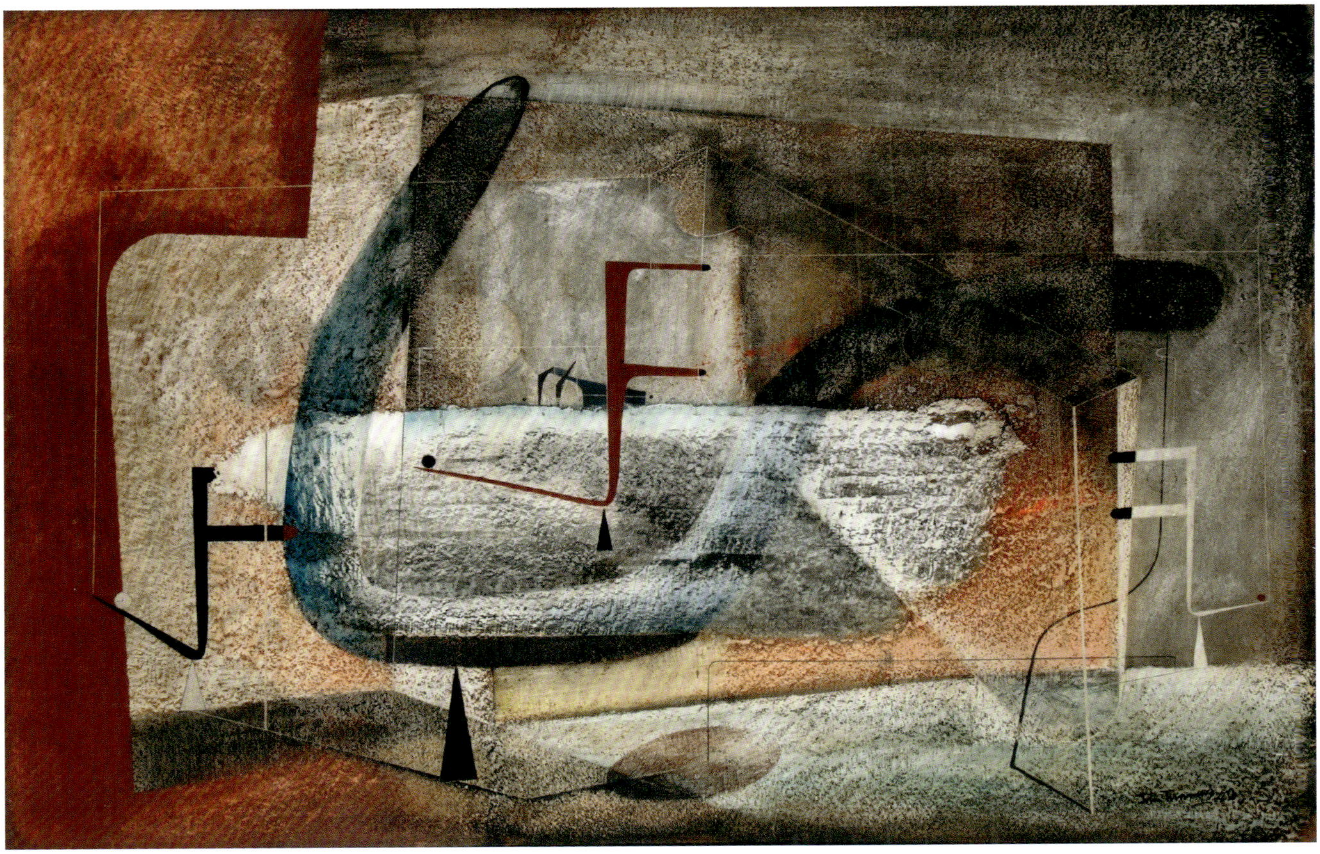

John Tunnard | *Anglo-Dutch* | 1942, Oil and tempera on board, 65 x 95 cm | © Imperial War Museum Art.IWMART LD16736

preferred to be engaged in camouflage work. In December 1940 Tunnard's article *The Life of a Coast Guard* was published in *Picture Post*, the photographs were taken by Humphrey Spender (1910–2005) whom he had known since the mid-1930s. He described his experiences on duty on the cliffs and at the Look-out Hut searching the sky for German aircraft. Tunnard explained that with the fear of fifth columnists all information, even the smallest detail, had to be reported. He continued to paint prolifically, his experiences having a profound effect on his work, the long periods watching the sea for ships in the hours of darkness on the alert for an invasion 'gradually shifted the emphasis of Tunnard's paintings away from the minutiae of the early abstract works and forward to the later panoramic works with their effective illusions of great distances and ultimately infinite space.'[96] The titles of some of his paintings unsurprisingly relate directly to the war, albeit they are not documentary records *per se*, such as *Sentinel* (1940) and *Assault* (1942). The *5th June 1944* (also known as *Eve of D-day*) was painted a few weeks before the Normandy landings; there likely being much speculation amongst his coastguard colleagues about a possible invasion of France.

Tunnard continued to exhibit throughout the war years and contributed to two exhibitions in 1942 staged to assist the war effort: *Artists Aid Russia* and *Artists Aid to China*. He also submitted work to the AIA *For Liberty* exhibition in March 1943. Exhibition spaces were difficult to find and it opened in the new basement canteen John Lewis's had constructed near the site of their Oxford Street store, which had been destroyed in a bombing raid. The centrepiece of the exhibition was paintings 'devoted to the "Four Liberties" of the Atlantic Charter: liberty of speech, liberty of worship, liberty from fear and liberty from want.' The themes for the other sections were: '"This is what we are fighting for", "This is how we are fighting" and '"This will happen unless"'.[97] Tunnard's *Focal Point*, which employs a range of methods including spray painting shows his affinities to Ben Nicholson and Barbara Hepworth. In July Tunnard had a successful solo exhibition at the Redfern Gallery selling 30 of the 33 works exhibited including *Anglo-Dutch* (1942) which was inspired by his coastguard duties. He was however much aggrieved when he received little by return from the gallery owing to their percentage share of the sales and the high rate of purchase tax levied by the wartime Government. *Anglo Dutch* was an ocean-going cargo ship; in the painting it floats as if inside a massive transparent structure, the deep red colour on the left of the composition suggesting rusting hulls, the maritime forms combine and a dark hook shape emerges suggestive of a rudder, and the triangular and circular symbols of navigational charts add to the nautical and abstract subject matter. Tunnard later explained how his practice developed:

> *I started certainly as a representational painter ... First, I suppose I was interested in merely trying to put down what I saw or thought I saw. Then, after that I was more interested in the dramatic content of the landscape ... and then ... with the geometrically dramatic content. By that I mean the dramatic movements of roads, of ruts sweeping into farmyards, of the lines of telegraph poles or the sweep of railings, and these I found myself exaggerating to get to the geometrically dramatic. Of course, I got to the stage when, confronted with a landscape, I felt that the only thing to do was invent. As soon as I started inventing I found that it was so much more exciting, and that inventing came gradually into what is called non-representational painting.*[98]

Post-war austerity hit the Tunnards hard and in 1947 he accepted a commission from Brenda Rawnsley (1916–2007), Director of The School Prints Ltd. to design a print for the series of original artists' lithographs, which aimed to give primary school children an understanding of contemporary art. For *Holiday*, the only print he ever produced, he received £85. It 'was certainly the most abstract print produced, it was nevertheless very popular, probably due to its bright colours and the cheerful exuberance which it radiates. The figures may well be strange and surreal, but they are by no means disconcerting and appear to be having a great deal of fun on a sunny beach as the waves roll in.'[99]

In 1953 following the death of Tunnard's mother he received a legacy, which enabled them to move to Lamorna, and buy 'Trethinick', a house in the Lamorna Valley, which had belonged to Dame Laura Knight. Freed from financial worries he was able to adopt a more relaxed approach to his artistic work. 'Most of the known works of the mid-1950s continued to reflect Tunnard's passion for natural history, but increasingly he became interested in the concept of space travel ...'.[100] In 1960 Tunnard had two works hung in the RA summer show, nearly three decades since his last appearance, hitherto he had declined believing the RA to have been less than progressive in its approach. His profile was in the ascendancy and his work in demand, but he never recovered from the shock of the death of Bob in May 1970 and he died in December 1971. ◆◆◆

KEITH VAUGHAN

(1912–77)

Vaughan was self-taught as an artist although his art master, Harold Rigby[101] (1879–1938) at Christ's Hospital School, Horsham, where he was a boarder from 1921–29 encouraged him and fostered his talent and interest in Frank Brangwyn, whose murals adorned the school chapel. A talented pupil he won school prizes for art and held his first public exhibition at the school of drawings of Cornwall. From 1931–39 he worked for the advertising agency Lintas.

Vaughan joined the St John Ambulance on the outbreak of war. In his journal which he kept from 25 August 1939 he noted the arrival of Canadians the following year on 14 April 1940, describing them as 'simple looking clumsy boys with gentle faces and soft eyes and a ready smile. They have come voluntarily to join in the mad house. … I cannot believe they want to kill people any more than I. Which is one reason which makes it impossible to be a CO.' Wrestling with his own stance Vaughan concedes 'It is more my reason that is offended by the war than my conscience. I can still postpone the decision a little while.'[102] On 12 August 1940 Vaughan appeared briefly before a Tribunal in Reading when, despite having rehearsed his responses, he agreed to serve in the RAMC, immediately regretting it, but to no avail. Just over four months later he received his call-up papers and on 2 January 1941 he went by train to Ilfracombe in Devon along with other recruits. The following day he was issued with his new khaki uniform with Non-Combatant Corps flashes on the shoulders.

In early February 1941 Vaughan found himself undertaking the first of a series of heavy, physical labouring jobs in Wiltshire and southern England which occupied him until mid-1943. Filling sand-bags with white and ochre clay on Salisbury Plain to reinforce a nearby pill-box Vaughan found his new life physically exhausting. A fellow recruit decided such work was against his conscience and was told to look after their kits instead. Vaughan was 'more concerned with keeping warm than with [his] conscience.'[103] In June, he worked on the land at Codford, having marched eighteen miles from Bulford Camp, spending the day reaping, he observed 'All this during a summer's day while the panzer divisions are marching against Russia.' Vaughan rued the 'Meaningless fatigues and kit-inspections after the day's work' and the fact that every few weeks his army companions were split up so that they did not become too contented. In between labouring Vaughan snatched a few moments to make a number of small pen and wash drawings in his sketchbook including one of the landscape near Bulford Camp (1941), and others depicting army life at Codford (1942). The following month he spent his days quarrying gravel with a pick axe at Melksham, being chivvied by NCOs with 'no idea of the beginning or end of a job or what its purpose is.' By 28 August 1941 Vaughan noted with some alarm that all talk was about 'the question of transferring; giving up our protected status and joining a combatant unit or volunteering for bomb disposal … '. Vaughan spent most of the winter living under canvas but by the New Year he was living 'in the luxury of Nissen huts' with a 'weirdly assorted lot with no common bonds or interests, except an unwillingness to kill strangers to order.' He wrote 'Our community is formed simply by military law.'[104] By June 1942 Vaughan was becoming restless at 'the aimless repetitive existence' and wondered what would happen if they had to restate their claims before a tribunal and public sentiment changed. Despite his restlessness he produced *Echo of the Bombardment* (1942), part of a series titled 'Destruction of the Human City' in response to the Blitz and other devastating air raids. This quasi-surrealist work with the simplified bombed out buildings with coiled forms emerging suggests inspiration from Samuel Palmer and William Blake and elements from other Neo-Romantic artists of the period. The War Artists' Advisory Committee bought eight watercolours from Vaughan in September 1942.

Vaughan journeyed north by train to Yorkshire in early July 1943 to find his new barracks, a disused mill, having marched with full kit five miles up what he described as 'virtually the side of a mountain'. He also spent time in

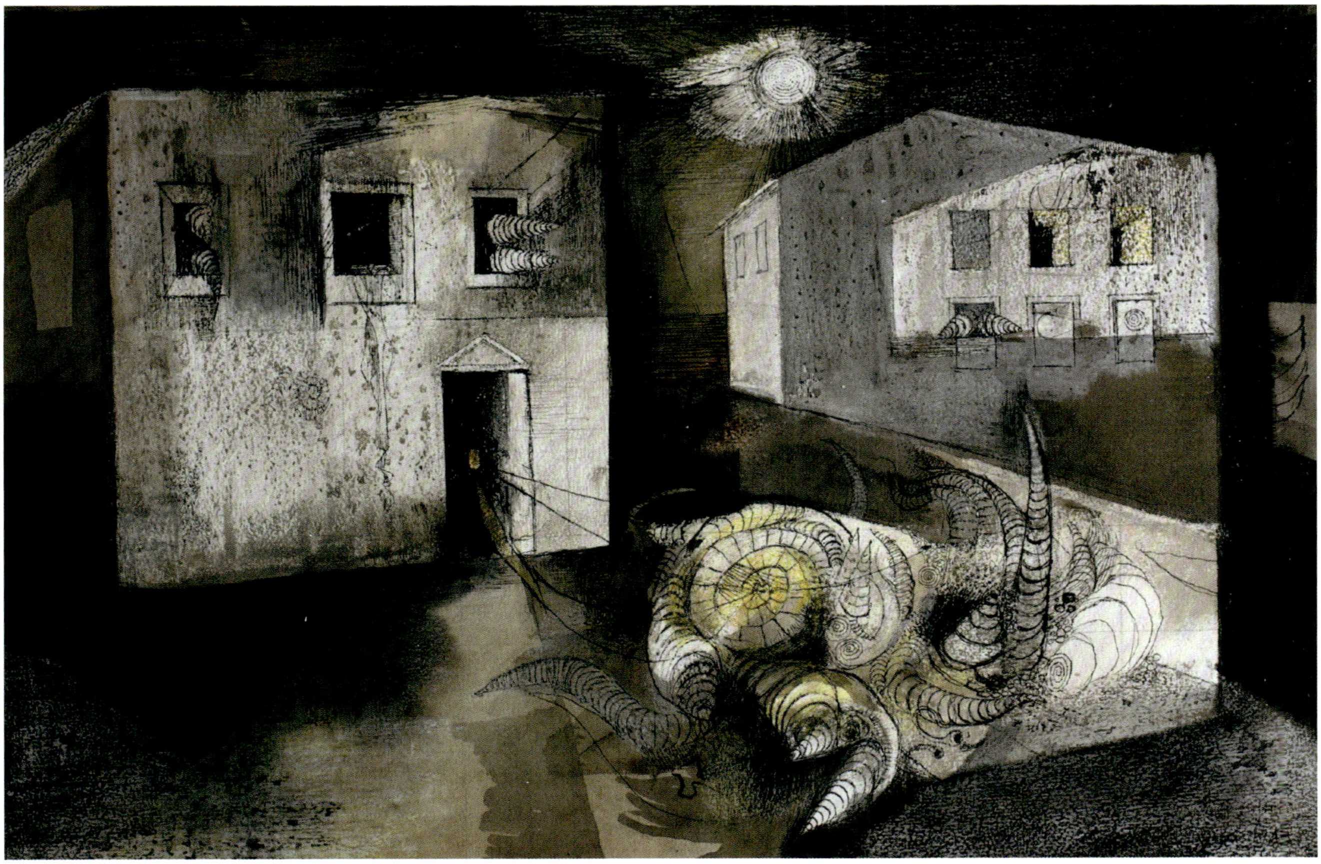

Keith Vaughan | *Echo of the Bombardment* | 1942, Watercolour, ink and crayon, 31.8 x 46.4 cm

Derby, before returning to London to receive training as a clerk-typist. In October 1943 he returned to Yorkshire to Eden Camp near Malton where he worked as an Orderly Room clerk and assistant German interpreter, knowing a little of the language, at the prisoner of war camp. He produced a number of highly charged gouaches and ink drawings of soldiers, interiors, and landscape working steadily, without a studio, making do with available materials. Gouache proved to be an attractive and versatile medium as it dried quickly and darker, and could be over-painted. Vaughan had by then met Graham Sutherland and drew inspiration from his work and ideas about painting and on occasion visited him in Kent when he had extended periods of leave. Vaughan also maintained his friendship with John Minton who was serving in the Pioneer Corps. In one of the few letters to Minton that survives he wrote in January 1945 about the difficulties caused by his work on his art and how he was:

> *... tired of finding drawings, continually fraternizing with filing cases and nominal rolls. I'm tired of messing about with pots of poster colour on pinned up pieces of tissue paper. I'm tired of having nothing to look at but barbed wire and flat fields full of waist high wheat, and grasses. I'm tired of always having to start when I'm tired.*[105]

He ended optimistically 'Actually I've been sparring around with some paintings lately.' Vaughan held his first solo show the previous May at The Lefevre Gallery, London in new premises in New Bond Street (as it had previously been bombed out). He shared the premises with work by the late Robert Bevan. *The Times*' art critic gave the show guarded praise identifying the influences of Picasso, Henry Moore, John Piper, and Sutherland amongst others remarking 'it is difficult to entangle the real Mr. Vaughan. His work however gives the feeling that something of his own may one day emerge.'

Demobbed in March 1946 Vaughan taught painting and illustration at Camberwell from autumn 1946–48; moving to the Central School 1948–57 and the Slade from 1954. Alongside his teaching he was commissioned to paint a mural (*Theseus*) for the Dome of Discovery on London's South Bank, for the Festival of Britain in 1951. He also produced distinctive book jackets and magazine illustrations. The main subject of Vaughan's work was the male figure, usually nude in landscape; in the 1950s he began a series of groups of male figures which he referred to as Assembly Figures; in some of his later work the images ended up more abstracted. As far as he was concerned the figure was the subject with which he was 'constantly, obsessively occupied'.[106] Vaughan remained troubled throughout his life about his ability as an artist despite considerable success during his lifetime and his sexuality and was forthright in his journals when homosexuality was illegal. ◆◆◆

ARTHUR WRAGG

(1903–76)

Wragg won a scholarship to Sheffield Art School when he was thirteen; however his father thought he would be better off in business and so he was unable to take it up immediately. In 1918 after having spent some time in the offices of a firm engaged in the production of munitions Wragg's determination to become an artist won through and he took up a place at the Art School. In 1923 he moved to London to become a commercial artist; his first commission was for Terry's Chocolates of York. He worked for a number of periodicals from 1924 including *Good Housekeeping, Nash's Magazine, Sunday Magazine, Woman's Journal, Woman's Pictorial* and *Tatler* and was briefly art-editor to *Opera and Ballet.*

In the interwar years Wragg wrote and illustrated a number of books with religious themes, which were published by Selwyn & Blount. *The Psalms for Modern Life* (1933), his first, was interpreted with bold and powerfully evocative black and white illustrations, and in common with his later work were 'closely related to modern conditions, full of pity and terror, and suffused with burning social criticism.'[107] The book contained a short, but telling Introduction by 'Dick' Sheppard (1880–1937), former Dean of Canterbury and popular radio broadcaster, who had at first refused to write the piece as he was rather old-fashioned about the Bible and feared either a series of 'arty' and painfully clever pictures, or else a number of goody-goody, sentimental drawings. Sheppard changed his mind after Wragg visited unannounced from Cornwall, (where he was living with Fred Johnson ['Essex' of *Punch*]), with his portfolio. On opening it Sheppard explained how he:

> *... gasped, because some of them seemed to pierce the soul like bullets. I remember turning aside lest Wragg should observe the lump in my throat. Many of his illustrations seemed to me wonderful and dreadful, very beautiful and very awe-ful, terribly vivid and yet perfectly simple; more, they seemed as true and yet for the most part as sincere as the voice of a prophet who will not cry Peace where no Peace is.*[108]

Sheppard believed that Wragg had something important to say and commended the work wholeheartedly though he feared that some readers who disliked this form of illustrating the Psalms would censure the work as being hysterical and sensational. Well-received it underwent numerous reprints, and by 1939 was in its 11th, including American and Dutch editions. The illustration most reproduced was for Psalm 94, the line taken for the caption was 'Understand, ye brutish among the people: and ye fools, when will ye be wise?' It shows a dead child apparently gassed lying on the pavement holding a doll with blood dripping into the drain, a newspaper advertising placard states 'When war is justified – more letters'.

Wragg's meeting with Sheppard led to an intense friendship that lasted until the latter's sudden death in 1937. Both ardent pacifists, Wragg drew the cover for the programme for a meeting called by Dick Sheppard at the Albert Hall in London in July 1935 for those men who had returned a postcard saying they renounced war. Known initially as 'Sheppard's Peace Movement' it became the Peace Pledge Union in 1936; a number of pacifist artists were members. Wragg's concern for social and political injustice continued to be reflected in his work, he contributed regularly to *Peace News*; designed election posters for the Labour party and the first eight covers for the socialist magazine *The Tribune*. His technical mastery was again demonstrated in *Thy Kingdom Come, a Prayer in Black and White for Ourselves and the World To-day* (1939) which was published after the outbreak of war, although he had executed and planned it in so called peace-time, it was dedicated to 'All those who still believe in something'. A note on the facing page pointed out that some of the drawings had been published earlier and employed 'both here and abroad in the raising of funds for welfare and humanitarian work, for public information, and for education or religious purposes.' Wragg in the introduction added a postscript, dated October 1939 in which he outlined when the drawings (they resemble woodcuts) were produced, and significantly he recorded his thanks to

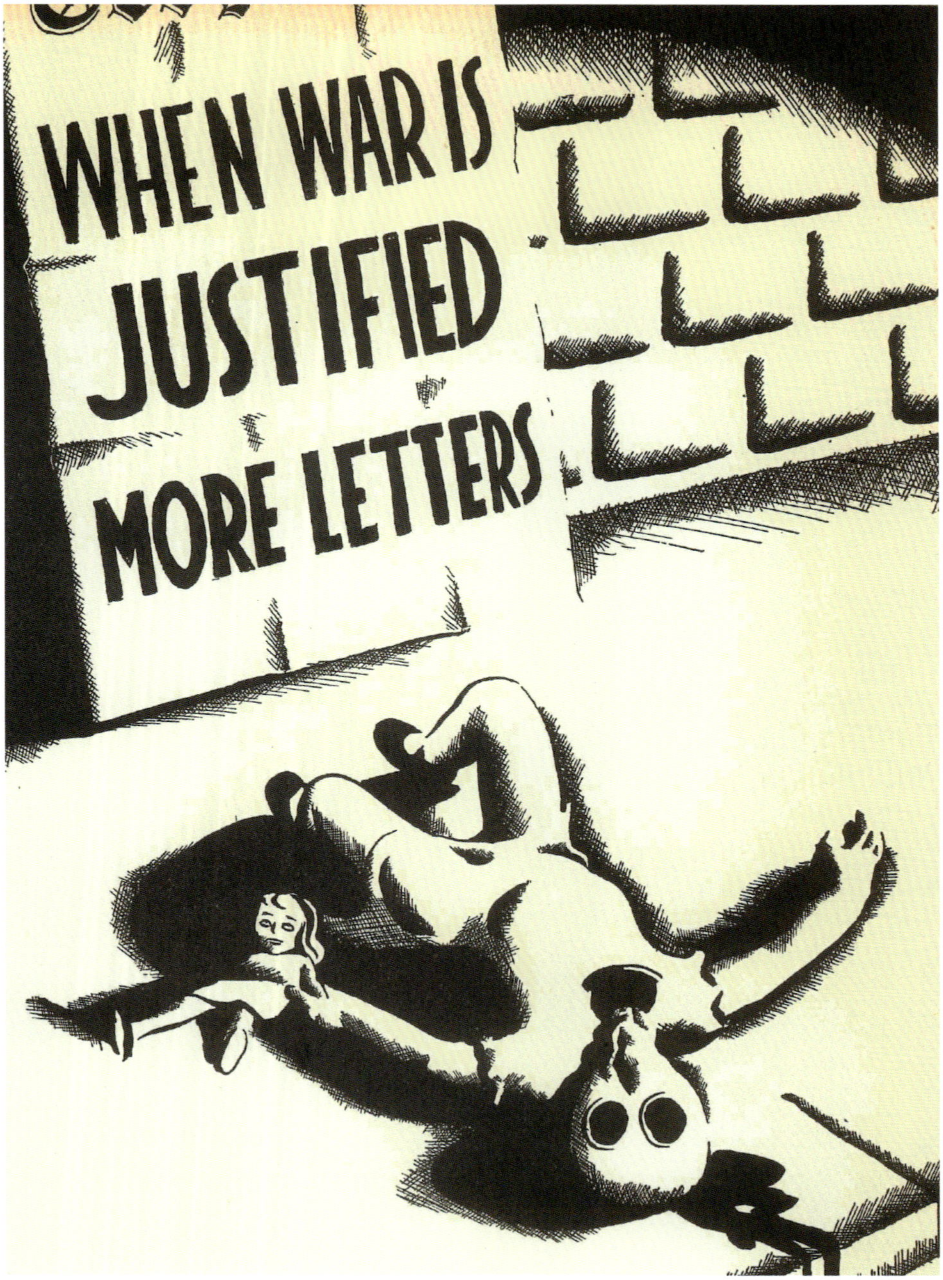

Arthur Wragg | *'Understand, ye brutish among the people: and ye fools, when will ye be wise?'*
Illustration of Psalm 94, from *The Psalms for Modern Life* (1933) | Selwyn & Blount Ltd

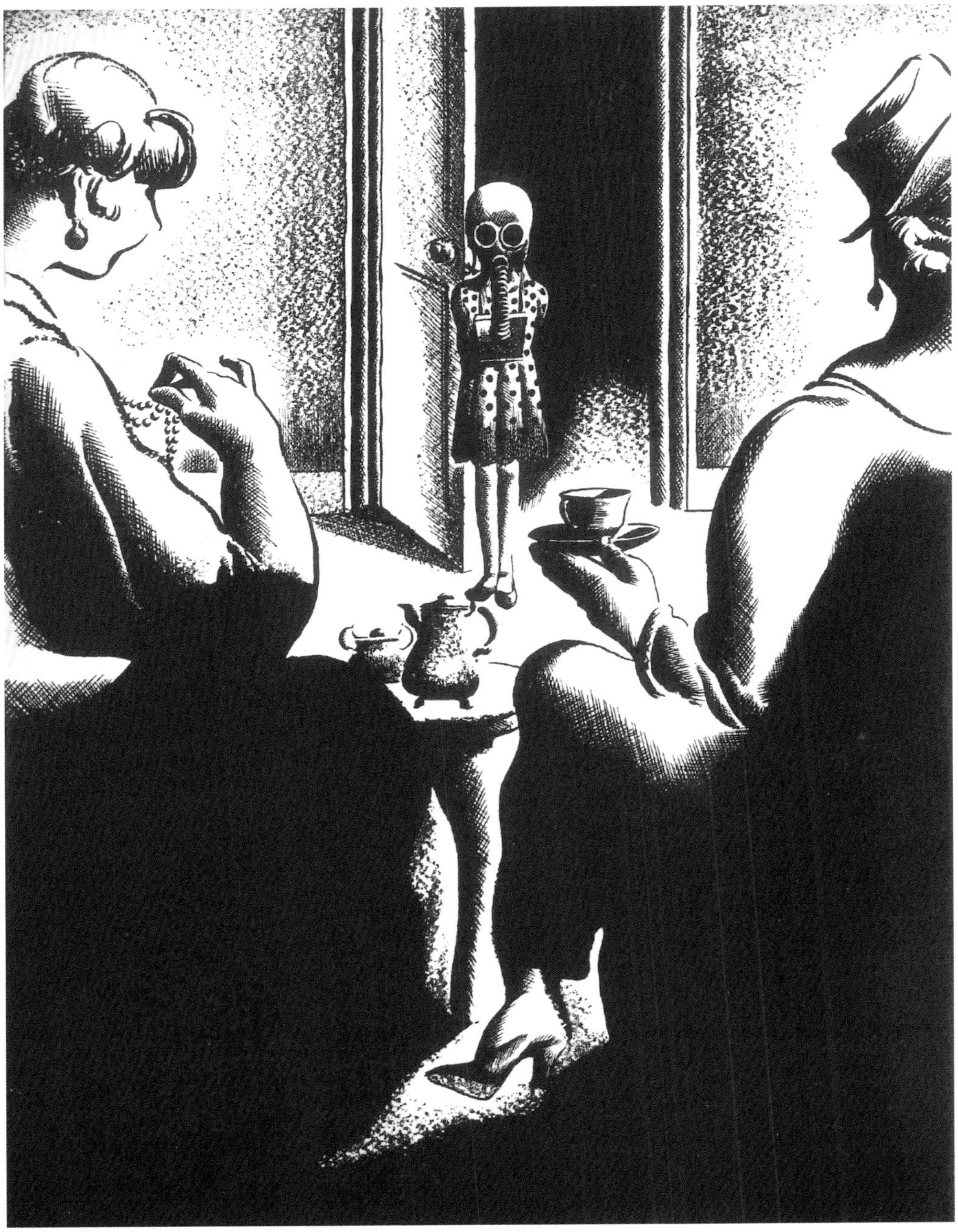

Arthur Wragg | *'Come, Effie, show Auntie you Nice New Gas-Drill'* | Illustration from *Thy Kingdom Come, a Prayer in Black and White for Ourselves and the World To-day* (1939) | Selwyn & Blount Ltd the community for being able to publish such a work even in times of war, recognising that his views were not shared by the majority. He closed by stating 'But sometimes it is both the duty and the privilege of a minority to contribute its views usefully to the community as a whole, a principle upon which democracy itself is based.'

For some six months in 1940 Wragg, a conscientious objector, taught drawing and painting at Wandsworth Gaol. The following year aged thirty-eight he received his call-up papers and in June 1941 he set out his deeply felt case at length to the South-Western Tribunal under Judge Wethered (1878–1975):[109]

> *I object to any kind of compulsory service which tends to continue the waging of war because it is contrary to my interpretation of Christian Teaching. …*
>
> *It is not my wish to juggle with Scriptural quotations in order to evade responsibility; my views have been expressed widely for many years in my published work (herewith submitted) and there seems no reason to burden the Tribunal with them here. …*
>
> *In my view a pacifist should, both in peace and war, do that which would otherwise not be done as far as his gifts allow. …*
>
> *For some time now I have been engaged on a 'Life of Christ' which … is intended as a contribution to the spiritual reconstruction necessary if the hatreds likely to arise in the post-war years are to be bridged. This work is for publication after the war and the Society of Friends Peace Committee are to be the guardians of the completed work, which I imagine will take me another two years. I am presenting the preliminary studies to the Government's pictorial war records for future use. This offer has been accepted. …*
>
> *… I was called to this work much as a priest is called to his. For nearly two years I have had to learn a new discipline in technique …*[110]

Wragg took to the Tribunal supporting statements as to his sincerity from various high profile figures, including those from George Bell, Bishop of Chichester who knew him well and had encouraged him to consider ordination and Vera Brittain, author of *Testament of Youth*, who had known him for several years and converted to pacifism in 1937 (for which Dick Sheppard was directly responsible). He was given exemption to continue with his work as artist and author and directed towards teaching as his war work. Wragg joined the staff of Beltane School as art master, which had been evacuated from Wimbledon to Shaw in Wiltshire in October 1941. During the war he also produced illustrations and book jackets, several for the series 'Modern Christian Revolutionaries' that included Eric Gill and wrote educational 'Letters to an Art Student' published in *The Artist* conveying aspects of his philosophy of art.

Post-war Wragg returned to London continuing to illustrate books, and in the 1950s he contributed a comic strip to *The People*. He retained his interest in politics to the last becoming preoccupied with the Cold War. He submitted political cartoons to the *Sunday Pictorial* in the 1960s. Wragg also designed illustrative record covers for Decca for the Argo series from 1954–76.[111] ◆◆◆

BRYAN WYNTER

(1915–75)

Wynter attended evening classes at Westminster School of Art from c.1936 having developed an interest in drawing from childhood, particularly animals. His family had intended he join the laundry business but eventually gave way and he took up a place at the Slade in 1938, where his contemporaries included Paul Feiler and Patrick Heron who, post-war, also based themselves in Cornwall. Wynter continued his studies in Oxford when the Slade was evacuated to share premises with the Ruskin in the Ashmolean Museum in October 1939. He was by then eligible to be called up for military service. When his papers arrived Wynter took the decision to register as a conscientious objector. 'The motives for his decision were complex but were clearly informed … by convictions to do with individual freedom and integrity.'[112] Wynter had made a detailed study of *Ends and Means: An Enquiry into the Nature of Ideals and into the Methods Employed for their Realization* (1937) by Aldous Huxley, and been drawn to his pacifist views about the nature of war, social reform and violence. Wynter appeared before a tribunal in Reading and was granted exemption on the grounds that he undertook work on the land. He was initially involved in land drainage, digging ditches along the Thames Valley and working as an agricultural labourer on a small holding at Noke, north-east of Oxford.[113] Then for a short time he worked as a Keeper for the monkeys being studied by zoologist Solly Zuckerman (1904–93) who was teaching anatomy at the University of Oxford and a leading authority on the social life of monkeys and apes. Wynter who found the work dispiriting fed and cleaned the monkeys' cages, preparing them for laboratory experiments together with fellow Slade student and conscientious objector Hugh Lyell Mellor, whose case for exemption was considered by the Lancashire Conscientious Objectors' Tribunal on 31 July 1941. The *Manchester Guardian* reported the case under the strap line 'AN ARTIST C.O. "No Strong Sense of Responsibility"'. Judge Burgis, who had gained a reputation for being uncompromising, said the applicant had most unfavourably impressed the tribunal, his life was selfish and shut and that he wanted to go on pursuing the comfortable, pleasant surroundings of Oxford. Mellor was ordered to perform non-combatant service.[114]

Wynter drew throughout the war years including landscape sketches and several Monkey House cartoons wherein monkeys and scientists exchange roles. He also attended a small informal Life Class in the city in Beaumont Street, run by Peter Greenham (1909–92) who taught in Magdalen College School. The room where the small group of subscribers worked was underground, warmed by a fire and an oil stove, and with a good electric light on the model.[115] Wynter moved to Cornwall as soon as he could around the end of June 1945 to where he had spent family holidays in the 1930s. He rented a near-derelict cottage on the hill above Zennor, which he bought in 1956; its position on the Moors had a marked effect upon his work and subject matter. 'By choosing to live in a remote, exposed place he submerged himself in an environment in immediate contact with weather and sea.'[116] The results were frequently small gouaches of Cornish landscapes and animals, noticeably birds. Wynter believed that some of his work produced post-war in the immediate aftermath of his labour in the laboratories was a reflection of his troubled state of mind at what he perceived was the cruelty of the wartime research. Earlier in the year he had been deeply disturbed by the emerging reports of the mass murders of Jews by the Nazis. He had, as a result, questioned his pacifist stance.

Wynter became more involved with the St Ives artistic community participating in the Crypt Group's first exhibition in 1946 and he was also a founder member of the Penwith Society in 1949. He also exhibited with the London Group. From 1951–56 Wynter taught at Bath Academy in Corsham where his colleagues included William Scott, Peter Lanyon, Adrian Heath and Kenneth Armitage. His work went through several phases and around 1956 he produced his first abstract leaving behind his early work that had been in part shaped by surrealism.[117] The subject matter, and size, changed. Wynter was once again inspired by Huxley's writings, specifically *The Doors of Perception*, which details his experience of taking the hallucinogenic drug mescaline. Wynter also experimented with the drug in order to experience its visual effects. Linked with his change in direction was his visit in January 1956 to the notable exhibition *Modern Art in the United States* at the Tate Gallery where he encountered the work of the Abstract Expressionists. In 1960 Wynter became interested in kinetics and from 1961 made a series of innovative kinetic mobiles, which he called IMOOS (Images Moving Out Onto Space) remaining dedicated throughout his life to the 'activities of the earth's surface.'[118] ◆◆◆

REFERENCES AND NOTES

1. See the section 'Sketchbooks and Studies' in Grieve, A. (1992) *Robert Adams, 1917–1984: A Sculptor's Record*, pp.22–23.
2. *The Times*, November 13, p.15.
3. http://www.gimpelfils.com/pages/exhibitions/exhibition.php?exhid=21&subsec=1, accessed 14/3/18.
4. Berlin, S. (1994) *The Coat of Many Colours*, Bristol: Redcliffe Press, p.91. I am grateful to Julia Berlin for drawing my attention to the fact that Sven Berlin's father was Swedish, and that he could have claimed exemption on this basis.
5. Berlin (1994) Ibid. and see Aarons, S. (2016) *Sven Berlin. Timeless Man*, Godshill: Millersford Press. I am grateful to Sonia and Anthony Green for their assistance.
6. Aarons (2016) Ibid., p.35.
7. Berlin (undated) 'In Cornwall', Chronology in *Sven Berlin: Paintings, Drawings and Sculpture* (1989), Belgrave Gallery, London, p.7.
8. Post-war Sven Berlin's commanding officer telephoned every Remembrance Sunday, a practice he continued until his death. He described Berlin 'as one of the bravest and fearless soldiers'. (Pers. comm. with Julia Berlin).
9. Buckman, D. (2006) *Artists in Britain since 1945*, vol. 1, A to L, Art Dictionaries Limited: Bristol, p.689.
10. Bridgeman, J. (2013) 'My father' in Michael, M.A. (Ed.) *Landscape to Sculpture: John Bridgeman 1916–2004*, Catalogue Leamington Spa Art Gallery & Museum, p.12.
11. http://www.gallery-pangolin.com/artists/john-bridgeman accessed 12/3/18.
12. See Henry Moore Institute Leeds, Archive catalogue.
13. Michael, M.A. (Ed.) (2013) *Landscape to Sculpture: John Bridgeman 1916–2004*, Catalogue Leamington Spa Art Gallery & Museum, p.66.
14. Michael (2013) Ibid. p.68.
15. Rosemary Butler (2000) in her interview for the *National Life Story Collection: Artists' Lives* discussed in detail Reg Butler's life and work. See The British Library Board http://sounds.bl.uk.
16. See Garlake, M. (2006) *The Sculpture of Reg Butler*, who states that they ran Lyfords Engineering Ltd. based in Liphook (some 6 miles from Iping).
17. See Burstow, R. (2014) 'Geometries of Hope and Fear: The Iconography of Atomic Science and Nuclear Anxiety in the Modern Sculpture of World War and Cold War Britain' in C. Jolivette (Ed.) *British Art in the Nuclear Age*, London: Ashgate, p.68.
18. Calvocoressi, R. (1983) 'Reg Butler: The Man and the Work' in *Reg Butler*, The Tate Gallery, p.13.
19. http://www.parkinfineart.co.uk/about1 accessed February 2018.
20. http://spitalfieldslife.com/2013/06/11/roland-collins-artist/accessed 24/7/17.
21. Lambirth, A. (2010) *A Critic's Choice. Selected by Andrew Lambirth*, London: Browse & Darby, unpaginated, see also his extended essay 'Introducing Roland Collins' in *Roland Collins Found Landscapes* (2012) curated by Nathaniel Hepburn at Mascalls Gallery, Paddock Wood, Kent.
22. The Downs was founded in 1900 by Herbert Jones, formerly headmaster at Leighton Park School.
23. Bury, S. (2004–11) Lawrence Gowing, *Oxford Dictionary of National Biography (ODNB)* entry.
24. Morris, L. and Radford, R. (1983) *The Story of the AiA: Artists International Association 1933–1953*, Oxford: Museum of Modern Art, Oxford, p.54.
25. Gowing, L. (1983) *Lawrence Gowing*, Arts Council of Great Britain, p.16.
26. Ibid., p.18.
27. Heron, P. (1978) *The Colour of Colour. E William Doty Lectures in Fine Art*, College of Fine Arts, The University of Texas at Austin, p.49.
28. Heron (1998) 'Interview with Martin Gayford' in Sylvester, D. (Ed.) (1998) *Patrick Heron*, Tate Gallery Publishing, p.22.
29. Heron (1978) Op. cit., pp.51–52 and also Gooding M. (1994) *Patrick Heron*, London: Phaidon Press, p.43.
30. See Heron's interview in the *National Life Story Collection: Artists' Lives* with Mel Gooding as referred to here (and Gooding 1994, Ibid.); in Heron's later interview with Gayford. Op. cit. in Sylvester (Ed.) (1998) he reverses the order of events before he goes to join Leach in St Ives.
31. See *Jonah Jones: An Artist's Life*, written by his son Peter Jones (2011), who worked as a letter cutter in his workshop.
32. Jones (2011) Op. cit., p.34. He took to the nickname and adopted the name completely after the war. He had been christened Leonard.
33. Jonah Jones (1987) cited in Jones (2011) Op. cit., p.34.
34. Stephens, M. (2004) Obituary, *The Independent*, 2 December, p.42.
35. Jonah Jones (c.1990s) 'The pacific fallacy?' cited in Jones (2011) Op. cit., p.25.
36. Hucker, S. (2004) *George Kennethson: A Modernist Rediscovered*, London: Merrell, p.15.
37. Hucker (2004) Ibid. p.16.
38. Kennethson quoted in *Translations from Life and Nature: Stone Carvings 1950–1985*, exhibition catalogue, Peterborough Museum & Art Gallery, unpaginated.
39. Dempsey, A. (1995) Arthur George Landseer Mackenzie (George Kennethson). Obituary. *Independent*, 23 January. Born MacKenzie he used the name Kennethson professionally in the early 1970s.
40. I am grateful to Elspeth Langsdale, Archivist, Oundle School for drawing my attention to this change.
41. Machin, A. (2002) *Artist of an Icon*, Kirstead: Frontier Publishing, p.65.
42. See the Sim Fine Art catalogue (2017) *Holding the Line. The Art of the War Years 1914–18 & 1939–45* for the 8th Annual War Art exhibition. I am grateful to Andrew Sim for his assistance re Ronald Fuller who produced a detailed record of an ambulanceman's life in the Blitz.
43. Berthoud, R. (1987) *The Life of Henry Moore*, London: Faber & Faber, pp.136, 137.
44. Bowness, A. (1995) *Bernard Meadows: Sculpture and Drawings*, London: Henry Moore Foundation in association with Lund Humphries, p.9.
45. Meadows, B. (1992) National Life Stories: Artists' Lives. British Library Oral History.

46. Meadows (1992) Ibid.
47. Meadows (1992) Ibid.
48. The other sculptors were Robert Adams, Kenneth Armitage, Reg Butler, Lynn Chadwick, Geoffrey Clarke, Henry Moore, Eduardo Paolozzi and William Turnbull.
49. Osborne Samuel (2017) *Aspects of Modern British Sculpture*, p.56.
50. Davies, P. (2005) Bernard Meadows. Obituary, *Independent*, 17 January.
51. Spalding, F. (2005) *John Minton: Dance till the Stars Come Down*, Aldershot: Lund Humphries, p.35.
52. Spalding (2005) Ibid., p.35.
53. See Gardiner, J. (2004) *History Today*, November, p.33.
54. Spalding (2005) Op. cit., p.46.
55. Spalding (2005) Op. cit., p.56.
56. See Yorke, M. (2001) *The Spirit of Place: Nine Neo-Romantic Artists and their Times*, London: Tauris Parke, p.180.
57. Forge, A. (Ed.) (1976) *The Townsend Journals. An Artist's Record of His Times 1928–51*, London: Tate Gallery, p.60.
58. Pasmore (1941) cited in *Victor Pasmore. Writings and Interviews* edited by A. Grieve (2010), Tate Publishing.
59. Pasmore (1941) Ibid.
60. Stourton, J. (2016) *Kenneth Clark. Life, Art and Civilisation*, London: William Collins, p.154.
61. Gieve (2010) Op. cit., pp.31, 32.
62. Craven, T. (1999) *The Euston Road School*, Southampton City Art Gallery, unpaginated
63. Walker, N. (Ed.) (2016) *Victor Pasmore. Towards a New Reality*, Lund Humphries in Association with Djanogly Gallery, Nottingham Lakeside Arts, p.28.
64. Lambirth, A. (2004–16) Victor Pasmore, *ODNB* entry.
65. I am grateful to Mick, David & Anna Petts for their help with the editing of this account.
66. Ronald John Petts (1987) IWM oral history.
67. The pen drawing *The Upland Team* (1944) was produced while Petts was working as a registered CO on Tyddyn Cynal farm in the Conwy Valley. I am grateful to Mick Petts for bringing this drawing by his father to my attention.
68. Garrett, A. (1978) *A History of Wood Engraving*, p.255.
69. The National Library of Wales in Aberystwyth.
70. Castle in 1958 wrote *Moral Education in Christian Times*.
71. See Vann, P. (2004) *Face to Face. British Self-Portraits in the Twentieth Century*, London, p.244. & Bristol: Piano Nobile & Sansom & Co.
72. See http://hugopowell.co.uk/biography/ accessed 1/3/18. I am grateful to Andrew Walton and Ruth Walton for sharing their family archive about Hugo Powell. See also Vann (2004) Ibid.
73. Gill was also a member of the Peace Pledge Union and a founder member of PAX, the first Catholic peace organisation in 1936.
74. John Allinson, Archivist, Leighton Park School kindly drew my attention to Powell's letter dated 15 November 1939.
75. Powell in L. Smith (1998) *Pacifists in Action*, York: William Sessions Limited, p.71.
76. The HSU was funded by Lady Hadfield; aged 77 she turned to her friend, novelist Mary Borden (later Lady Spears) to run a mobile hospital.
77. Powell. Op cit., p.129.
78. Powell had not completed his college course and as a CO it was not easy to find employment as a teacher.
79. Powell letter to E. B. Castle, 25 November 1947, Leighton Park School archives.
80. See Pretty, T. & Foster, A. (2012) Conservation of the 1948 Olympic Roll of Honour Plaques, *Journal of Architectural Conservation*, 18, 2, pp.7–22. I am grateful to Liz Hirst, Hirst Conservation for supplying the article and for providing further detail re the conservation. When Wembley Stadium was demolished in 2003, the plaques were extracted, conserved and housed in Brent Museum.
81. Pretty & Foster (2012) Ibid., p.11.
82. Peter Reddick, Obituary. *The Times*. 16 October, 2010, p.82.
83. Garrett (1978) Op. cit., pp.308–09.
84. Brett, S. (2010) Peter Reddick. Obituary. *Guardian*. 24 November.
85. Kenneth Rowntree (1996) National Life Stories: Artists' Lives, British Library.
86. Macmillan, Chairman of the Pilgrim Trust (1946), 'Introduction', *Recording Britain*, 1, Oxford University Press in association with the Pilgrim Trust, p.v.
87. Rowntree letter to Dickey, April 2, 1940. IWM ART/WA2/03/071.

88. See Clarke, G. (2012) *Randolph Schwabe*, Bristol: Sansom & Co., for further details re the scheme.
89. Calvocoressi, R. (1997) Kenneth Rowntree, Obituary, *Independent*. 5 March.
90. Extract from text written by artist and Camberwell teacher Christopher Pemberton (1923–2010) in 2006 for Scott's Highgate Gallery exhibition.
91. See Darnley Fine Art catalogue *Gordon Scott 11th - 18th November 2017.*
92. Pemberton (2006) Op. cit.
93. Trevelyan came from a pacifist background and detested all things military.
94. See *John Tunnard: Inner Space to Outer Space* (2010) by Simon Martin with a chronology by Brian Whitton and Alan Peat, Chichester: Pallant House Gallery. Tunnard was exceedingly knowledgeable about entomology and collected specimens of insect life for what was then the British Museum of Natural History.95. Trevelyan, J. (1957 reprinted 1996) *Indigo Days: The Art and Memoirs of Julian Trevelyan*, Aldershot: Scolar Press, pp.126–27.96. Peat, A. and Whitton, B. (1997) *John Tunnard. His Life and Work*, Aldershot: Scolar Press. I am grateful to Brian Whitton for sharing his knowledge and writing on Tunnard.97. See Morris and Radford (1983) Op. cit., p.67.
95. Trevelyan, J. (1957 reprinted 1996) *Indigo Days: The Art and Memoirs of Julian Trevelyan*, Aldershot: Scolar Press, pp.126-27.
96. Peat, A. and Whitton, B. (1997) *John Tunnard. His Life and Work*, Aldershot: Scolar Press. I am grateful to Brian Whitton for sharing his knowledge and writing on Tunnard.
97. See Morris and Radford (1983) Op. cit.
98. Glazebrook, M. (1977) 'Developments and Influences' in *John Tunnard 1900–1971*, Arts Council, p.22.
99. Marshall, S. (2015) 'Strange Tides' in Clarke, G. and Marshall, S. (Eds) *Shorelines: Artists on the South Coast*, Bristol: Sansom & Co., p.107.
100. Peat and Whitton (1997) Op. cit., pp.121–22.
101. Rigby, who trained at the RCA is credited with revolutionising the teaching of art at the school, his approach gained national attention, many coming to consult him on his methods. He died in post. I am grateful to Laura Kidner, Museum Curator, Christ's Hospital Museum, for drawing my attention to this.
102. Vaughan, K. (1966) *Journal & drawings 1939–65*, London: Alan Ross Ltd., p.21.
103. Vaughan Ibid., p.43.
104. Vaughan Ibid., pp.44–46 and 49–50.
105. Vaughan (1945) 7 January. http://www.thekeithvaughansociety.com/2017/03/29/keith-vaughan-john-minton/accessed 9/3/18.
106. Vaughan (1964) in Barber, N. (1964) *Conversations with Painters*, London: Collins, p.79.
107. Grimsditch, H.B. (1936) Artists of Note: Arthur Wragg, *The Artist*, July, pp.151–52.
108. Sheppard, H.R.L. (1933) 'Introduction' in Wragg, A. *The Psalms for Modern Life.* Interpreted with drawings by Arthur Wragg, London: Selwyn & Blount, Ltd., unpaginated.
109. I am grateful to Sue Hibberd for allowing me access to her father's papers. Frederick Walker (1912–2000) was a CO and Member of the Religious Society of Friends (Quakers) from 1942–2000. His Tribunal in September 1940 was also held in Bristol under Judge Wethered.
110. Wragg cited in Brook, J. (2001) *Arthur Wragg: Twentieth-century Prophet and Jester*, Sansom and Co., pp.100–01.
111. Brook (2001) Ibid., p.157 and p.159.
112. Bird, M. (2010) *Bryan Wynter*, Farnham: Lund Humphries, p.31.
113. See Bird (2010) Ibid., pp.31–2.
114. Newspaper cutting pasted into Randolph Schwabe's Scrapbook and see Schwabe's edited diaries, Clarke (2016).
115. Ibid., 29 March, 1943, 5 June 1944, 7 May 1945.
116. Cross, T. (2008/1994) *Painting the Warmth of the Sun: St Ives Artists 1939–1975*, Wellington, Somerset: Halsgrove, p.73.
117. See Bird (2010) Op.cit., chapter 5 'A New Painting Consciousness': the Abstract High Noon, 1955–9.
118. Cited in Alan Bowness's 'Foreword' to *Bryan Wynter 1915–1975. Paintings, Kinetics and Works on Paper*, Hayward Gallery, London. Exhibition catalogue.

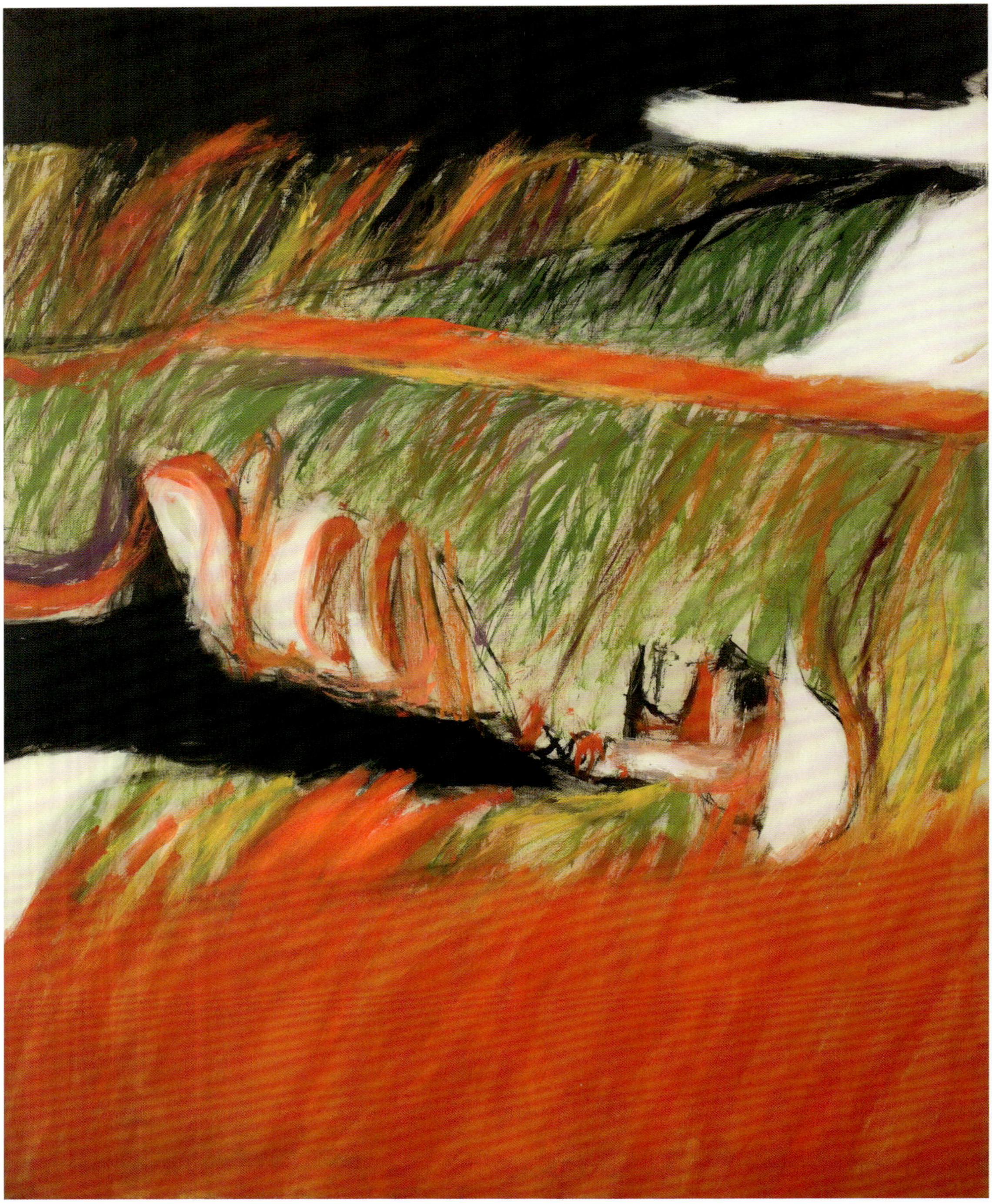

William Crozier | *Bourlon Wood* | 1962, Oil on canvas, 154 x 123 cm

CODA

THE LEGACY OF WAR AND PEACE

Conflicting Views: Pacifist Artists has sought to draw attention to the diverse experiences of artists who faced with compulsory military service were war resisters whether as conscientious objectors or pacifists. The accounts demonstrate the importance of seeing war as more than just the battlefields or trenches of the Western Front (or elsewhere) and offer an alternative vantage point to assess the impact of war on artists and their artistic careers. The diverse work of the artists in most cases eschews the brutality of conflict but nonetheless demonstrates the role of artists as moral witnesses and points to the value of portraying the myriad of ways in which war is experienced.

To illustrate the profound and lasting impact of the First and Second World War on artists particularly after the latter's abrupt ending in 1945 with the dropping of atomic bombs on Hiroshima and Nagasaki, it is apposite to turn to the work of Scottish-Irish artist William Crozier (1930-2011) as it was the catalyst for his pacifism. Crozier's imagination was to be haunted throughout his life, with images from the Holocaust seen as a teenager in Scotland at the local cinema when Pathé newsreels of the Allies liberation of the prison camps were shown.[1] 'The enormity of that horror'[2] was something he never fully dealt with. Too young to serve Crozier took his pacifist stance when called up for National Service in 1953,[3] which at the time meant *de facto* active service in Korea.

Bourlon Wood (1962) one of Crozier's most memorable paintings, completed when he was widely seen as one of the most exciting artists of his generation;[4] encapsulates the very essence of his painterly and philosophical concerns. The motivation for his work came from the conjoining of his deeply held pacifist and existentialist beliefs. 'He used photographs of World War I and the concentration camps of Bergen-Belsen and Auschwitz for paintings such as *Bourlon Wood* … to depict a traumatized humanity, the consequence … of the two world wars…'.[5]

Crozier's evocative, expressionist *Bourlon Wood* portrays the blood-stained, ravaged landscape in northern France in the darkness, at the foot of a ridge lies a skeletal soldier wearing a tin-hat. It is significantly more than just a comment on the horrors of war, and 'catches the metaphysical idea of death, "the skull beneath the skin"'.[6 7]

Bourlon Wood remains a potent image and serves as a compelling reminder of the brutality of warfare and the ever-present need to strive for the maintenance of peace and freedom. ◆◆◆

REFERENCES AND NOTES

1. See Crouan, K. (2017) 'Fellow Celts, After All' in Crouan, K. and Kissane, S. (Eds) *William Crozier. The Edge of Landscape*, Irish Museum of Modern Art, Oxford: Piano Nobile Publications.
2. Crozier's (1969) comment was written after a visit to Bergen-Belsen, cited in Crouan, K. (2016) *William Crozier. Rainbow's End*, Quinnipiac University, p.5.
3. National Service intake ceased in December 1960. The last conscripts were discharged in 1963.
4. See W. Laffan's (2010) Introduction to *William Crozier: Early Work*, London: Pyms Gallery.
5. Crouan, K. (2016) Op. cit., p.4.
6. Crouan, K. (Ed.) (2007) *William Crozier*, Aldershot: Lund Humphries, p.70. The contributors importantly draw attention to Crozier's wide ranging work over some 50 years, however my focus here is on the period when he incorporated skeletal figures into his work and hence does not seek to place it in wider European traditions.
7. 'Crozier was not alone in this absorption in the First World War. The 60s marked 50 years after the start of the war. He knew and admired Joan Littlewood whose musical 'Oh! What a Lovely War' opened in 1963 and in 1964 the BBC broadcast 'The Great War'. The opening credits showing a skeleton in uniform, recall Bourlon Wood.' (Crouan pers. comm. to the author 28 March, 2018). I gratefully acknowledge Katharine Crouan's guidance in the writing of this Coda.

PACIFIST ARTISTS
A SELECTED LISTING

FIRST WORLD WAR

Adrian Allinson
Maxwell Armfield
Claude Francis Barry
Arthur Cotterell
James Cowie
Ronald Ossory Dunlop
Mark Gertler
Duncan Grant
Percy Horton
(George) Leslie Hunter
Harold Knight
Haydn Mackey
William McCance
George Peace Micklewright
Job Nixon
Claughton Pellew
Ernest Procter
Eric Robertson
Joseph Southall
Walter Spradbery
Ethelbert White
Donald Wood

SECOND WORLD WAR

Robert Adams
Sven Berlin
John Bridgeman
Reg Butler
Roland Collins
Lawrence Gowing
Patrick Heron
Jonah Jones
George Kennethson
Arnold Machin
Bernard Meadows
John Minton
Victor Pasmore
John Petts
Hugo Powell
Peter Reddick
Kenneth Rowntree
Gordon Scott
John Tunnard
Keith Vaughan
Arthur Wragg
Bryan Wynter

ACKNOWLEDGEMENTS

Conflicting Views: Pacifist Artists is dedicated to John Sansom and pays tribute to his longstanding and steadfast championing of British artists both well- and lesser-known.

In researching and writing *Conflicting Views: Pacifist Artists* there have been many people who have provided advice, encouragement and support and to whom I extend my thanks. While space precludes my naming them all I am particularly grateful for the assistance received from many archivists, curators and librarians, amongst those who have provided invaluable help are: staff at the British Library; London Library; The Library of the Religious Society of Friends in Britain, Friends House, London; Wellcome Library; Emsworth Library; Kay Munro, College of Social Sciences Library, University of Glasgow; St Andrews University Special Collections; Christopher Whittick, Kate Elms, The Keep, East Sussex Record Office, Brighton; John Allinson, Archivist, Leighton Park School, Reading; Alastair Cook, Headmaster, Simon Mellor, Head of Art, The Downs School, Malvern; Elspeth Langsdale, Archivist, Oundle School, Peterborough; Jan Melichar, CO Project Coordinator, Peace Pledge Union; Charlotte Hall, Peace Museum, Bradford; Laura Kidner, Museum Curator, Christ's Hospital Museum; Bristol Museum & Art Gallery; Swindon Museum & Art Gallery and Steve Marshall, St Barbe Museum and Art Gallery, Lymington.

The following also assisted in various ways: Julia Berlin; Lois Bibbings; Jane Bridgeman; Rosemary Butler; David Capps; Ronald Clark, Chairman Essex Art Club; Ruth Christie; Katharine Crouan; Jeremy Gardiner; Penny Gay; Laura Gowing; Sonia and Anthony Green; Sue Hibberd; Liz Hirst, Hirst Conservation; Alan Lygobaker; Margaret McCance; George MacBride; Chris Martin; John and Lena Morgan; John Pasmore; Cyril Pearce; Mick, David and Anna Petts; Helen Power; Gordon Samuel, Tania Sutton, Osborne Samuel Gallery; The Scottish Gallery; Peyton Skipwith; Elizabeth Malet Spradbery; Edward Starkie; Leeds Quakers and in particular Susan Robson, Robert Keeble, Veronica O'Mara and Pat Gerwat; Andrew Walton; Ruth Walton and Alison Wilcox.

Any errors of fact and or interpretation arising out of these various communications are of course, all mine.

I gratefully acknowledge the support of a publication grant from the Marc Fitch Fund and Rachel Sharman Charitable Trust.

It has been a pleasure to work once more with The Otter Gallery Team. I am particularly grateful to Mike Carter for sourcing the images and associated photography and copyright clearance; Julie Peachey for expediting financial matters, and the assistance of Charlie Alexander, Gallery Officer.

The exhibition would not have been possible without the cooperation of the following: Melissa Atkinson, Religious Society of Friends (Quakers) in Britain; Imperial War Museum, London; Government Art Collection; Helen Scott, City Art Centre, Museums & Galleries, Edinburgh; Andrew Sim, Sim Fine Art; Adrian Pett, Darnley Fine Art; Hilary Chapman Fine Prints; Robert Travers, Piano Nobile Works of Art Ltd; Paul Liss and Sacha Llewellyn, Liss Llewellyn Fine Art; Sir Peter and Lady Coulson; Brian Whitton; University of Leeds Special Collections; The Downs School and those private lenders who preferred to remain anonymous.

Finally, I should like to thank Sarah Gilroy – as ever I have benefitted greatly from her support and insightful comments on *Conflicting Views: Pacifist Artists*.

GILL CLARKE
Visiting Professor & Curator, The Otter Gallery,
University of Chichester

INDEX

ABOUT THE AUTHOR

Gill Clarke is Visiting Professor and Curator at the Otter Gallery, University of Chichester. Her books include *Evelyn Dunbar: War and Country* (2006); *The Women's Land Army: A Portrait* (2008); *Randolph Schwabe: A Life in Art* (2012); *Shorelines: Artists on the South Coast* (2015); *The Bishop Otter Art Collection: A Celebration* (2016). In 2016 she also completed editing *The Diaries of Randolph Schwabe: British Art 1930-48*, which he kept while Head of the Slade School of Art. She has contributed to publications on British artists including 'Gluck: A Life in Art', which appears in *Gluck: Art and Identity* (2017) edited by Amy de la Haye and Martin Pel and published by Yale University Press. In addition she has guest curated at St Barbe Museum and Art Gallery, Lymington and most recently in 2016 at Pallant House Gallery for the exhibition of the Bishop Otter Art Collection.